Multilingualism as a Resource and a Goal

Marianne Turner

Multilingualism as a Resource and a Goal

Using and Learning Languages in Mainstream Schools

Marianne Turner
Faculty of Education
Monash University
Clayton, VIC, Australia

ISBN 978-3-030-21590-3   ISBN 978-3-030-21591-0   (eBook)
https://doi.org/10.1007/978-3-030-21591-0

© The Editor(s) (if applicable) and The Author(s) 2019
This work is subject to copyright. All rights are solely and exclusively licensed by the Publisher, whether the whole or part of the material is concerned, specifically the rights of translation, reprinting, reuse of illustrations, recitation, broadcasting, reproduction on microfilms or in any other physical way, and transmission or information storage and retrieval, electronic adaptation, computer software, or by similar or dissimilar methodology now known or hereafter developed.
The use of general descriptive names, registered names, trademarks, service marks, etc. in this publication does not imply, even in the absence of a specific statement, that such names are exempt from the relevant protective laws and regulations and therefore free for general use.
The publisher, the authors and the editors are safe to assume that the advice and information in this book are believed to be true and accurate at the date of publication. Neither the publisher nor the authors or the editors give a warranty, express or implied, with respect to the material contained herein or for any errors or omissions that may have been made. The publisher remains neutral with regard to jurisdictional claims in published maps and institutional affiliations.

Cover illustration: lunagraphica / Getty Images

This Palgrave Macmillan imprint is published by the registered company Springer Nature Switzerland AG.
The registered company address is: Gewerbestrasse 11, 6330 Cham, Switzerland

Para Ángel Luis, Héctor y Leo. Mi corazón es vuestro.

Acknowledgements

The writing of this book would not have been possible without the input of principals, teachers, students and parents. Although I cannot mention them by name—they have been de-identified in the studies as part of the ethics process—I am extremely grateful for their participation. The passion and dedication of the teachers and principals with respect to the affirming and leveraging of students' language practices and/or to the teaching and learning of languages at school were inspirational. Especial thanks to the students who contributed their beautiful artwork. Thank you to Anne De Kretser and Jennifer Brown-Omichi for helping me to combine teachers' professional learning with research, and to Hiroki Kurihara and Gwyn McClelland for early discussions about content and language integrated learning (CLIL). In my wrestling with theoretical ideas, I am very grateful for the translanguaging conversations I had with Angel Lin, a discussion with Ester de Jong and Mark Pacheco about my book during a long car ride, and the two days I spent with Jacqui D'Warte, Yvette Slaughter, Russell Cross and Julie Choi discussing translanguaging and communicative repertoire. Ester was also very generous in her advice and feedback on Chap. 2, and Jacqui's work on language maps was key to the study I discuss in Chap. 5 and the English-medium classes in Chap. 6. Any omissions and errors in the book are, of course, my own.

Contents

1	**Introduction**	1
1.1	What the Book Is About	1
1.2	A Monolingual View of Language	5
1.3	Communicative Repertoires	7
1.4	Languages Across the Curriculum	9
1.5	Teaching and Learning Objectives	10
1.6	Structure of the Book	12
	References	13

Part I	**Foundations**	17

2	**Language and Multilingualism**	19
2.1	Language as a Social Construct	19
2.2	Language as a Political Tool	23
2.3	Bi/Multilingualism	25
2.4	Translanguaging	27
2.5	The Nature of Linguistic Repertoire	30
2.6	Widening the Lens	33
2.7	Conclusion	38
	References	38

ix

x   Contents

3 Use of Languages Across the Curriculum   45
3.1   Introduction   45
3.2   Instructional Separation of Languages   46
3.3   Flexibility in the Use of a Target Language   50
3.4   Incorporating Students' Languages into English-Medium
      Classrooms   55
3.5   Language-Related Pedagogies: Learning Through the
      Target Language   58
      3.5.1   Form-Focused Instruction   58
      3.5.2   Functional Language   60
      3.5.3   Language Scaffolding   62
3.6   Crosslinguistic Pedagogy   65
3.7   Conclusion   69
References   69

4 Opportunities to Learn (Through) Languages   79
4.1   Introduction   79
4.2   Opportunities to Learn from a Sociocultural Perspective   80
4.3   Multilingual Stance   83
4.4   Student Engagement with Languages   89
4.5   Institutional Structures   94
4.6   A Multilingual Practices Framework   98
4.7   Conclusion   100
References   101

Part II Application   109

5 Primary Schools with Heritage-Language Students   111
5.1   Introduction   111
5.2   The Study   112
      5.2.1   Aims   112
      5.2.2   Participants and Data Collection   113
5.3   Lesson Sequences   114
5.4   Summary of Findings   118

5.5	Multilingual Stance		119
	5.5.1	What It Means to Be Bilingual	119
	5.5.2	Literacy Practices	121
5.6	Student Engagement With Languages		122
	5.6.1	Connecting Home and School	123
	5.6.2	Heritage Languages at School	125
5.7	Institutional Structures and Pedagogies		127
	5.7.1	Professional Learning and Teacher Collaboration	128
	5.7.2	Student-Centred Learning, Inclusion of the Community and Crosslinguistic Pedagogy	128
5.8	Opportunities to Learn (Through) Languages		131
	5.8.1	Heritage Languages as Central to Learning	131
	5.8.2	Heritage Languages as Relevant to Learning	133
	5.8.3	Monolingual Students	135
5.9	Discussion		135
5.10	Conclusion		138
References			138

6 A Whole-School Primary Bilingual Programme

			141
6.1	Introduction		141
6.2	The Study		142
	6.2.1	Aims	142
	6.2.2	Participants and Data Collection	143
6.3	Lessons and Lesson Sequences		145
6.4	Summary of Findings		147
6.5	Multilingual Stance		148
	6.5.1	Heritage Languages	148
	6.5.2	Learning Japanese	150
6.6	Student Engagement With Languages		152
	6.6.1	Japanese	153
	6.6.2	(Other) Heritage Languages	155
6.7	Institutional Structures and Pedagogies		156
	6.7.1	Consistency and Student-Centred Learning	157
	6.7.2	Language-Related Pedagogies	159

xii   Contents

6.8   Opportunities to Learn (Through) Languages   162
  6.8.1   The Japanese-Medium Classroom   163
  6.8.2   Heritage Languages in the English-Medium
           Classroom   163
6.9   Discussion   165
6.10 Conclusion   167
References   168

7   Teacher-Driven CLIL Initiatives in Secondary Schools   169
7.1   Introduction   169
7.2   The Study   170
  7.2.1   Aims   170
  7.2.2   Participants and Data Collection   171
7.3   Units of Work   172
7.4   Summary of Findings   174
7.5   Multilingual Stance   175
  7.5.1   Advocacy and Relevance   175
  7.5.2   Japanese/French Language Use   177
7.6   Student Engagement With Languages   179
  7.6.1   Increasing the Capital of Linguistic and
           Cultural Knowledge   179
  7.6.2   Japanese/French   180
7.7   Institutional Structures and Pedagogies   182
  7.7.1   Collaboration, Professional Learning and
           Cross-curricular Priorities   183
  7.7.2   Language-Related Pedagogies   184
7.8   Opportunities to Learn   189
  7.8.1   Leveraging Language to Learn Content   190
  7.8.2   Leveraging Content to Learn Language   191
7.9   Discussion   192
7.10 Conclusion   194
References   195

8   A Structured, Opt-In Secondary CLIL Programme   197
8.1   Introduction   197

		Contents	xiii

8.2	The Study		198
	8.2.1	Aims	199
	8.2.2	Participants and Data Collection	199
8.3	Lessons		201
8.4	Summary of Findings		203
8.5	Multilingual Stance		204
	8.5.1	Challenge	204
	8.5.2	Japanese/Italian Language Use	206
8.6	Student Engagement With Languages		208
	8.6.1	Exposure to CLIL Language Outside School	209
	8.6.2	Non-CLIL Students	210
	8.6.3	CLIL Versus Acceleration	211
8.7	Institutional Structures and Pedagogies		212
	8.7.1	Logistics and Professional Learning	213
	8.7.2	Language-Related Pedagogies	214
8.8	Opportunities to Learn		217
	8.8.1	Opportunities for Non-CLIL Students	218
	8.8.2	Leveraging Language to Learn Content	219
	8.8.3	Leveraging Content to Learn Language	220
8.9	Discussion		222
8.10	Conclusion		225
References			225

Part III Synthesis — 227

9 Teaching and Learning Objectives — 229

9.1	Introduction	229
9.2	Celebrating and Valuing Multilingual Identities	233
9.3	General Learning and Instruction	235
9.4	Reflecting Critically on Linguistic Hierarchies and Social Structures	237
9.5	Learning Content-Related Target Language in Different Subject Areas	239

xiv Contents

9.6	Learning Language in the Language Classroom Via Cross-curricular Content	242
9.7	Using a Target Language for Everyday Communication	244
9.8	Conclusion	246
References		246

10 Multilingual Practices and Opportunities to Learn — 251

10.1	Introduction	251
10.2	Multilingual Stance	254
10.3	Student Engagement with Languages	257
10.4	Institutional Structures and Pedagogies	260
10.5	Crosslinguistic and Translanguaging Pedagogy	262
10.6	Differentiation	264
10.7	Innovation	268
10.8	Language Hierarchies	270
10.9	Conclusion	272
References		273

Conclusion — 277

References — 281

Index — 305

List of Figures

Fig. 4.1	Multilingual practices framework	99
Fig. 5.1	Findings according to multilingual practices framework	118
Fig. 5.2	Examples of language maps	130
Fig. 6.1	Findings according to multilingual practices framework	147
Fig. 6.2	Excerpt from Year 1 student's Father's Day card	149
Fig. 6.3	Writing sample 1 (Year 6 student)	151
Fig. 6.4	Writing sample 2 (Year 5 student)	151
Fig. 6.5	Year 5/6 classroom activity: Venn diagram 1	155
Fig. 6.6	Year 5/6 classroom activity: Venn diagram 2	156
Fig. 6.7	Language map—foundation student	161
Fig. 6.8	Language map—Year 5 student	161
Fig. 7.1	Findings according to multilingual practices framework	174
Fig. 7.2	Excerpt from advanced Year 8 students' language assessment at Cassia	185
Fig. 7.3	Excerpt from Year 7 assessment at Acacia	186
Fig. 7.4	Excerpt from Year 10 'Me, my career and Japan' unit at Banksia	187
Fig. 7.5	A reading text used for the Japanese community project unit at Banksia	188
Fig. 7.6	Excerpt from PowerPoint slides used for the Japanese geographical features unit at Banksia	188
Fig. 8.1	Findings according to multilingual practices framework	203

xvi   **List of Figures**

Fig. 8.2	Extracts from the Italian CLIL Year 9 assessment (two different students)	207
Fig. 8.3	Weekly planner—Japanese CLIL Year 8 visual arts	215
Fig. 8.4	Excerpt from Japanese CLIL Year 8 visual arts assessment	216
Fig. 8.5	Excerpts from Japanese CLIL Year 8 science presentation	217
Fig. 8.6	Excerpts from Year 7 Italian non-CLIL students' humanities worksheets	218
Fig. 8.7	Example of students' note-taking in the Year 9 Italian CLIL humanities class	221
Fig. 10.1	Multilingual practices framework	253
Fig. 10.2	Degree of school commitment to the cross-curricular use of a target language	262

List of Tables

Table 5.1	The three phases of the study	113
Table 5.2	Participants and data collection	114
Table 5.3	Investigating students' language practices	115
Table 5.4	Leveraging students' language practices	116
Table 6.1	Teacher participants	144
Table 6.2	Observed lessons	144
Table 6.3	Investigating students' language practices in the English-medium classes	145
Table 6.4	Leveraging students' language practices	146
Table 6.5	Foundation lesson plan—Japanese	160
Table 7.1	Summary of participants and data collection	171
Table 7.2	Summary of units of work	173
Table 8.1	Number of students at each year level studying CLIL	199
Table 8.2	Summary of participants and data collection	200
Table 8.3	Observed lessons	202

1

Introduction

1.1 What the Book Is About

As the world becomes increasingly interconnected, schools are both engaging with, and attempting to prepare students for, ever-greater diversity. Language lies at the heart of this preparation because it is the way people communicate with each other and express themselves to the world. Language is also central to teaching and learning (e.g., Halliday, 1993; Vygotsky, 1987), but one language—and rather limited ways of speaking it—can be taken for granted and preside over others. Also, the norm, or standard by which students are measured tends to be monolingual rather than multilingual (e.g., García & Li, 2014; Rymes, 2010), meaning that multilinguals' ability to speak a language is judged by monolingual communication. Together, language dominance and monolingual standards reward monolinguals of a dominant language, and this can significantly influence the learning of languages both in the community and at school.

In Australia, the context of this book, English is overwhelmingly dominant as an institutional language, and other languages are generally considered in relation to their functional benefits, especially Asian languages (see Lo Bianco, 2014). This fits with a neoliberal kind of reasoning that Australian institutions, similar to so many other institutions around the

© The Author(s) 2019
M. Turner, *Multilingualism as a Resource and a Goal*,
https://doi.org/10.1007/978-3-030-21591-0_1

world, have adopted. The reasoning highlights what Dardot and Laval (2013, p. 3) termed existence in 'a world of generalized competition' where success requires a competitive advantage. However, only considering languages in relation to their utility may not have a marked effect on their current marginal status; English is widely understood to be a prestigious lingua franca, and can therefore be considered sufficient in a country like Australia (Djité, 2011). There are many other ways students can gain a competitive advantage in the workplace, not only through their language skills. Viewing languages through a narrow neoliberal frame does not do justice to all the benefits of engaging with them. An effort to broaden the frame is clear in the rationale for the first Australian national curriculum for languages:

> Being able to communicate proficiently gives learners essential communication skills in the target language, an intercultural capability, and an understanding of the role of language and culture in human communication. It provides the opportunity for students to engage with the linguistic and cultural diversity of humanity, to reflect on their understanding of human experience in all aspects of social life, and on their own participation and ways of being in the world. (Australian Curriculum and Reporting Authority, 2011)

The rationale highlights the value of language as a resource for learning as well as for communication. It has been found, for example, that learning another language promotes the ability to give a variety of solutions to a problem (divergent thinking) and the ability to find original solutions (creative thinking) (see Baker & Wright, 2017 for a review). Rather than only focusing on the functional aspects of language, the rationale additionally highlights human interactions in a broader sense, and the way languages give access to a qualitative appreciation of different kinds of interactions and ways of knowing. It also allows for a critical study of the way language is part of our positioning, or our participation in the world. Languages offer a concrete way of reflexively engaging with both inequity and diversity, of seeing what may be similar and different from the inside out, of learning in different, constructive, engaging and identity-affirming ways.

The aim of this book is to apply the rationale to languages spoken in the community, as well as to languages that are taught at school, and generate an overarching framework that can be used for the inclusion of both across the curriculum in schools. Separating the use and learning of heritage languages (languages students 'inherit' as part of their cultural/linguistic background) and school-based target languages can be artificial, and this will be clear in the settings discussed in the book. My hope is to offer a framework that links the leveraging and expanding of students' language resources in a practical, student-centred and theoretically coherent way that also prioritises spaces for the critiquing and disrupting of linguistic hierarchies.

The Australian context is one of institutional monolingualism and student diversity, and is the backdrop against which I consider cross-curricular language use and learning. In this context, student diversity not only relates to the rich variety of languages students speak, but also to their diversity of experiences with language. They may speak a heritage language fluently, have limited exposure to it (grandparents might speak it but parents might not) or only have exposure to English outside school. Languages taught in schools, referred to in this book as target languages, may or may not be students' heritage languages. The context can be considered—rather loosely—one of elective bilingualism (Valdés, 2003). Elective bilinguals choose to learn a language and circumstantial bilinguals are required to learn a language through circumstance—they may have moved to a country where their language is not spoken outside the home or community domain. A great number of students with a heritage language are born and raised in Australia and, if they are fluent in English, they can frequently choose whether or not to engage with their heritage. As Valdés (ibid.) pointed out, over time, circumstantial bilinguals may shift to the dominant language and lose the minority language. This language attrition can worsen with subsequent generations (see Eisenchlas, Schalley, & Guillemin, 2013).

A multilingual approach for *all* students, even in situations where teachers do not speak the language(s) entering the classroom, is the position taken in the book. In the words of Lo Bianco (2014, p. 17), 'acknowledging multilingualism and multi-literacy throughout the academic and administrative operations of education can enhance the quality, seriousness and equity of education for all learners, not just for those who were brought up multilingually'. The following question shows how this acknowledgement (and affirmation) can be related to contexts where institutional monolingualism predominates:

> How do we promote multilingualism in mainstream schools where the pursuit of another language may be considered a benefit but not a priority in wider society, and heritage language attrition is common?

The approach taken in the book is inclusive of various kinds of exposure to different languages. The terms 'heritage' and 'foreign' are used as a way of showing in a very broad sense whether or not students have a connection to the language outside of school: 'heritage' indicates that they do and 'foreign' indicates that they do not. This connection sits more comfortably on a continuum than in distinct categories; the terms are only employed to highlight the significance of differences in access to (and identification with) a language outside school. The terms are also reflective of different ways language can be approached in schools. For example, heritage languages may be discouraged at school as part of a de facto English-only policy and foreign languages may be studied as a subject area rather than used as a cross-curricular resource and/or mode of communication. Understanding language differently can be a useful step in formulating a school language policy (or a classroom policy for a teacher) that takes a systemic approach to multilingualism. A systemic approach refers to the use and learning of languages across the curriculum for different purposes but with a common thread. This thread is called multilingual stance in the book, and its implementation is a core theme.

The framework explained in the book, a multilingual practices framework, shows the relationship between a multilingual stance (or a school/classroom-based language policy), student engagement with languages and institutional structures and pedagogies. These three dimensions interact to produce opportunities to learn. The framework is embedded in stakeholder experiences with—and understanding of—language, and also the learning environment. The influence of identity and power dynamics on the use and learning of language is also taken into account. The framework was designed to assist in considering what kinds of structures and pedagogies may be beneficial in different kinds of mainstream settings when taking a multilingual stance and working with a great range of student (and community) engagement. In generating the framework, I sought to understand what I was seeing in Australian schools through the lens of sociocultural and sociolinguistic theories, and with the assistance of literature on bilingual education, teaching English to speakers of other languages (TESOL) and second-language acquisition research.

The theories and research that influenced the thinking behind the framework are set out in Part One of the book. The application of the framework to four different studies I conducted across different settings in the Australian mainstream school context is the subject of Part Two. These settings include (1) generalist primary classrooms with a high number of heritage-language students, (2) a whole-school primary bilingual programme, (3) teacher-driven secondary content-and-language-integrated learning (CLIL) initiatives and (4) a structured, secondary CLIL programme. The diversity of the student cohorts, widely varying degrees of language proficiency in different languages, the mainstream (non-selective) nature of programmes and the degree to which the dominant language—English—was used as the medium of communication by students were similar in all the settings. Part Three discusses different teaching and learning objectives and ways in which the multilingual practices framework can assist in grasping opportunities to learn from a student-centred perspective.

1.2   A Monolingual View of Language

The promotion of multilingualism in mainstream, institutionally monolingual settings is a move away from monolingual views of language that have traditionally prevailed in formal learning environments. A monolingual view of language is not limited to people who identify as monolingual—bi/multilinguals can also hold the view in that they understand their languages to be separate. Cummins (2007) referred to this idea as the 'two solitudes', and García (2009a) also discussed the rather counterintuitive notion of being monolingual in two or more languages.

6   M. Turner

She framed the desired outcome as 'either proficiency in the two languages according to monolingual norms for both languages, or proficiency in the dominant language' (p. 115). In cases where one language is dominant in schools, there is a well-established view that languages need to be kept separate according to different domains of use. In the institutional domain, monolingual norms for one particular language often inform how students are taught and assessed. Other languages may be encouraged but can be considered to belong to the community domain and/or the foreign language classroom. This view can lead bi/multilinguals to perceive monolingual norms in one particular language to be central to teaching and learning.

In Australia, as Scarino (2014) pointed out, there is a need to 'unlearn monolingualism' because schools strongly evidence monolingual educational structures (Scarino, 2014; Spence-Brown, 2014). The norm is for languages to be taught as a subject, and cross-curricular use of these languages is considered to be a bonus rather than a requirement. Further, a foreign language is not compulsory in senior secondary school. Emerging bi/multilingual students are also commonly expected to speak English in class without resorting to other languages. For example, pre-service teachers have anecdotally reported to me that, on practicum, they have been asked not to use a language they share with students in the classroom, and also that some schools have a formal English-only policy. The result of these monolingual educational structures is that students may be leaving mainstream schooling with limited opportunities to speak in a language other than English and/or to discover ways to (openly) leverage a language they speak in ways that further their learning.

The empirical focus of the book is on Australia, but it is fair to say that no one country has a monopoly on a monolingual view of language. This language may be English but, in other countries, there may be a different language that is institutionally dominant, eclipsing others. For example, in Tsung's (2014) book on multilingual education in China, she explained that, in many cases, the ultimate objective of bilingual education for ethnic minorities is for them to speak Chinese, and even in programmes that are called bilingual programmes, the minority language is considered to be supplementary. The discussion in this book aims to resonate with mainstream settings where encouraging students to speak different languages (or teachers to promote different languages strategically) across the curriculum can be a struggle, especially in contexts where the student cohort is diverse.

1.3 Communicative Repertoires

Global mobility and the innumerable ways in which languages are harnessed for the purposes of interaction have assisted in breaking down monolingual views of language. Sociolinguists in particular have offered ways of thinking about language that reflect the incredible diversity of interactions which take place, even in what we might label as one language. Blommaert (2010) spoke of the 'supervernacular' that is English, for example, with all its modalities and dialects around the world. Rymes (2010, 2014, p. 290) discussed the way we express ourselves in terms of a communicative repertoire, rather than some kind of 'pure' form of language. This repertoire includes the way one dresses, comports oneself and other non-linguistic forms of communication: 'multiple languages, multiple ways of speaking the "same" language and many other features beyond language can serve as part of an individual's communicative repertoire' (see also Canagarajah, 2013; Li, 2011; Pennycook, 2017). This notion of repertoire is not aimed at perfecting an area of expertise, and positions mastery as an impossible goal. Blommaert (2010) viewed all repertoires as truncated because we cannot possibly know all there is to know about a language. However, for him, there is nothing wrong with 'partial competence': 'no one needs all the resources that a language potentially provides' (p. 103).

In the book, under the overarching banner of communicative repertoire, I focus on multiple languages. We are all multilingual in a sense: even if we identify as only speaking one language, we use different styles, modes, registers and non-linguistic cues in different contexts. However, I use multilingualism to refer to the leveraging and expanding of students' communicative repertoires through the inclusion of different languages across the curriculum. Bilingual learners are included in this idea of multilingualism because they are learning/using more than one language, and they are 'developing multiple linguistic repertoires at home and at school' (de Jong, 2011, p. 18). By framing language as repertoire, I aim to show connections and explore students' language resources in a holistic way. Situated knowledge of a school-based standardised form of a dominant language is still necessary to do well academically in a majority of contexts around the world, and showing how the notion of repertoire can connect with this reality is an aim of the book. I discuss repertoire as multilingual—under a communicative umbrella—because non-linguistic features and different ways of speaking one language were not a direct focus of the empirical studies included in the book.

Viewing language through the lens of repertoire is also a way to validate students' linguistic knowledge and to disrupt language hierarchies. These objectives take up the work of sociolinguists, both in the UK and the US (e.g., Creese & Blackledge, 2010; García & Li, 2014; Li & Zhu, 2013) and in former colonial contexts (Lin & Lo, 2017; Lin & Wu, 2015). The most powerful element of this hierarchy in institutionally monolingual settings is the dominant language versus all the others, but there are hierarchies between other languages too. Pennycook (2001, p. 215), in his discussion on de facto language policy, maintained that 'when we fight in support of a community-based language program, when we allow or disallow the use of one language or another in our classrooms, when we choose which language to use in Congress, conversations, conferences, or curricula, we are making language policy'. Choosing one language over another to study in our classrooms is a form of hierarchy—this language is worthy of study, whereas this other one is not quite so important. However, if we did not make these kinds of choices, it would be difficult for us to teach any language, thereby failing to expand students' linguistic repertoire and engagement with different ways of thinking.

In Australia, language classrooms are dominated by languages which are attached to economically powerful, culturally prestigious and/or geopolitically important countries. These languages include—but are not limited to—Japanese, Italian, French, Chinese, German and Indonesian. The diversity of student cohort means that some students speak at home (to varying degrees of proficiency) a language taught in their school, some students speak a language that is similar in some way (for example, they speak Chinese and study Japanese) or a language they speak at home is very different from that which is being taught at school. In the studies covered in this book, the languages taught at school were Japanese, Italian and French. Findings of the studies revealed that hierarchies between these languages and students' heritage languages could play out in nuanced ways, and this will be discussed in the final chapter.

1.4 Languages Across the Curriculum

The benefits that accrue from cross-curricular use of different languages have been well documented. Over the past three decades, there has been an increasing focus on the advantages of bringing languages that students speak at home into the classroom to assist with their learning (Cummins & Swain, 1986; González, Moll, & Amanti, 2005; Schecter & Cummins, 2003). Efforts have also been made to shift the view of languages as discrete entities by questioning language separation in bi/multilingual brains (García & Li, 2014). A shift from a deficit view of 'English language learners' as coming to class with nothing of value, to a recognition of their linguistic resources and emerging bi/multilingual status has also been documented (e.g., Gee, 2004; Lankshear & Knobel, 2003). There has been a growing normalisation of multilingualism, referred to as the 'multilingual turn' (Conteh & Meier, 2014; May, 2014) in both the fields of bilingual education and TESOL, and a focus on pedagogies which explicitly leverage these resources to help students learn (García & Li, 2014; Velasco & García, 2014).

Using language to convey meaning, as opposed to a sole focus on language as a system, has also long been considered beneficial for language learning (see Ellis & Shintani, 2014). A cross-curricular approach to the teaching and learning of a target language, for example, is based on the understanding that students' ability to communicate in a language will improve if they are taught different subject areas in that language. Within this cross-curricular approach, the range of language distribution can extend from one subject being taught using the target language to 50 per cent or more of school time being conducted in that language. Much research, including studies on how to draw students' attention to language structures while teaching different subject areas, has come from Canadian French immersion (e.g., Lyster, 2007; Swain, 1985, 2000), and also immersion contexts in the United States (e.g., Lindholm-Leary, 2005; Potowski, 2004; Tedick & Young, 2017), where the target or minority language is used for 50 per cent or more of school time. More recently, research has also come from European CLIL programmes (see Pérez-Cañado, 2012 for a review of CLIL; see also San Isidro, 2018), where there is more flexibility around language distribution.

The dominance of English in literature on cross-curricular language use is clear, both in relation to English-as-an-additional-language (EAL) students in English-speaking countries and also to content-based instruction for majority language speakers. In the case of the latter, English is a common target language chosen in CLIL programmes, in Asia (e.g., Cho, 2012; Lin, 2008) as well as in Europe (Dalton-Puffer, Llinares, Lorenzo, & Nikula, 2014). In situations where English is *not* the target language—in Canadian French immersion, for example—English dominance is also apparent. Ballinger, Lyster, Sterzuk and Genesee (2017) urged caution when thinking about bringing English into the French classroom as a pedagogical tool. This indicates that English language dominance has been at the root of either arguing for the presence of a minority students' language resource or for thinking very deeply about how (and if) English can be used to further students' learning of a different target language. Pedagogies are likely to differ depending on the extent to which students are expected to be able to communicate in a target language at school, and teaching and learning objectives are a major theme of the book.

1.5 Teaching and Learning Objectives

In the book, I discuss cross-curricular use of heritage languages and languages chosen for study by schools because the diverse nature of contemporary student cohorts in mainstream schools can make links between the two very useful. This diversity is not only relevant to Australia, but is a reality for many schools in countries which are home to different ethnic languages, to an immigrant population and/or encourage the participation of international students in mainstream schooling. I take stakeholders' language experiences as a starting point in order to reflect on ways that context-sensitive, systemic changes can be made to monolingual educational structures, and the potential benefits of these changes. Although some of the settings I discuss are referred to as CLIL, there was a great deal of variation in teachers' use of the target language across the different contexts. The discussion in the book will be linked to different pedagogies, and Chap. 3 is dedicated to explaining pedagogies (and approaches) relevant to the empirical studies.

Cenoz (2015), in her argument that there is no real pedagogical distinction between the umbrella terms of content-based instruction (used frequently in the US) and CLIL (used frequently in Europe), stated that both focused on teaching content through the medium of another language. In the book, I aim to promote the idea that use of different languages across the curriculum can happen bottom-up as well as top-down, and bottom-up includes a kind of leaking of languages from the community domain or from the language classroom. This 'leaking' is student-driven and students may bring a language to class which a teacher (and other students) may not understand. Considering the bottom-up approach to be teaching content through the medium of another language is potentially misleading because the latter connotes teachers' own target language use. In the book, cross-curricular language(s) use is linked to different teaching and learning objectives—increasing student proficiency in a language that has entered the classroom is an objective, but not the only one. Use of languages use is also viewed as a resource for students' general learning, for example.

Harnessing the use of languages for various teaching and learning objectives thus relates to the leveraging of students' existing language resources as much as it does to developing these resources. Literature on bringing students' languages into English-medium classrooms mainly comes from the field of teaching English to minoritised students in English-speaking countries, and this will be referenced in the book. In the empirical studies under discussion, students were not observed to struggle to understand the English they needed for school and a great majority were born in Australia. However, the objectives are just as relevant to EAL learners as they are to students whose fluency in English can render invisible a wider linguistic repertoire. In Australia, EAL learners commonly receive some kind of sheltered instruction, in the form of intensive language classes and/or withdrawal classes. Aside from this, their schooling is spent in mainstream classes. A systemic and strategic implementation of multilingualism as a resource and a goal for all students can assist in the notion of language enrichment, as opposed to a deficit view; the EAL students know something important, not irrelevant, to institutional learning.

1.6 Structure of the Book

The book has three parts. In Part One, I discuss the main ideas and approaches that inform the promotion of multilingualism in mainstream schools. In Chap. 2, I begin by discussing ways of thinking about language, and the significance of this thinking to learning (and maintaining) different languages. Chapter 3 then covers structural and pedagogical approaches to bilingual education and/or EAL students in English-medium classrooms. Chapter 4, the last in this part, is dedicated to directly theorising the dimensions of a multilingual practices framework. I explain the thinking behind opportunities to learn, a multilingual stance, student engagement with languages and institutional structures/pedagogies. In Part Two, I then map the findings of empirical studies, conducted in four different settings, against the dimensions of the framework; generalist primary classrooms with a high number of heritage-language students, a whole-school primary bilingual programme, teacher-driven secondary CLIL initiatives and a structured secondary CLIL programme. Finally, in Part Three, I discuss the teaching and learning objectives that were generated when considering the studies through the lens of the multilingual practices framework. The final chapter is dedicated to a discussion of the three framework dimensions with a special focus on pedagogies related to the planned use of more than one language in the classroom. Differentiation, innovation and language hierarchies are also discussed as important aspects of opportunities to learn from a student-centred perspective.

References

Australian Curriculum, Assessment and Reporting Authority (ACARA). (2011). *The shape of the Australian curriculum: Languages.* Retrieved from http://docs.acara.edu.au/resources/Languages__Shape_of_the_Australian_Curriculum_new.pdf

Baker, C., & Wright, W. E. (2017). *Foundations of bilingual education and bilingualism* (6th ed.). Bristol: Multilingual Matters.

Ballinger, S., Lyster, R., Sterzuk, A., & Genesee, F. (2017). Context-appropriate crosslinguistic pedagogy: Considering the role of language status in immersion education. *Journal of Immersion and Content-Based Language Education, 5*(1), 30–57.

Blommaert, J. (2010). *The sociolinguistics of globalization.* Cambridge: Cambridge University Press.

Canagarajah, S. (2013). *Translingual practice: Global Englishes and cosmopolitan relations.* New York: Routledge.

Cenoz, J. (2015). Content-based instruction and content and language integrated learning: The same or different? *Language, Culture and Curriculum, 28*(1), 8–24.

Cho, D. W. (2012). English-medium instruction in the university context of Korea: Trade-off between teaching outcomes and media-initiated university ranking. *Journal of Asia TEFL, 9*(4), 135–163.

Conteh, J., & Meier, G. (Eds.). (2014). *The multilingual turn in languages education: Opportunities and challenges.* Bristol: Multilingual Matters.

Creese, A., & Blackledge, A. (2010). Translanguaging in the bilingual classroom: A pedagogy for learning and teaching? *The Modern Language Journal, 94*, 103–115.

Cummins, J. (2007). Rethinking monolingual instructional strategies in multilingual classrooms. *Canadian Journal of Applied Linguistics (CJAL), 10*(2), 221–240.

Cummins, J., & Swain, M. (1986). *Bilingualism in education: Aspects of theory, research and practice.* Harlow: Longman.

Dalton-Puffer, C., Llinares, A., Lorenzo, F., & Nikula, T. (2014). 'You can stand under my umbrella': Immersion, CLIL and bilingual education. A response to Cenoz, Genesee & Gorter (2013). *Applied Linguistics, 35*(2), 213–218.

Dardot, P., & Laval, C. (2013). *The new way of the world: On a neoliberal society.* London: Verso.

de Jong, E. J. (2011). *Foundations for multilingualism in education: From principles to practice.* Philadelphia, PA: Caslon Publishing.

Department of Education and Training, Victoria. (2016). *Languages provision in Victorian Government schools, 2016.* Retrieved February 26, 2018, from http://www.education.vic.gov.au/Documents/school/teachers/teachingresources/discipline/languages/2016_Languages_provision_report.pdf

Djité, P. G. (2011). Language policy in Australia: What goes up must come down? In C. Norrby & J. Hajek (Eds.), *Uniformity and diversity in language policy: Global perspectives* (pp. 53–67). Bristol: Multilingual Matters.

Eisenchlas, S., Schalley, A., & Guillemin, D. (2013). The importance of literacy in the home language: The view from Australia. *SAGE Open, 3*(4), 1–14. https://doi.org/10.1007/2158244013507270

Ellis, R., & Shintani, N. (2014). *Exploring language pedagogy through second language acquisition research.* London: Routledge.

García, O., & Li, W. (2014). *Translanguaging: Language, bilingualism and education.* New York: Palgrave Macmillan.

Gee, J. P. (2004). *Situated language and learning: A critique of traditional schooling.* New York: Routledge.

González, N., Moll, L. C., & Amanti, C. (Eds.). (2005). *Funds of knowledge: Theorizing practices in households, communities and classrooms.* Mahwah, NJ: Lawrence Erlbaum.

Halliday, M. A. K. (1993). Towards a language-based theory of learning. *Linguistics and Education, 5*(2), 93–116.

Lankshear, C., & Knobel, M. (2003). *New literacies: Changing knowledge and classroom learning.* Buckingham: Open University Press.

Li, W. (2011). Moment analysis and translanguaging space. *Journal of Pragmatics, 43*, 1222–1235.

Li, W., & Zhu, H. (2013). Translanguaging identities and ideologies: Creating transnational space through flexible multilingual practices amongst Chinese university students in the UK. *Applied Linguistics, 34*(5), 516–535.

Lin, A. M. Y. (2008). Code-switching in the classroom: Research paradigms and approaches. In K. A. King & N. H. Hornberger (Eds.), *Encyclopedia of language and education: Vol. 10. Research methods in language and education* (pp. 273–286). New York: Springer.

Lin, A. M. Y., & Lo, Y. Y. (2017). Trans/languaging and the triadic dialogue in content and language integrated learning (CLIL) classrooms. *Language and Education, 31*(1), 26–45.

Lin, A. M. Y., & Wu, Y. M. (2015). 'May I speak Cantonese?'—Co-constructing a scientific proof in an EFL junior secondary Science classroom. *International Journal of Bilingual Education and Bilingualism, 18*(3), 289–305.

Lo Bianco, J. (2014). Foreword. In J. Conteh & G. Meier (Eds.), *The multilingual turn in languages education: Opportunities and challenges* (pp. 16–17). Bristol: Multilingual Matters.

Lyster, R. (2007). *Learning and teaching languages through content: A counterbalanced approach*. Amsterdam: John Benjamins.

May, S. (Ed.). (2014). *The multilingual turn: Implications for SLA, TESOL and bilingual education*. London: Routledge.

Pennycook, A. (2001). Lessons from colonial language policies. In R. D. González (Ed.), *Language ideologies: Critical perspectives on the official English movement* (Vol. 2, pp. 195–219). Urbana, IL: National Council of Teachers of English.

Pennycook, A. (2017). Translanguaging and semiotic assemblages. *International Journal of Multilingualism, 14*(3), 269–282.

Pérez-Cañado, M. L. (2012). CLIL research in Europe: Past, present, and future. *International Journal of Bilingual Education and Bilingualism, 15*(3), 315–341.

Rymes, B. (2010). Classroom discourse analysis: A focus on communicative repertoires. In N. Hornberger & S. McKay (Eds.), *Sociolinguistics and language education* (pp. 528–546). Buffalo, NY: Multilingual Matters.

Rymes, B. (2014). Communicative repertoire. In C. Leung & B. V. Street (Eds.), *The Routledge companion to English studies* (pp. 287–301). London: Routledge.

San Isidro, X. (2018). Innovations and challenges in CLIL implementation in Europe. *Theory Into Practice, 57*, 185–195.

Scarino, A. (2014). Situating the challenges in current languages education policy in Australia—Unlearning monolingualism. *International Journal of Multilingualism, 11*(3), 289–306.

Schecter, S., & Cummins, J. (Eds.). (2003). *Multilingual education in practice: Using diversity as a resource*. Portsmouth, NH: Heinemann.

Spence-Brown, R. (2014). On rocky ground: Monolingual educational structures and Japanese language education in Australia. In N. Murray & A. Scarino (Eds.), *Dynamic ecologies, Multilingual education* (pp. 183–198). Dordrecht: Springer.

Swain, M. (1985). Communicative competence: Some roles of comprehensible input and comprehensible output in its development. In S. Gass & C. Madden (Eds.), *Input in Second Language Acquisition* (pp. 235–253). Rowley, MA: Newbury House.

Swain, M. (2000). French immersion research in Canada: recent contributions to SLA and Applied Linguistics. *Annual Review of Applied Linguistics, 20*, 199–212.

Tsung, L. (2014). *Language power and hierarchy: Multilingual education in China*. London: Bloomsbury Academic.

Valdés, G. (2003). *Expanding definitions of giftedness: The case of young interpreters from immigrant communities*. Mahwah, NJ: Lawrence Erlbaum.

Velasco, P., & García, O. (2014). Translanguaging and the writing of bilingual learners. *Bilingual Research Journal, 37*(1), 6–23.

Vygotsky, L. S. (1987). *The collected works of L. S. Vygotsky. Volume 1: Problems of general psychology. Including the volume thinking and speech* (N. Minick, Ed. & Trans.). New York: Plenum.

Part I

Foundations

Part I of this book introduces key concepts and research relevant to the using and learning of languages across the curriculum in mainstream schools. The section is divided into three chapters. In Chap. 2, ways in which language is theorised and understood are summarised. An emerging theory of language—translanguaging—is also discussed in relation to the promotion of multilingualism at school. The backdrop of this book is the institutional dominance of one language (English) and structures of power that lie at the heart of translanguaging theory. In Chap. 3 different approaches to cross-curricular language use and language-related pedagogies are both addressed. Approaches are considered in relation to language distribution, or the instructional time allotted to target languages, as well as students' languages in English-medium classrooms. Language-based pedagogies appear in the same chapter but separately because they are not unique to different kinds of language distribution. Finally, in Chap. 4, a multilingual practices framework developed to explore the leveraging and expanding of students' linguistic repertoire in mainstream schools is explained and discussed.

2

Language and Multilingualism

2.1 Language as a Social Construct

Language is mankind's greatest invention—except, of course, that it was never invented. (Deutscher, 2005)

Language is a social construct in that we, collectively, decide the nature of language. We breathe it into existence and it connects us with other human beings. We can change its properties, but a group consensus is important, since we use language to interact with others. Groups can vary in size; for example, twins making up their own way of talking to each other, or Mandarin Chinese speakers—the largest group of first language speakers of what is considered to be one language in the world. However, for widespread beliefs around the nature of language(s), some institutions (made up of people) are far more influential than others. Everyone has the power to change the properties of language, but the power to convince others to adopt them differs significantly. Dictionaries are a case in point—they can be extremely influential in guiding people's thinking around what words mean. To illustrate, the word 'language' can be defined as 'the method of human communication, either spoken or written, consisting of the use of words in a struc-

© The Author(s) 2019   **19**
M. Turner, *Multilingualism as a Resource and a Goal*,
https://doi.org/10.1007/978-3-030-21591-0_2

tured and conventional way', 'a system of communication used by a particular country or community' and 'the style of a piece of writing or speech' (adapted from the Oxford English Dictionary, 2018).

This definition appears to be straightforward, but it buckles under lived experience. Is language only the domain of the 'structured and conventional'? If this is the case, how do changes in languages occur? When people are creative, at what point are they no longer using language? How are boundaries around a particular system of communication determined? When can a community claim that they are speaking a different language from their surrounding communities or simply a dialect? If a system of communication is used by a particular country or community, does this mean that they can determine language 'rules' or norms if people in other countries or communities engage in a similar system of communication?

Dictionary definitions of language are commonly based on studies of linguistics throughout the twentieth century that were profoundly influenced by the linguist Saussure, who differentiated between what he called *parole* and *langue*. *Parole* refers to what people do with language on a daily basis and *langue* refers to structures and socially shared conventions of language internal to different systems. Saussure understood *parole* to be difficult to study, and chose to focus on *langue*. According to Bourdieu (1991, p. 33), 'the entire destiny of modern linguistics was determined by Saussure's inaugural act through which he separates the "external" elements of linguistics from the "internal" elements […] reserving the title of linguistics for the latter'. The earlier dictionary definition of language is strongly influenced by the concept of *langue* in that it highlights the structures and systems of language rather than what people do with language in their day-to-day lives.

Chomsky, another theorist who has been influential in the field of linguistics, also focused on studying what was less variable when it came to language. He distinguished between *competence* and *performance*, positioning competence as individual, internal and less variable than performance, which he considered to be social, and variable (1986). Chomsky's understanding of more fixed linguistic knowledge was different from Saussure's because it lacked the social element of *langue*, or 'a fund accumulated by the members of the community through the practice of speech' (Saussure, 1983, p. 13). Language learning from a Saussurian viewpoint was an apprenticeship into a social system, whereas Chomsky (2000, p. 7) considered language acquisition to be similar to 'the growth of organs' or 'something that happens to the child, not that the child does'. Saussure's and Chomsky's perspectives demonstrate how language was traditionally more associated with less variable 'internal' elements, and how the nature of these elements has been much debated.

More context-sensitive ways of thinking about language became conspicuous in the second half of the twentieth century. For example, Hymes (1962) argued against Chomsky's (1957) focus on the formal structure of language and for variation and the importance of cultural and social factors in communication. As Hymes (1972, p. 277) said, 'a normal child acquires knowledge of sentences, not only as grammatical, but also as appropriate. He or she acquires competence as to when to speak, when not, and as to what to talk about with whom, when, where, in what manner'. Halliday's later influential theory of language is complementary to this idea of appropriateness and competence but rests on the idea that language is primarily about making meaning and that there is a system of choices which are available to the speaker (see Halliday, 1993). Similar to Hymes' view, for Halliday, a context of culture determines the potential to make meaning. There is also a context of situation, which refers to the day-to-day interactions and practices in which choices are made. As Van Lier (2004) pointed out, Halliday is particularly accessible to educators. From a Hallidayan perspective, language is organised into three macro functions: ideational (the content, the ideas or the substance that is being communicated), interpersonal (the relationship between the participants, including any differences in status) and textual (the way language is organised in order for it to be interpreted in particular ways) (Halliday, 1993, 2009). This understanding of language is inherent in the notion of *register*, which is used to help teachers guide students' understanding of different kinds of texts. Register is made up of field, tenor and mode, and these map against the three macro functions respectively (ibid.).

Another theory of language that has been increasingly influential is that of Bakhtin. He proposed that language 'for the individual consciousness' lay 'on the borderline of oneself and the other' (1981, p. 293). When we speak, we are always responding to what has gone before and antici-

22   M. Turner

pating what will come after, seeking to imprint ourselves on the language we choose. For Bakhtin (1981), there is an ongoing tension between more fixed, sociohistorically situated forms of language and what he termed *heteroglossia*—the way we are creative with language, making it our own. Heteroglossia is now used as a theoretical base for the argument that speakers draw from one linguistic repertoire, rather than from separate languages, and make choices depending on the social interactions in which they find themselves (e.g., Creese & Blackledge, 2010; García & Li, 2014; Li & Zhu, 2013). Bakhtin understood heteroglossia to occur within one language, but this is theoretically consistent with bi/multilingualism if we think of different languages as belonging to one linguistic repertoire that contains 'multiple co-existing norms' (García, 2009, p. 117). Bakhtin's dialogic view of language as inclusive of tension-filled creativity and transformation on the part of the individual consciousness helps develop our understanding of language(s)-as-social-practice. Like Halliday, Bakhtin's theory involves choices that people constantly make about language, but the dialogic nature of these choices is highlighted above all—the push towards self-expression and the pull towards what's gone before.

More recently, Thibault (2011) has also theorised the relationship between language-as-social-practice and language-as-system by focusing on what speakers do. He used the term *first-order languaging* to describe speakers' social practices and *second-order language* to refer to 'stabilised cultural patterns on longer, slower cultural timescales' (Thibault, 2011, p. 216). Thibault was clear that his primary focus was on social practice (by calling it first-order languaging) and also showed that language-as-a-system (second-order language) is subject to change, but over a longer period of time. It is, therefore, possible to consider that second-order language can be harnessed as a way to expand people's linguistic repertoire, or what they are able to do with language. Thibault discussed second-order language only in relation to one language (English), but these stabilised cultural patterns can also be considered to exist for other languages.

2.2 Language as a Political Tool

Language is an invention. (Makoni & Pennycook, 2007)

Theories of language thus show increasing engagement with the day-to-day social interactions that make up people's language use. Alongside research into language practices has come an understanding of language as political and firmly entrenched in structures of power. Language can become a deliberate invention (as opposed to Thibault's more gradual patterns) when the extent of the agency—or power—of some groups of humans is taken into account. This is particularly apparent in colonial contexts where European powers decided what were to be considered languages. Given the political nature of this naming and boundary-making, Makoni and Pennycook (2007) called for the 'disinvention' and reconstitution of languages. Lemke (2016) also pointed out that political programmes of control and homogenisation created national languages and that the linguistic definition of a language variety 'depends on an imagined and exaggerated homogeneity of usage among speakers'. Prescribing boundaries is openly acknowledged by linguists to be problematic. For example, a look at the Ethnologue (2018) website showed the number of languages spoken globally to be 7099, but the writers add a caveat. They state that this number is notional since what we understand languages to be is constantly changing, and also cite the speed at which we continue to lose what have been officially categorised as distinct languages.

However, even with this caveat, the social construction of languages as discrete and separate is an extremely powerful one in our minds. This is perhaps most clearly encapsulated in the notion of a 'native' speaker, and the idea that only a privileged group of people can properly speak a language. The privileged group of people then act as gatekeepers for the language, officially as well as unofficially. For example, in English-speaking countries, tests such as the International English Language Testing System (IELTS) and the Test of English as a Foreign Language (TOEFL) have

24   M. Turner

enormous influence on international students' opportunities to study in higher education institutions, and can also be a requirement for different visas. If there are any discrepancies between different *Englishes* or ways to structure communication, then these tests are commonly upheld as conforming to a perceived ideal standard. Unofficially, the way that people and institutions talk about the language of native speakers as a model to follow shows the power of this imagined ideal. The native/non-native debate has predominantly focused on speakers of English (Holliday, 2006) because discussion has principally occurred as a result of the issue of political inequality (e.g., Canagarajah, 1999; Holliday, 2006; Pennycook, 1994). However, political inequality also extends beyond English to other languages of prestige—Creese, Blackledge and Takhi (2014, p. 938) considered the notion of 'native speaker' to refer to 'speakers of economically powerful languages with a secure national base'. This might not always be the case (see, for example, Ó Murchadha & Flynn, 2018, for a discussion on varieties of Irish), but the idea of prestige is key to native speakerism. From a pedagogical perspective, the task of teaching native-speaker norms is also an artificial enterprise; there is so much variation in the way so-called native speakers communicate—they do not conform to one set standard (see Kramsch, 1997).

Along with the issues of gatekeeping and artifice, native speakerism has been questioned on linguistic and pragmatic grounds (Árva & Medgyes, 2000). In linguistic terms, it does not make sense to call a speaker 'non-native' if they speak the language fluently, it is a common language in their country and they have always spoken it. Is a French speaker hailing from Cameroon a native or non-native French speaker, for example? In some people's minds, the native speaker group might be more flexible and incorporate a wider range of speakers, whereas in other people's minds, it might be more inflexible. Also, growing up with more than one language may preclude an individual from being considered a native speaker. The pragmatic, or practical, contestation of the native/non-native dichotomy refers to individual confusion in contexts of diversity where children of immigrants may be unsure about whether or not they are native speakers of their parents' language(s)—from the children's point of view, what level of fluency does this require?—and/or a societal language in which they communicate as they grow up.

Even though the native/non-native categorisation is no longer accepted in any rigorous academic sense, it maintains currency, having 'evolved from some roughly intuitive generalization of perceived differences among people with a diversity of expertise and experience as language users' (Moussu & Llurda, 2008, p. 318). This intuitive generalisation is understandable and to ignore it is counterproductive. If the objective of language education, for example, is to learn language, however we conceptualise this, it is helpful to recognise that some people have more expertise and experience with particular languages than others. It is also helpful to recognise that, even if we try to deconstruct native speakerism, we may still be left with what Kramsch (2012) referred to as 'imposture', or individuals struggling with feelings of inauthenticity and illegitimacy because they do not know how and if they fit in, and may not even be certain that they want to. The idea of imposture will be discussed further in relation to students' engagement with languages in Chap. 4.

2.3 Bi/Multilingualism

Our understanding of the nature of language, including its social construction, impacts on the way we think about bi/multilingualism and how we use what we identify as different languages. Perhaps the most influential aspect of how we think about bi/multilingualism is our positioning of boundaries between languages and our subsequent views on mastery. The political construct of the native/non-native speaker discussed earlier is a very good illustration. The two ways of thinking about bi/multilingualism that I will explore in this section have different foci. The first, the monoglossic view (also known as monolingual and fractional), has a greater emphasis on language as a bounded system. The second, the heteroglossic view (also known as holistic), has a greater emphasis on language-as-social-practice. The second view has been gaining a lot of ground in literature on TESOL and bilingual education. However, the first is still very conspicuous in the way language teaching and learning is understood and implemented in real-world contexts.

First, the monoglossic view of bi/multilingualism draws on the understanding that each language is a system that is to be kept separate from

26   M. Turner

other systems. A speaker's ability to achieve cognitive separation of languages is a priority since this separation is the closest approximation possible to a monolingual speaker—the monolingual speaker is the point of reference (Baker & Wright, 2017). Terms such as symmetrical, maximal and balanced are used to describe the objective of 'native-like' proficiency in two languages (de Jong, 2011, p. 51). A focus on varying skill levels is evident in terms such as dominant bilingual, receptive bilingual, productive bilingual and semi-bilingual (Li, 2000). The word 'semi-lingual' has also been around since the 1970s and this word refers to unequal ability in two languages. Both the term semi-lingual and associated terms have been found to be disparaging and connotative of failure (Baker & Wright, 2017).

The monoglossic perspective is understood to be both subtractive and additive. A subtractive framework supports language shift, or a transition to the majority language. Speaking the majority language is the goal and it is not considered important whether or not a speaker retains her/his original language (García, 2009). This can be considered a deficit model in that the speaker's competence is attached only to the majority language under study and not any other language the speaker might know. An additive framework supports the learning of another language while maintaining a first language. Similar to the subtractive framework, García (2009) considered an additive framework to be monoglossic in that the languages are considered to be compartmentalised and speakers are viewed as operating in two distinct languages and cultures, or as learning within a separatist paradigm. However, this has recently been critiqued by Cummins (2017) because much of the literature on additive bilingualism has focused on the use of home language in minority contexts aimed to help language minority speakers bring all their linguistic resources to bear when learning a majority language. Cummins proposed the term 'active bilingualism' so that this 'additive bilingualism' literature could be understood as aligning with a heteroglossic perspective.

The heteroglossic perspective primarily takes Bakhtin's idea of heteroglossia to focus on what people do with language. In this view, interlocutors are considered to draw on one linguistic repertoire: 'the language practices of bilinguals are complex and interrelated; they do not emerge in a linear way or function separately since there is only one linguistic system' (García & Li, 2014, p. 14). From this it follows that context or domains of use are very important. Discussions of language proficiency need to take into account where the language is used (de Jong, 2011). Complete mastery is not possible because no one can take part in every type of social interaction, and language competence is tied to situated practices, such as playing/socialising with friends, working and studying. As Baker and Wright (2017, p. 12) put it, from this perspective 'a bilingual is a complete linguistic entity, an integrated whole'.

The monoglossic and heteroglossic views reflect the notion of languages as relatively closed systems and as fluid social practices respectively. These views also show different levels of engagement with social inequity and the way that languages are inextricably linked to their speakers. However, institutional realities commonly call for language standardisation and measurement against this standardisation. A succinct summary of the issues related to this institutional standardisation is offered by Gajo (2014, p. 136) in his discussion on the complexities of the plurilingual focus in Europe. He saw a heteroglossic focus mainly as 'related to everyday or "street" language […] and in the negotiation of complex identities', and 'as not necessarily [able to] capture the specific features and constraints of institutional contexts, in which actors are supposed to use given codes and are considered as more or less competent'. Working with the features and constraints of institutional contexts (mainstream schools), whilst moving towards a heteroglossic understanding of language in the classroom, does not have to be mutually exclusive, and this idea is explored in the book.

2.4 Translanguaging

One way to move towards a heteroglossic view of language is to draw on translanguaging theory. Originally, the term translanguaging was used to show how two languages could be structured into teaching and learning in Welsh–English bilingual education in Wales. Students received input in one language and generated output in the other and then the process was reversed so that students used the two languages both receptively and productively (Baker, 2003; Williams, 1994). García (2009) borrowed the term and linked it to a heteroglossic way of thinking. Translanguaging

28   M. Turner

theory was then generated in the context of minority speakers in a learning environment where English prevailed as a dominant language (e.g., García & Li, 2014; García & Lin, 2016; Li & Zhu, 2013).

A translanguaging perspective offers a way of thinking that counteracts the deficit view of emergent bilinguals in particular, and focuses in increasingly targeted ways on the sophistication of what speakers can already do with language. Showing what bilinguals and emerging bilinguals can do is important because monoglossic understandings of language have historically hidden this. De Jong (2011, p. 54), for example, drew attention to the problematic nature of testing bilingual children using their 'stronger' language, noting that 'it is unlikely that children acquire their languages under exactly the same conditions or that they are exposed to the same language patterns in both languages'. Minority speakers can further be judged to be 'at risk' even when they are capable of the same range of grammatical features as more fluent speakers (Valadez, MacSwan, & Martínez, 2002).

The social imperative to confront inequity experienced by minority language speakers has led to translanguaging being conceptualised as a political act (Flores, 2014), and also as being linked to circumstantial bilingualism, or speakers who are bilingual (or emerging bilingual) through circumstance rather than choice (see Valdés, 2003). Drawing on Derrida's understanding of being born 'into' speaking different languages, García and Li (2014, p. 18) maintained that 'the term *translanguaging* offers a way of capturing the expanded complex practices of speakers who could not avoid having had languages inscribed in their body, and yet live between different societal and semiotic contexts as they interact with a complex array of speakers'. These language practices do not only include named languages but also language varieties, such as informal and formal, and different kinds of regional *Englishes* (García, 2009) and other languages (for example, see Zentella, 1997 for the complexity of Latinx linguistic codes).

Translanguaging can be applied in the classroom for different kinds of purposes. For example, it can help students to co-construct knowledge and also to display it (e.g., Gumperz & Cook-Gumperz, 2005; Martin-Beltrán, 2014), promote metalinguistic awareness and develop language resources (e.g., García & Kano, 2014; Lewis, Jones, & Baker,

2012; Martin-Beltrán, 2014), affirm multilingual identities (e.g., Cenoz & Gorter, 2011; Lin & He, 2017) and support social justice and critical reflection on language inequality (e.g., Flores & García, 2017; García & Li, 2014). This final purpose can be related to an understanding of power and privilege as integral to social relationships, of the structured nature of inequity, and of how we are positioned in relation to these structures (Freire, 1970). When offering their pedagogical goals for translanguaging, García and Li (2014) also differentiated instructional goals (the construction and demonstration of knowledge) for monolingual, bilingual and emergent bilingual students and highlighted the flexibility of language practices and the development of background knowledge. They broadly categorised translanguaging pedagogical goals as the appropriation and communication of knowledge, the development of new practices and the maintenance of old practices, and the interrogation of inequality through identity affirmation and critique (ibid.).

From a translanguaging perspective, the language practices of the speaker, rather than named languages such as English, Chinese and Italian, are highlighted, and linguistic repertoire is referred to as an 'idiolect' (Otheguy, García, & Reid, 2015). Given that the questioning of linguistic inequality is an important goal of translanguaging (Blackledge & Creese, 2010; García, 2009; Hornberger & Link, 2012; Lin & Lo, 2017), the emphasis on the speaker's idiolect is a way to move the principal focus away from named languages and associated hierarchies of power. Taking the speaker as a linguistic point of departure, as opposed to a particular language, also highlights the dynamics of identity: translanguaging is understood to be identity performance (Blackledge & Creese, 2010; García & Li, 2014).

In the context of formal schooling, however, operating within language hierarchies is usually a reality. In their discussion on translanguaging in the classroom, Hornberger and Link (2012, p. 243) emphasised the benefits of a translanguaging perspective, but drew attention to potential constraints. Working in the US, they asked themselves: 'In the current US education policy climate of homogenized curricula and assessment practices, how might educators resist the pressure to subordinate translanguaging and eschew it as a teaching tool?' In response to this question, they devised a 'continua of biliteracy' framework. This framework provided a set of lenses to help educators think about the combination of bilingualism and literacy in the classroom in relation to hierarchies and power structures. In this framework, Hornberger and Link (2012) understood the three factors—micro, oral and bi(multi)lingual—to be traditionally less powerful than their counterparts—macro, literate and monolingual. They also showed in the framework that the macro, literate, monolingual focus was reflected in the importance attributed to decontextualised writing (writing for an unknown audience) and the separation of languages, which they referred to as successive, as opposed to simultaneous, exposure to languages.

Hornberger and Link (2012) pointed out that, although translanguaging is associated with the traditionally less powerful language practices, it can be implemented and promoted in the classroom in beneficial ways. Attaching value to what students do with their language and the contexts of language use can help move students towards different learning objectives because the teacher is simultaneously validating what the students know and gaining an understanding that can then help them leverage student knowledge for subsequent learning. The political sense of the translanguaging concept is important given the need to tackle the language deficit view towards minority speakers that is so prevalent in monoglossic views of language, and so influential in the abandonment of heritage languages.

2.5 The Nature of Linguistic Repertoire

Translanguaging theory embraces students' linguistic resources as intrinsically valuable and not just a way to transition to a dominant language. This validation and celebration of what the students bring with them to the classroom has been conspicuous in TESOL literature for the past 30 years, and will be discussed in Chap. 3 in relation to this literature. The novel, and more recent, assertion associated with translanguaging is the deconstruction of monolingual, bounded understandings of 'named' languages such as English, Japanese and French, and a focus on language as emerging from one linguistic repertoire. This assertion has resulted from sociolinguists doubting whether or not discrete languages exist (e.g., Blommaert, 2010; Harris, 1981; Heller, 2007; Kravchenko, 2007; Makoni & Pennycook, 2007). Historically, the alternation of different language resources has taken discrete languages as a point of departure and been named code-switching, code-switching which implies that languages are codes with relatively stable boundaries (see Lin, 2013). For translanguaging theorists, translanguaging is not code-switching because speakers are not drawing from different language systems but from one unitary system (e.g., Otheguy et al., 2015). An important issue when considering how translanguaging theory can be applied to the idea of language learning in particular is conceptualising how to expand—or add to—this system. Previously, a student would expand their knowledge of, and ability to use, a particular bounded system associated with a particular language. From a translanguaging perspective, what does this now look like?

The idea of different systems for different languages can be an intuitive one, as can the notion of linguistic distance and proximity. For example, learning Japanese (as an adolescent) and Spanish (as an adult), any direct translations I hazarded from English to Spanish were generally better understood than those from English to Japanese. MacSwan (2017) discussed this idea of similarity and difference between languages in relation to mental grammars. He argued against the idea that bi/multilinguals have fully discrete linguistic systems attached to each language they speak, but also against the translanguaging idea of a unitary model in which bi/multilinguals were only drawing upon one system. For MacSwan (ibid.), mental grammars can be both shared and discrete. Linguistic resources used by bi/multilinguals can be understood to overlap, but not always. While endorsing the translanguaging project of allowing minority children full access to their linguistic repertoire, MacSwan also emphasised the importance of viewing our linguistic knowledge—or internal rule systems that create linguistic patterns—as 'internally diverse'. If we think of everyone's linguistic resources as emerging from one system, the linguistic diversity of students who are bi/multilingual is difficult to discuss, celebrate and promote. It is also difficult to encourage the expansion of linguistic repertoire without the recognition of rule systems that govern the way we talk, even when we are being creative and using the full breadth of our resources. Research on code-

32   M. Turner

switching has revealed that some things sound more 'right' to bilinguals than others when they are using different kinds of language resources in the same sentence, and this led MacSwan (ibid., p. 181) to assert that 'bilingualism is psychologically real—that is, an actual part of our linguistic knowledge'.

MacSwan was thus not arguing that languages are bounded and discrete, but rather offering an understanding of internal rule systems, and how these systems apply to bi/multilingual language practices. If we take an even wider view, it is not only these rule systems that may be guiding language practices, but also an individual's experiences in the world. Lemke, in an interview with Lin (Lin, Wu, & Lemke, forthcoming, p. 3), discussed this idea in relation to translanguaging performances, which he understood to be 'not as tightly structured as formal written grammars would dictate, but [...] not so loosely structured that anything is possible, any mix is possible'. Lemke viewed translanguaging performances (and language performances in general) as something that occur as a result of what has happened to an individual. Taking a physics perspective that emphasises dynamic processes over material objects, Lemke conceptualised the individual as the nexus of language that has passed, or flowed, through her/him, and as part of different communities 'in which these various resources and meanings and ways of speaking have connected you to other people, connected you to written texts, connected you to just walking around in the world, in an ecosystem' (Lin et al., forthcoming, p. 10).

Familiarity with particular language resources may be important, but only in relation to the performances that arise from one's positioning in (and connections with) the world. The effort involved in gaining this familiarity is well known to those amongst us who were born and raised with one language and came to bi/multilingualism late, and now appears to be supported by neuroimaging research conducted on the representation and processing of two or more languages (see Del Maschio & Abutalebi, 2018 for a review). The neural network responsible for language has been found to process different languages in a similar fashion for people considered to be highly proficient bilinguals, but variations have been found to occur as a result of differences in proficiency. When proficiency in a language is low, greater neural activity has been found, including outside the usual language network in areas related to executive control (Del Maschio & Abutalebi, 2018). This indicates that language is processed differently when it has not yet been automatised, and is more demanding before this time, possibly because of the need to suppress the more familiar language/languages (ibid.). The finding supports the idea that the expansion of linguistic repertoire may require effort, and the automatisation of language performances may be an important factor in language use in any form.

2.6 Widening the Lens

Translanguaging theory currently focuses more strongly on bi/multilinguals' language practices and their richness, rather than helping them arrive at these practices if their linguistic resources are mainly associated with a dominant language. It is a theory that is concerned with structures of power and disrupting the language deficit view so often attached to minority language speakers. So how is it beneficial when we are thinking about leveraging and expanding the linguistic repertoire of all students, including those who have limited or no exposure to another language? Additionally, even if this is beneficial, how does it speak back to unequal power structures? In this section, I will attempt to address these questions, first in relation to the potential of translanguaging to help students communicate using different languages, and then in relation to the potential diversity of students' language experiences. I will approach the second sub-question on a more societal level, in relation to social cohesion, but I will also discuss the challenge at the root of social inequity.

First, the potential of translanguaging for speakers with little or no exposure to any other language than the dominant one at school lies in its focus on linguistic repertoire rather than on the learning of named languages. This focus allows a side-stepping of the unattainable deficit-oriented goal of becoming a native speaker in a language, and instead can help highlight the use of named languages as a tool to expand students' language resources. Students can then learn French, for example, to increase their linguistic repertoire—the main focus being on the extension of their language practices, rather than on French. They still learn

34   M. Turner

French but this change of focus means that the students (what they currently do and want to do with language in general) are central and French becomes the tool to expand their linguistic range.

Thinking about language in this way can help us consider the diversity of students' and teachers' language experiences. For example, if we take the teaching and learning of Japanese in Australia—the main target language that appears across the settings in the book—in a class where the learning of *kanji* (Chinese characters) is the focus, the linguistic repertoire of a Chinese international student may not be expanding to the same degree as that of a student who only speaks English at home. Rather than thinking of these *kanji* as either Japanese or Chinese, we can simply think of them as part of the international student's language resources, and something the other student is learning for the first time. Expanding the linguistic repertoire for these two students may look different even though both students may have approximately the same degree of spoken proficiency in Japanese.

This kind of issue is particularly conspicuous when considering cross-curricular use of different languages. In language classrooms, a structured, developmental approach to language learning allows the Chinese international student to sit back and take a nap while everyone else learns the curriculum-specified *kanji* that she/he already knows. However, ways to use languages across the curriculum can be less clear, given both uneven proficiency and the often limited proficiency of majority language speakers in a target language chosen by the school. A translanguaging perspective can help determine relevant and realistic objectives that promote language use to stakeholders, especially to those who might be somewhat confronted with the idea of different languages across the curriculum and/or be disengaged with language learning in general. Languages can be embedded in what students do, and specific objectives can either directly or indirectly show the expansion of linguistic repertoire.

It is important to note that a focus on the expansion of linguistic repertoire does not always need to include moving between different languages (and language varieties) in class. If the student is only exposed to the target language at school, this language may need to be promoted in strategic ways. The neuroimaging research discussed in the previous section indicates that the use of non-automatised language is effortful, and may therefore be avoided by students—the relevance of motivation to language use is discussed in Chap. 4. In their discussion on the role of language status in immersion education, Ballinger, Lyster, Sterzuk and Genesee (2017) were cautious about the use of a majority language in a minority language classroom. Translanguaging has been attracting much attention from teachers and researchers, and Ballinger et al. argued that 'multiple uses of the term render it vague for many in the field of second language education, which can lead to misunderstandings' (2017, p. 36). In this book, I am most interested in the creation of opportunities where the *faculty* to translanguage is enhanced, or where all students' repertoires have the potential to be expanded in situated contexts of use.

Translanguaging theory addresses the significant influence of language hierarchies on the education of bi/multilingual and emergent bi/multilingual students, and these language hierarchies also apply to majority language speakers if multilingualism is to be promoted in mainstream schools. In order to include different student profiles in the discussion, I use Ballinger et al.'s (2017) term *crosslinguistic pedagogy* when I discuss how languages are structured into the classroom. Working with majority language speakers in an immersion context, Ballinger et al. (2017, p. 36) stated that '[w]e use the term "crosslinguistic pedagogy" to refer to practices that may, or may not be, grounded in translanguaging theory'. In the book, when discussing how teachers structure languages into the classroom, I use the term to refer to practices that are not necessarily grounded in translanguaging but I also emphasise, through discussion, how working towards translanguaging pedagogical goals can be conceptualised for all students. Any school-based activity that involves the planned use of more than one language is referred to as crosslinguistic pedagogy. A strategic focus on meaning-making through the inclusion of practices from more than one language is conceptualised as translanguaging: crosslinguistic pedagogy is used as an umbrella term under which translanguaging sits. Examples of what does and does not constitute translanguaging (taken from García & Li, 2014) are provided in the final section of Chap. 3.

By considering the expansion of majority language speakers' linguistic repertoires, my intention is not to dilute an important point of departure of translanguaging theory, which is the social inequity that is intrinsic to linguistic hierarchies. However, it can be difficult to value what you have not experienced. If students only engage with the dominant language, it is difficult for them to have any real sense of what bi/multilinguals know. At a societal level, this might also lead people to understand the use of more than one language to be a problem, especially in institutional domains. Use of other languages has long been framed in this way. For example, in 1917, Theodore Roosevelt understood the perpetuation of different languages to be contrary to American interests and, in the 1980s, Ronald Reagan supported this view by directly naming bilingual education programmes as anti-American (see Baker & Wright, 2017). This language-as-problem view is alive and well, as attested by a website dedicated to making English the official language of the US (http://www.usenglish.org/).

In order to make sense of different language-related ideologies, Ruiz (1984) offered three orientations: language-as-problem (the orientation stated earlier), language-as-right and language-as-resource. The second orientation—language-as-right—focuses on the minority speakers and their basic human rights. This orientation emphasises that there is no place for language discrimination and prejudice in democratic societies. The language-as-problem orientation, therefore, takes a view of social cohesion from a majority perspective—cohesion is strengthened if we all speak the majority language. The language-as-right positions social cohesion from the minority perspective: cohesion needs to take into account how we treat people, and languages are intrinsically connected to who people are. The final orientation offered by Ruiz (1984) is language-as-resource and, in this orientation, Ruiz seeks to show the connections between majority and minority speakers. The language-as-resource orientation focuses on the benefits of bi/multilingualism for groups and individuals, or how the ability to communicate with different groups of people (and think differently) is beneficial in a range of ways. Lo Bianco (2001) further breaks these benefits down into six dimensions: cognitive, cultural, economic, social, civic participation and language rights. Within the orientation as a whole, social cohesion is conceptualised as the coexistence of national unity and linguistic diversity: 'tolerance and cooperation between groups may be possible with linguistic diversity' and

2 Language and Multilingualism 37

'would be unlikely when such linguistic diversity is repressed' (Baker & Wright, 2017, p. 380).

In this book, I take a language-as-resource approach to social cohesion, which complements translanguaging pedagogies and practices for minority students (see Baker & Wright, 2017). More specifically, I take a multilingualism-as-resource orientation. This is an orientation developed from Ruiz' (1984) and Lo Bianco's (2001) thinking on language-as-resource by de Jong, Li, Zafar, and Wu (2016), and it highlights the lived multilingual realities of bi/multilingual students. My aim is to explore multilingualism for all students, which includes expanding students' linguistic repertoires as well as validating, fostering and leveraging existing repertoires. Thus, I explicitly position multilingualism as a goal as well as a resource. Multilingualism as a resource and a goal promotes the idea of bi/multilingualism—all students learning and using more than one language, including the majority language. Given the power of the language-as-problem orientation, majority speakers may have minority speaker parents who have not taught them their heritage language(s). The overarching multilingual practices framework I discuss in the book was generated to help deal systemically with the diversity of backgrounds that is so often a reality in mainstream schools.

However, it is important to note that hierarchies of power and status are not only linguistic. The interactions in which the hierarchies reside are inherently social, and favour some groups over others. Providing majority speakers with more opportunity to learn languages—one field in which minority speakers who also speak English can have an advantage—may result in inequity; for example, if the minority speakers lose this relative advantage, and are passed over for future jobs. Flores and García (2017) draw attention to the issue of inequity in their critique of dual-language immersion programmes in the US (to be discussed in the next chapter) as favouring white middle-class students over lower-income Latinx students. They view a move from bilingual education in racialised basements, to which Latinx students were previously relegated, to 'boutique' programmes that included majority language speakers, as perpetuating racial hierarchies (ibid.). The idea of seeking to help *all* students, rather than having a sole focus on minoritised students, has been linked to 'interest convergence', or an overlapping of the interests of minority and majority students (Bell, 1980). Mutual benefit is key: the interests of majority language speakers should not be prioritised over those of minority speakers (see Zitlali Morales & Maravilla-Cano, 2019). An interrogation of power structures is important, and translanguaging theory is applied in this book as a way to emphasise the sociopolitical dimensions of language learning and use at school. A fundamental goal is to work towards equity as much as possible and have it as an organising principle in the learning and leveraging of languages (e.g., Palmer, Cervantes-Soon, Dorner, & Heiman, 2019; Zitlali Morales & Maravilla-Cano, 2019).

2.7 Conclusion

Language-as-social-practice offers a useful frame for thinking about language learning and use across the curriculum in mainstream schools because it takes the speaker, rather than different language systems, as the point of departure. Translanguaging theory and its origins offer a way of thinking about language holistically, and richly, as linguistic repertoire. Translanguaging has mainly been aimed at minority speakers, but I expand the lens to include majority language (English) speakers who have limited—or no—exposure to a language other than English outside school. This includes students with a heritage language they do not speak. I aim to retain an important foundation of translanguaging theory, which positions bi/multilinguals as sophisticated language users. A significant part of this aim is to disrupt the monolingual notion that languages need to be kept separate by exploring how students' linguistic resources may be beneficial to the learning of language, to different subject areas and—not least—to student engagement.

References

Árva, V., & Medgyes, P. (2000). Native and non-native teachers in the classroom. *System, 28*, 355–372.

Baker, C. (2003). Biliteracy and transliteracy in Wales: Language planning and the Welsh national curriculum. In N. H. Hornberger (Ed.), *Continua of biliteracy: An ecological framework for educational policy, research, and practice in multilingual settings*. Clevedon: Multilingual Matters.

Baker, C., & Wright, W. E. (2017). *Foundations of bilingual education and bilingualism* (6th ed.). Bristol: Multilingual Matters.

Bakhtin, M. M. (1981). *The dialogic imagination: Four essays by M.M. Bakhtin* (C. Emerson & M. Holquist, Trans. & M. Holquist, Ed.). Austin, TX: University of Texas Press.

Ballinger, S., Lyster, R., Sterzuk, A., & Genesee, F. (2017). Context-appropriate crosslinguistic pedagogy: Considering the role of language status in immersion education. *Journal of Immersion and Content-Based Language Education, 5*(1), 30–57.

Bell, D. A. (1980). Brown v. board of education and the interest convergence dilemma. *Harvard Law Review, 93*, 518–533.

Blackledge, A., & Creese, A. (2010). *Multilingualism: A Critical Perspective*. London, UK: Continuum.

Blommaert, J. (2010). *The sociolinguistics of globalization*. Cambridge: Cambridge University Press.

Bourdieu, P. (1991). *Language and symbolic power*. London: Polity Press.

Canagarajah, S. (1999). *Resisting linguistic imperialism*. Oxford: Oxford University Press.

Cenoz, J., & Gorter, D. (2011). Focus on multilingualism: A study of trilingual writing. *The Modern Language Journal, 95*, 356–369.

Chomsky, N. (1957). *Syntactic structures*. The Hague: Mouton.

Chomsky, N. (1986). *Knowledge of language: Its nature, origin and use*. New York: Praeger.

Chomsky, N. (2000). *New horizons in the study of language and mind*. Cambridge: Cambridge University Press.

Creese, A., & Blackledge, A. (2010). Translanguaging in the bilingual classroom: A pedagogy for learning and teaching? *The Modern Language Journal, 94*, 103–115.

Creese, A., Blackledge, A., & Takhi, J. (2014). The ideal 'native speaker' teacher: Negotiating authenticity and legitimacy in the language classroom. *The Modern Language Journal, 98*(4), 937–951.

Cummins, J. (2017). Teaching minoritised students: Are additive approaches legitimate? *Harvard Educational Review, 87*(3), 404–425.

de Jong, E. J. (2011). *Foundations for multilingualism in education: From principles to practice*. Philadelphia, PA: Caslon Publishing.

de Jong, E. J., Li, Z., Zafar, A. M., & Wu, C. (2016). Language policy in multilingual contexts: Revisiting Ruiz's 'language-as-resource' orientation. *Bilingual Research Journal, 39*(3–4), 200–212. https://doi.org/10.1080/1523 5882.2016.1224988

de Saussure, F. (1907/1983). *Course in general linguistics*. La Salle, IL: Open Court.

Del Maschio, N., & Abutalebi, J. (2018). Neurobiology of bilingualism. In D. Miller, F. Bayram, J. Rothman, & L. Serratrice (Eds.), *Bilingual cognition and language: The state of the science across its subfields* (pp. 325–345). Amsterdam: John Benjamins Publishing.

Deutscher, G. (2005). *The unfolding of language*. London: Macmillan.

Ethnologue. (2018). *Languages of the world*. Retrieved February 26, 2018, from https://www.ethnologue.com/

Flores, N. (2014). *Let's not Forget that Translanguaging is a Political Act*. Retrieved 12 November, 2018, from https://educationallinguist.wordpress.com/2014/07/19/lets-not-forget-that-translanguaging-is-a-political-act/

Flores, N., & García, O. (2017). A critical review of bilingual education in the United States: From basements and pride to boutiques and profit. *Annual Review of Applied Linguistics, 37*, 14–29.

Freire, P. (1970). *Pedagogy of the oppressed*. New York: Herder & Herder.

Gajo, L. (2014). From normalization to didactization of multilingualism: European and Francophone research at the crossroads between linguistics and didactics. In J. Conteh & G. Meier (Eds.), *The multilingual turn in languages education: Opportunities and challenges* (pp. 131–175). Bristol: Multilingual Matters.

García, O. (2009). *Bilingual education in the 21st century: A global perspective*. Malden, MA: Wiley-Blackwell.

García, O., & Kano, N. (2014). Translanguaging as process and pedagogy: Developing the English writing of Japanese students in the U.S. In J. Conteh & G. Meier (Eds.), *The multilingual turn in languages education: Benefits for individuals and societies* (pp. 258–277). Clevedon: Multilingual Matters.

García, O., & Li, W. (2014). *Translanguaging: Language, bilingualism and education*. New York: Palgrave Macmillan.

García, O., & Lin, A. M. Y. (2016). Translanguaging in bilingual education. In O. García, A. M. Y. Lin, & S. May (Eds.), *Bilingual and multilingual education (Encyclopedia of language and education)* (pp. 117–130). Cham: Springer.

Gumperz, J. J., & Cook-Gumperz, J. (2005). Making space for bilingual communicative practice. *Intercultural Pragmatics, 2*(1), 1–23.

Halliday, M. A. K. (1993). Towards a language-based theory of learning. *Linguistics and Education, 5*(2), 93–116.

2 Language and Multilingualism   41

Halliday, M. A. K. (2009). *The essential Halliday*. London: Continuum.

Harris, R. (1981). *The language myth*. London: Duckworth.

Heller, M. (2007). *Bilingualism: A social approach*. New York: Palgrave Macmillan.

Holliday, A. (2006). Key concepts in ELT: Native-speakerism. *ELT Journal, 60*(4), 385–387.

Hornberger, N., & Link, H. (2012). Translanguaging in today's classrooms: A biliteracy lens. *Theory Into Practice, 51*, 239–247.

Hymes, D. H. (1962). The ethnography of speaking. In T. Gladwin & W. C. Sturtevant (Eds.), *Anthropology and human behavior* (pp. 15–53). Washington, DC: Anthropological Society of Washington.

Hymes, D. H. (1972). On communicative competence. In J. B. Pride & J. Holmes (Eds.), *Sociolinguistics: Selected readings* (pp. 269–293). Harmondsworth: Penguin.

Kramsch, C. (1997). The privilege of the nonnative speaker. *PMLA, 112*, 359–369.

Kramsch, C. (2012). Authenticity and legitimacy in multilingual SLA. *Critical Multilingualism Studies, 1*, 107–128.

Kravchenko, A. V. (2007). Essential properties of language, or, why language is not a code. *Language Sciences, 29*(5), 650–671.

Lemke, J. L. (2016). *Translanguaging and flows*. Unpublished research manuscript.

Lewis, G. W., Jones, B., & Baker, C. (2012). Translanguaging: origins and development from school to street and beyond. *Educational Research & Evaluation, 18*, 641–654.

Li, W. (2000). Dimensions of bilingualism. In W. Li (Ed.), *The bilingualism reader* (pp. 3–25). New York: Routledge.

Li, W., & Zhu, H. (2013). Translanguaging identities and ideologies: Creating transnational space through flexible multilingual practices amongst Chinese university students in the UK. *Applied Linguistics, 34*(5), 516–535.

Lin, A. M. Y., & He, P. (2017). Translanguaging as dynamic activity flows in CLIL classrooms. *Journal of Language, Identity & Education, 16*, 228–244. https://doi.org/10.1080/15348458.2017.1328283

Lin, A. M. Y. (2013). Classroom code-switching: Three decades of research. *Applied Linguistics Review, 4*(1), 195–218.

Lin, A. M. Y., & Lo, Y. Y. (2017). Trans/languaging and the triadic dialogue in content and language integrated learning (CLIL) classrooms. *Language and Education, 31*(1), 26–45.

Lin, A. M. Y., Wu, Y. M., & Lemke, J. L. (forthcoming). 'It takes a village to research a village': Conversations with Jay Lemke on contemporary issues in

42   M. Turner

translanguaging. In S. Lau & S. V. V. Stille (Eds.), *Critical plurilingual pedagogies: Struggling toward equity rather than equality.* Cham: Springer. http://www.grape.uji.es/wordpress/wpcontent/uploads/2018/11/Lin-Wu-Lemke_Conversations-with-Jay-Lemke-on-Translanguaging_Clean-Version-1.pdf

Lo Bianco, J. (2001). *Language and literacy policy in Scotland—SCILT.* Retrieved from http://www.scilt.org.uk/Portals/24/Library/publications/languageandliteracy/Language%20and%20literacy%20policy%20in%20Scotland_full%20document.pdf

MacSwan, J. (2017). A multilingual perspective on translanguaging. *American Educational Research Journal, 54*(1), 167–201.

Makoni, S., & Pennycook, A. (2007). Disinventing and reconstituting languages. In S. Makoni & A. Pennycook (Eds.), *Disinventing and reconstituting languages* (pp. 1–41). Clevedon: Multilingual Matters.

Martin-Beltrán, M. (2014). What do you want to say? How adolescents use translanguaging to expand learning opportunities. *International Multilingual Research Journal, 8*, 208–230.

Moussu, L., & Llurda, E. (2008). Non-native English-speaking English language teachers: history and research. *Language Teaching, 41*(3), 315–348.

Ó Murchadha, N., & Flynn, C. J. (2018). Educators' target language varieties for language learners: Orientation toward 'native' and 'nonnative' norms in a minority language context. *The Modern Language Journal, 102*(4), 797–813. https://doi.org/10.1111/modl.125140026-7902/18

Otheguy, R., García, O., & Reid, W. (2015). Clarifying translanguaging and deconstructing named languages: A perspective from linguistics. *Applied Linguistics Review, 6*(3), 281–307.

Oxford English Dictionary. (2018). *Definition of 'language'.* Retrieved February 26, 2018, from https://en.oxforddictionaries.com/definition/language

Palmer, D. K., Cervantes-Soon, C., Dorner, L., & Heiman, D. (2019). Bilingualism, biliteracy, biculturalism and critical consciousness for all: Proposing a fourth fundamental goal for two-way dual language education. *Theory Into Practice, 58*(2), 121–133. https://doi.org/10.1080/00405841.2019.1569376

Pennycook, A. (1994). *The cultural politics of English as an international language.* London: Longman.

Ruiz, R. (1984). Orientations in language planning. *NABE Journal, 8*(2), 15–34.

Thibault, P. J. (2011). First-order languaging dynamics and second-order language: The distributed language view. *Ecological Psychology, 23*(3), 210–245.

2 Language and Multilingualism   43

Valadez, C., MacSwan, J., & Martínez, C. (2002). Toward a new view of low achieving bilinguals: A study of linguistic competence in designated 'semi-linguals. *Bilingual Review, 25*(3), 238–248.

Valdés, G. (2003). *Expanding definitions of giftedness: The case of young interpreters from immigrant communities.* Mahwah, NJ: Lawrence Erlbaum.

Van Lier, L. (2004). *The ecology and semiotics of language learning: A sociocultural perspective.* New York: Kluwer Academic.

Williams, C. (1994). *Arfaniad oDdulliau Dysgu ac Addysgu yng Nghyd-destun Addysg Uwchradd Ddwyieithog [An evaluation of teaching and learning methods in the context of bilingual secondary education].* Unpublished Doctoral Thesis, University of Wales, Bangor.

Zentella, A. C. (1997). The Hispanophobia of the official English movement in the US. *International Journal of Society and Language, 127,* 71–86.

Zitlali Morales, P., & Maravilla-Cano, J. V. (2019). The problems and possibilities of interest convergence in a dual language school. *Theory Into Practice.* https://doi.org/10.1080/00405841.2019.1569377

3

Use of Languages Across the Curriculum

3.1 Introduction

The use of languages other than a societally dominant, or majority, language has been conceptualised in many different ways in schools. Broadly, language use can be viewed in relation to degrees of exposure to a target language in cross-curricular teaching and learning and/or the ways in which students' languages are incorporated into lessons taught in a majority language. For example, instructional language separation, or the teachers' sole use of a target language in designated classes, provides students with a high level of language exposure. The idea of language separation as a way to protect the target language from the majority language will be discussed in the chapter in relation to one-way and dual-language immersion programmes because they have historically had this focus (see Fortune & Tedick, 2008; Hamman, 2018). Flexibility in the use of an instructional language, or differences in the amount of time teachers dedicate to a target language in class, will be addressed in relation to CLIL, which has been taken up in ways that can allow for highly varying degrees of language exposure. The incorporation of students' languages in lessons

© The Author(s) 2019
M. Turner, *Multilingualism as a Resource and a Goal*,
https://doi.org/10.1007/978-3-030-21591-0_3

taught in a majority language will then be addressed by discussing TESOL literature on the teaching and learning of emergent bi/multilinguals.[1]

Language-related pedagogies are the focus of the second part of the chapter and are distinguished from the degree of exposure to a target language and/or the incorporation of students' languages because they can be used across settings with different kinds of language distributions. Nevertheless, the pedagogies can differ depending on whether or not there is a focus on (1) learning language in a developmental way, (2) ensuring understanding of—and ability to produce—the language of a subject area, and (3) bringing students' linguistic resources to bear holistically on the learning of language in particular and learning in general. Three pedagogies are addressed together in the same section—form-focused instruction (FFI), functional pedagogies and general language scaffolding—because they all relate to learning through the medium of the target language, including through the medium of English for EAL students. The final section on crosslinguistic pedagogy is subsequently dedicated to the leveraging of students' knowledge of other languages, or the third focus.

3.2 Instructional Separation of Languages

Immersion programmes where 50 per cent or more of instruction is delivered in a minority/foreign language used at school have been extensively researched in North America. This is especially true of French immersion programmes in Canada, where research has been conducted for four decades on programme organisation, pedagogy and student outcomes—since the first programme at St Lambert began in 1965 (Genesee, 2015). In the US, the first (Spanish–English) dual immersion programme was established in Miami, Florida in 1963 (de Jong, 2016). In dual immersion, the immersion is aimed at two target populations attending the same classes—majority language speakers of English immersed in a minority language (e.g., Spanish) and minority language

---

[1] The contexts are chosen for discussion based on their relevance to the settings in Part Two. Indigenous programmes in particular are a notable omission, but these lie outside the scope of the studies.

speakers (e.g., from Spanish-speaking backgrounds) immersed in the majority language (English). It was not until the 1980s that dual immersion programmes began to increase in popularity—a catalyst for renewed interest was the success of the French immersion programmes in Canada (Genesee, 2004, as cited in de Jong, 2016). Dual-language immersion programmes also began to be perceived as assisting social interactions between minority and majority language speakers (Baker & Wright, 2017).

In research on one-way, dual and indigenous immersion, Fortune and Tedick (2008, p. 10) emphasised the following characteristics:

* Instructional use of the immersion language (IL) to teach the subject matter for at least 50 per cent of the preschool or elementary day (typically up to Grade 5 or 6); if continued at the middle/secondary level a minimum of two-year-long content courses is customary, and during that time all instruction will occur in the IL.
* Promotion of additive bi- or multilingualism and bi- or multilingual literacy with sustained and enriched instruction through at least two languages.
* Employment of teachers who are fully proficient in the language(s) they use for instruction.
* Reliance on support for the majority language in the community at large for majority language speakers and home language support for the minority language for minority language speakers.
* Clear separation of teacher use of one language versus another for sustained periods of time.

As evidenced by these characteristics, instructional language separation is considered important for at least 50 per cent of the time. This understanding of immersion takes enrichment as an aim, not transition from a minority to a dominant language, and instructional language separation is a protection mechanism against overuse of the latter (and subsequently limited learning of the former). In Canadian immersion programmes, full immersion traditionally refers to a period of 100 per cent immersion in French before moving to 50 per cent of teaching time in English, and partial immersion refers to 50 per cent of teaching time in the target language from the beginning of the immersion programme (Reid, 1996).

48   M. Turner

There is also an age component, in that immersion programmes can start at different ages and this can affect student outcomes—a distinction is drawn between early immersion (early primary), delayed immersion (mid-primary) and late immersion (the beginning of secondary school). Students enrolled in early immersion programmes have generally been found to achieve greater target language proficiency than their counterparts who start later, especially in oracy (Genesee, 1987; Lapkin, Hart, & Swain, 1991; Turnbull, Lapkin, Hart, & Swain, 1998). However, it is possible for students enrolled in late immersion programmes to perform just as well in their reading and writing as their early immersion counterparts, even though they have less exposure to the language (Genesee, 1981). Some reasons given for this finding are that the older students can transfer the knowledge and skills acquired in their dominant language to the target language, tend to be self-selecting at this age and are more committed and motivated to learn the language (Lindholm-Leary & Genesee, 2014).

The added complexity of teaching students with different language backgrounds in dual immersion programmes has led to greater variation in time spent in the two languages. In the US, there are two main models: 50:50 and 90:10 (Baker & Wright, 2017). The 90:10 model begins with the minority language used 90 per cent of the time, and then the ratio changes to 50:50 around Grade 4. In the 50:50 model, this ratio is frequently present from the beginning. Nevertheless, there are programmes that give the minority language more time and this may be different depending on whether the student is a minority or majority language speaker. For example, in Marian, Shook, and Shroeder's (2013) study on student achievement in Spanish–English dual immersion compared with mainstream programmes in the US, all the students studied the same curriculum, but language distribution differed according to the students' language background. The programme separated the majority and minority students during their study of reading and writing and kept them together for all the other subjects. This helped to prioritise Spanish for the Spanish speakers in the early years and gradually reduce Spanish language use to 40 per cent in upper primary. More English was included for the English speakers in early primary, but this changed to 100 per cent Spanish for English speakers in the third grade. From Grade 4, Spanish use was decreased to 80 per cent for this majority language group. Marian et al.

3 Use of Languages Across the Curriculum 49

(2013) found that the majority students' performance in reading (English) and mathematics was higher than that of their mainstream peers and minority students had caught up to mainstream students in reading (English) by fourth grade—at which time they surpassed them. The minority students consistently outperformed their mainstream minority peers in mathematics. This finding supports other studies which have also found that dual-language immersion programmes benefit both majority and minority students academically (e.g., Collier & Thomas, 2004; Genesee, 1983; Lindholm-Leary, 2005; Lindholm-Leary & Howard, 2008; Thomas & Collier, 2002).

One-way and dual-language immersion programmes have also been found to be beneficial for students' language proficiency in that students become more proficient in the less familiar language than if they were studying in a mainstream foreign language programme or an EAL (English-only) setting for minority students (Lindholm-Leary & Genesee, 2014). Nevertheless, even though language exposure does often appear to result in greater uptake of that language, some studies on both 50:50 and 90:10 programmes have also shown that students' language proficiency in the minority language can be quite limited (e.g., Kovelman, Baker, & Petitto, 2008; Tedick & Young, 2016), and differences in receptive and productive abilities have been documented. Students have been found to attain a higher proficiency level in reading and listening than in writing and speaking (Lyster, 2007). Their production of language can contain inaccuracies and be inappropriate from a sociolinguistic perspective (e.g., Fortune & Tedick, 2015; Genesee, 1987; Tedick & Young, 2016). This can be related to Swain's (1985) 'output hypothesis', which proposes that students need to have the opportunity to produce an extensive amount of the immersion language in order to process accurate and appropriate language forms.

A desire for students to produce the immersion language has led to immersion researchers' concern around the implementation of crosslinguistic pedagogy (Ballinger, Lyster, Sterzuk, & Genesee, 2017). In the context of Canadian immersion, it has been found that students may often prefer to speak in English with each other (Tarone & Swain, 1995), and that students' use of the immersion language can decrease around Grade 4, at a time when their oral language proficiency might be plateauing

50   M. Turner

(Fortune & Tedick, 2015; Lapkin et al., 1991). This preference for English has also been noted in dual-language immersion programmes (Potowski, 2007), where linguistic support is conceptualised ideally as equitable for both majority and minority speakers (de Jong & Howard, 2009; Palmer, Ballinger, & Lizette, 2014).

Finally, the issue of student diversity in immersion programmes is beginning to be recognised, especially in relation to dual immersion programmes. In dual immersion, there is an assumption—inherent in the name—that there are two target populations—'native' speakers of each of the languages in the programme. However, diversity in the programmes has been increasing, and de Jong (2016) noted that the Centre for Applied Linguistics in the US reported 59 per cent of dual immersion programmes as having more than 25 per cent of English-speaking ethnic minority students enrolled. Also, speakers of the minority language in the programme may speak different language varieties at home (ibid.). For example, the epithet 'native Portuguese speakers' can refer to people who speak Portuguese in Portugal, Brazilian Portuguese speakers or Cape Verdean Creole speakers (see Rubinstein-Avila, 2002). Based on this diversity of languages and language varieties, de Jong (2016) advocated that teachers avoid labelling students linguistically in ways that do not reflect their lived realities (see also Durán & Palmer, 2014; Fitts, 2006; Potowski, 2004).

3.3 Flexibility in the Use of a Target Language

Content and language integrated learning (CLIL) is a cross-curricular approach that is inclusive of programmes in which students can receive relatively limited exposure to the target language. CLIL was originally endorsed by the European Commission as a way to tailor successful Canadian French immersion programmes to the European context (2002). 'Situational and operational variables' which the Commission understood to be drivers for adaptation included Canadian students' relative homogeneity in target language proficiency, their socioeconomic status and schools' access to bilingual teachers (ibid.). CLIL was viewed as a pragmatic, cross-curricular way to facilitate the learning of languages—a

3 Use of Languages Across the Curriculum 51

pressing imperative in Europe (Marsh, 2002)—and enabled the incorporation of existing bilingual programmes in different European countries to be redefined as CLIL programmes (Beatens Beardsmore, 2009). CLIL has been broadly considered to be an integrated approach 'where both language and content are conceptualized on a continuum without an implied preference for either' (Coyle, 2007, p. 545). In Europe, the transferability of CLIL in different kinds of schools and across various countries has been understood as key to its operational success (see Coyle, Hood, & Marsh, 2010), and its capacity for transfer has relied on a certain degree of flexibility.

Given such flexibility, more concrete definitions of CLIL can differ in their focus. Although learning content through the use of a target language is central to CLIL, researchers have tended to define CLIL either according to how it can be implemented or according to its actual implementation in Europe. In the case of the former, CLIL is referred to as a way of teaching: 'an innovative methodological approach' (Eurydice, 2006, p. 7). Perhaps the most well-known pedagogy associated with CLIL is what is known as the 4Cs: content (subject matter), communication (language), cognition (thinking and learning skills) and culture/citizenship (Coyle, 2007, p. 550). The learning principles underlying these 4Cs are that content knowledge and skills are constructed (rather than acquired) by the learner, explicit attention to thinking skills can help learners participate in their learning in an active way, social interactions and learning language in context are an intrinsic part of the learning process, and culture and language have a complex relationship (Coyle, 2007).

CLIL has also been conceptualised in relation to choices stakeholders have made around its implementation. Informed by empirical research conducted in the European context, Dalton-Puffer, Llinares, Lorenzo, and Nikula (2014, p. 215) proposed three prototypical characteristics of CLIL: (1) target languages are *linguae francae*, with English dominating; (2) foreign language classrooms continue to exist—they are not replaced by CLIL; and (3) CLIL takes place in (assessed) content lessons taught by teachers qualified in that subject area. Dalton-Puffer et al. (2014) understood that the implementation of CLIL can vary widely, and transferring research findings between contexts should be done in a critical fashion, just as with any kind of comparative educational research. However, for these researchers, variation in CLIL did not include what they positioned as 'misappropriations', one of which is occurring in 'the foreign language industry, which sells conventional foreign language textbooks with so-called CLIL add-ons' (ibid., p. 215). In these foreign language textbooks, CLIL is envisaged as an approach in a foreign language classroom, or to be language- rather than content-driven (Banegas, 2014).

An understanding of CLIL from a pedagogical perspective does allow it to take place in a language classroom, however, and thus does not fulfil the latter two of Dalton-Puffer et al.'s (2014) three prototypical characteristics of CLIL in Europe. For example, CLIL has been considered to involve various kinds of implementation, such as immersion programmes, one or more subjects using the target language, study-abroad, student exchanges, CLIL camps and language showers in which students are exposed to the language in intensive sessions (see Mehisto, Marsh, & Frigols, 2008). In some of these cases, the programme may be language-driven but still conform to the 4Cs through an additional focus on learning content. Cenoz, Genesee, and Gorter (2014, p. 245) contended that this lack of specificity was unhelpful: 'A view of CLIL that embraces such wide variation in content and language instruction is problematic because it is difficult to imagine a traditional non-CLIL L2/foreign language class with a less than 10 percent focus on some type of content. Such a flexible definition makes CLIL very broad, but arguably overly inclusive'. Although Dalton-Puffer et al. (2014) offered the three prototypical characteristics of CLIL in response to Cenoz et al.'s (2014) concerns, a pedagogical understanding of CLIL continues and has been instrumental in its uptake in settings such as Australia.

In Australia, there has been a push for terminological clarification, but with pedagogy at the core. Cross (2015, p. 6) referred to CLIL as a 'flexible pedagogical approach', for example:

CLIL-based programs can take a variety of forms (e.g., units of work within standard languages programs, standalone subject options within larger school programs), or CLIL can be the pedagogical basis for regular bilingual programs (i.e. where the whole school curriculum is organized for

3 Use of Languages Across the Curriculum 53

instruction in the medium of another language, using CLIL pedagogy). [...] A key point of distinction between CLIL and similar content-related pedagogies is the explicit dual focus in CLIL on developing both new content and language, rather than a focus on content while teaching through the medium of another language, or using content to simply frame language around particular themes or topics that might only be an incidental to the teaching of language.

Cross' (2015) explanation of CLIL takes pedagogy as its point of departure but states the importance of developing new content knowledge; lessons are driven by content to some degree, thus separating CLIL classes from the traditional foreign language class in which content is used solely as a vehicle through which language can be learned.

In Europe, pedagogies associated with teaching content in another language, or the integration of the two, are a significant focus of CLIL literature. The 'integration' part of the acronym has been foregrounded by challenging the separation of language and content into distinct categories (e.g., Meyer, Coyle, Halbach, Schuck, & Ting, 2015; Nikula, Dafouz, Moore, & Smit, 2016). For example, Meyer et al. (2015, p. 52) offered a pluri-literacies model which highlighted 'the growing ability of individual learners to "language" subject-specific concepts and knowledge in an appropriate style using appropriate genre moves for the specific purpose of communication in a range of modes'. Nikula, Dafouz, et al. (2016, p. 10) viewed integration in a similar way, stating that 'integrated classes can be seen as featuring new teaching scenarios with content teachers planning their maths or science tasks within language sensitive frameworks that include some sort of communicative practice in the L2'. These language-sensitive frameworks also include the idea of functional and genre-based approaches to language; these will be discussed later in this chapter. Nikula et al. (ibid.) considered language teachers to play a collaborative role in order to 'produce a joint scheme that gives a sense of structure to the class' (p. 12). For Meyer et al. (2015) also, linguistic development in language learning was important, but this development could be embedded in subject progression rather than treated as something separate. The latter authors further challenged the idea that students needed to reach a certain communicative level in a target language in order to succeed in subject-area classrooms.

Literature on CLIL has additionally begun to engage with translanguaging. Working in the Hong Kong context, Lin (2015) argued that CLIL could be differentiated from other cross-curricular approaches by attributing flexibility to the use of languages in the classroom. Lin viewed monolingual ideologies to be particularly prevalent in South East Asia and viewed CLIL as a vehicle that could potentially help deconstruct these ideologies by attributing a role to students' first language (L1) (ibid.). In the CLIL context, Lin (2015, p. 86) viewed this role as planned:

> When we adopt a balanced and open-minded stance towards the potential role of L1 in CLIL, there is a lot of systemic planning and research that we can do to try out different kinds of combinations of different L1 and L2 everyday resources (together with multimodal resources) that can scaffold the development of L1 and L2 academic resources.

In the European context, Moore and Nikula (2016) also referred to the monolingual orientation of much of CLIL research in their discussion on translanguaging in CLIL. Citing Dalton-Puffer and Smit (2013), they understood the typical CLIL classroom to differ from classrooms with minority speakers growing up in bi/multilingual settings because students have limited exposure to the target language outside class. Nikula, Dalton-Puffer, Llinares, and Lorenzo (2016, p. 21) additionally drew attention to the large number of 'non-native' CLIL teachers who shared a language with their students, and were therefore positioned well to use more than one language in order to enrich 'students' content and language engagement in the classroom'. Here, translanguaging can be viewed as a strategic choice of languages. In their own research, Moore and Nikula (ibid.) saw the target language as dominating but bilingual resources being used in a meaningful and functional way. Similar to Lin's (2015) view of planned language(s) use, they also mentioned that it is important to avoid a *laissez-faire* attitude towards translanguaging, and understood it to be a pedagogical tool (Moore & Nikula, 2016, p. 233).

3.4 Incorporating Students' Languages into English-Medium Classrooms

The inclusion of migrant and international students' linguistic backgrounds in their learning in English-medium classrooms can overlap with CLIL because the CLIL target language can often be English. However, the idea of students speaking different languages at home than those of their class-mates—and their teacher—is more prevalent in EAL literature (in English-speaking countries) than in literature on CLIL. In EAL, it is well established that home languages can be positioned as a resource for students rather than something to be avoided at school (e.g., Cummins & Swain, 1986; Lucas & Katz, 1994; Moll, Amanti, Neff, & Gonzales, 1992; Schecter & Cummins, 2003; Teo, 2008). Literacy education in English-speaking countries has also focused on the importance of understanding that students come to school with cultural and linguistic knowledge that can assist them in their learning (e.g., Kalantzis & Cope, 2008; The New London Group, 1996). However, as mentioned in the previous chapter, unexamined assumptions around language separation and either explicit or de facto English-only language policies have led to minority language speakers being positioned as deficient in English rather than linguistically sophisticated emergent bi/multilinguals (e.g., de Jong, 2011; Valadez, MacSwan, & Martínez, 2002), and monolingual goals and ideologies can still be very pervasive in institutional contexts (see Martínez-Roldan, 2015).

Empirical studies taking into account sociolinguistic diversity within classrooms and schools have explored the implementation of multilingual practices and noted different kinds of uptake and positioning among both teachers and students. French (2016), for example, found that migrant students in a secondary school in Australia had a very positive attitude towards their multilingual resources, and demonstrated metalinguistic awareness, hybrid language practices and knowledge of *linguae francae* other than English. Along with students' engagement with—and pride in—their linguistic repertoire, French noted that the most common positioning among the teachers was one she termed 'passive acceptance', meaning that the teachers allowed the students to draw on their linguistic resources without actively incorporating these

56 M. Turner

resources into their own pedagogical practices. This passive positioning is a move towards the incorporation of home languages into the classroom, but does not necessarily lead to systemic change (e.g., Canagarajah, 2011; Cummins, 2006).

In another study, Pacheco (2018) found that two teachers in different primary schools in the US were actively encouraging the students to use their linguistic resources in class and not just English, but the positioning of the teacher was important. In one classroom, languages were brought into the class in a teacher-directed way; the teacher asked students for translations and examples in Spanish and Arabic, but she was then uncertain about how to evaluate this language use. In the other classroom, students' Spanish and Arabic language practices were used by the students with each other in order to make meaning in a comprehension activity. In this case, the teacher was able to negotiate meaning with the students by being a 'peripheral participant', or a novice who was open to learning language in her interaction with the students. Rather than a passive acceptance of her students' language use, she was actively engaged in their practices: 'She attempted to leverage student expertise and shared understandings of texts and her own bilingualism to work toward and structure new goals in comprehension activities' (Pacheco, 2018, p. 23). For the first teacher, the teacher-directed format limited students' opportunities to negotiate ways to engage. As Pacheco (ibid., p. 22) commented, 'student use of [other languages] did not then create opportunities for her to investigate language with them or for her to develop her own emerging bilingualism, but challenged her status as a central member of an English-centric community of practice'.

Blair, Haneda, and Nebus Bose (2018) were also interested in how teachers who were predominantly monolingual could engage in heteroglossic practices to encourage learning in English-medium classrooms. Like Pacheco (2018), they reported on two primary schools in the US, and both of these were considered to be positive examples that facilitated students' multilingual language practices. In the first school, the teacher's inquiry-based approach, as well as a science experiment, gave two of her Chinese-heritage newcomer students an implementational space where they could use an expanded range of semiotic resources, including Chinese: 'throughout the year, [the two students] repeatedly referred to this experiment as the occasion when they first felt empowered in the classroom' (Blair et al., 2018, p. 524). The teacher and bi/multilingual children also led the class on bilingual read-alouds. In these read-alouds, the teacher was able to explicitly value students' language practices by targeting how valuable it was to know more than one language, and monolingual students additionally benefited from increased language awareness.

In the other primary setting, there was a whole-school heteroglossic approach. In this school, more than 50 per cent of students were considered to be emergent bi/multilingual and 70 per cent were economically disadvantaged (Blair et al., 2018). Collaboration, co-planning and co-teaching were all school structures that lent themselves to opening up spaces for children to use their language resources in a systemic way. The school had a developmental bilingual programme in Spanish and English, but there were also students from a variety of backgrounds. There was a shared 'assets-based philosophy', and the principal's 'familiarity with the school's evolving student population with regard to language background, country of origin, refugee status, length of time in the country, socioeconomics, and other characteristics, was the starting point for "responsiveness to the individual students and responsiveness to the larger group"' (ibid., p. 530). This led the teachers to value students' home language development and receive systemic support for the incorporation of language practices into everyday teaching and learning. Although the two cases discussed by Blair et al. (2018) differed in scope, the authors highlighted similarities that related to the feasibility of incorporating languages that were not understood by the teacher or—necessarily—by peers. They found that 'heteroglossic spaces were co-created by students and teachers together' and that 'teachers strategically orchestrated opportunities for student-led work'.

Other literature also shows how both monolingual teachers and their bi/multilingual students can be guided towards an understanding of the significance of language practices in which the students engage in their everyday lives, and leverage this understanding in concrete ways in mainstream classrooms (e.g., D'Warte, 2014, 2015; García, Ibarra Johnson, & Seltzer, 2017; Somerville, D'Warte, & Sawyer, 2016). For example, D'Warte (2014) reported on a study conducted in Australian primary

58 M. Turner

schools in which teachers were supported in planning and delivering lessons that encouraged students to investigate their own language practices and visually 'map' these practices. The language maps will be discussed later in the chapter under crosslinguistic pedagogies. Both bi/multilingual and monolingual students shared their practices, and they were leveraged by teachers to work towards planned curriculum objectives. In the study, the 'classroom space became a shared place of inquiry' and 'multilingualism was normalised [...] as students documented their language resources' (D'Warte, 2014, p. 28). This was also reported by all students and teachers to have 'a powerful effect on students' identity, confidence and the classroom culture' (ibid.).

3.5 Language-Related Pedagogies: Learning Through the Target Language

Cross-curricular language-based pedagogies can cut across different kinds of programmes and more than one kind of pedagogy may be in evidence in a class. The three pedagogies to be discussed in this section—form-focused instruction, functional pedagogies and general language scaffolding—can all be used as a way to focus on learning (or learning through) a target language, including in English-medium classes for EAL students. These pedagogies do not necessarily draw on students' knowledge of other languages. They all focus on ensuring understanding of—and ability to produce—the language of the subject area, when they are used across the curriculum. The first two pedagogies also have the potential to include a developmental language trajectory if the teacher takes this into account when planning how to use language when teaching a subject area. General language scaffolding addresses students' understanding of the content of the lesson.

3.5.1 Form-Focused Instruction

Form-focused instruction (FFI)—a focus on language and how it works—is a pedagogy that has emerged from a strong communicative emphasis on meaning-making in a target language. FFI has been particularly relevant to a language-teaching approach known as task-based language teaching (TBLT). A task has a primary focus on meaning—requiring inference, the communication of an opinion or the transmitting of some kind of (unknown/novel) information. The target language is used by students to achieve a clearly defined (non-linguistic) outcome (Ellis & Shintani, 2014). FFI was put forward as a way to address issues and critiques of TBLT that commonly relate to the prioritisation of meaning over the explicit teaching of language, and the way this can have a negative impact on students' language learning (e.g., Seedhouse, 1999, 2005; Swan, 2005). It is argued that attention to form is a significant element in whether or not TBLT can work as a way to teach languages (see Ellis & Shintani, 2014). A focus on form in the context of meaningful communication is relevant to the learning and using of languages across the curriculum, especially in contexts—such as Canadian immersion discussed earlier in the chapter—where students' speaking and writing abilities have been found to be lower than their listening and reading (see Lyster, 2007).

Taking Ellis' (2001, pp. 1–2) definition of FFI as 'any planned or incidental instructional activity that is intended to induce language learners to pay attention to linguistic form', Lyster (2004) analysed an FFI intervention in five studies of Canadian French immersion classrooms. He found that a distribution of focus on noticing, awareness-raising and targeted practice in the studies was an effective way for students to improve their productive language abilities. The idea of noticing can be related to Schmidt's (1983, 1990) Noticing Hypothesis where he emphasised the importance of this ability for language acquisition to occur. Ortega (2009, p. 63) referred to noticing as 'the brain registering the new material, with some fleeting awareness at the point of encounter that there is something new, even if there is no understanding of how the new element works, and possibly even if there is no reportable memory of the encounter at a later time'. Lyster (2004) maintained that a mostly receptive emphasis on noticing could help guide students' attention to linguistic accuracy in their speaking and writing.

Awareness-raising as another aspect of FFI refers to the explicit inclusion of language analysis, such as investigating grammatical rules relevant

60   M. Turner

to the language needed for communication in the content-based lesson; for example, gender (Harley, 1998; Lyster, 2004), the conditional mood (Day & Shapson, 1991) and the past/past continuous tenses (Harley, 1989). Awareness-raising not only needs to be proactive, or planned into lessons; it can also be reactive in the form of teachers' corrective feedback to students in an immersion classroom (Lyster & Ranta, 1997). Targeted practice is the third aspect of FFI. Chosen linguistic features are central to this practice; that is to say, the students cannot complete the task without these features being reinforced (Lyster, 2007).

Cross-curricular approaches to language learning can be viewed as task-based, given the strong focus on the contextualised and meaningful use of a target language. However, it is important to note that practising linguistic forms and structures may be perceived by the teacher as competing with time on content. Teachers' own knowledge about language is also important given that FFI can have a direct focus on language analysis. In their study in a Spanish–English dual-language immersion setting in the US, Tedick and Young (2017) found that pedagogical limitations impeded student engagement with FFI, and also detracted from students' engagement with content. As Tedick and Young (2017, p. 13) stated, 'before developing FFI activities, teachers need to spend time understanding the linguistic forms and developing ways to explain those forms to different learners with clarity and consistency'.

3.5.2   Functional Language

In addition to FFI, there are also language-related pedagogies that focus on the function of language in particular contexts of use. In her discussion on Halliday's (1993) theory of language (see Chap. 2), Derewianka (2011) explained that language is a meaning-making resource that is highly situated in culture and therefore not neutral. Derewianka (ibid.) also maintained that the language we use is dependent on aspects of context, such as with whom we are interacting, the subject matter and the medium of communication, and studying the way language is put together in different contexts can help students use language more effectively.

3 Use of Languages Across the Curriculum   61

A functional pedagogy called genre-based pedagogy (e.g., Christie, 2005; Martin, 1985, 2009; Rose & Martin, 2012) has been developed from this understanding of language, and focuses on ways in which texts are formed. Initially a research focus in Australia, genre-based pedagogy aimed at guiding the production of a variety of school genres (Martin, 1991). Genre-based pedagogy has been applied in EAL contexts, and also in countries such as the US (e.g., Schleppegrell, 2004) and China (Lin, 2016), and the notion of genre from a Hallidayan perspective is conspicuous in the general English Curriculum in Australia (Australian Curriculum and Assessment Reporting Authority, 2018). In genre-based pedagogy, genres are text types that fulfil such functions as informing, entertaining, explaining, instructing and persuading (Derewianka & Jones, 2016). Within each genre, there are also considered to be different registers, or variations in the field, tenor and mode (see Chap. 2). For example, a story genre that has the purpose of entertaining may be a romance, horror or adventure, may be written for children, and may be oral, printed or digital-interactive (ibid.) Genre-based pedagogy focuses on the language choices associated with particular purposes in order to make those choices explicit to students, thus guiding them to comprehend and use language in the context of school-based learning. A teaching–learning cycle, in which students build their understanding of what they need to write about (and are supported in their reading on relevant topics), work with models of a relevant genre/text-type, jointly construct a text with their teacher and then write a text independently (e.g., Derewianka & Jones, 2016), is an example of this kind of pedagogy.

Genre-based pedagogy addresses the issue that students are expected to intuitively apply genre and register after learning grammar, or being exposed to a bottom-up approach where linguistic knowledge is developed from the micro to the macro level (Rose, 2015). Some students may be able to do this but others may not. Rather than replace 'micro-level' linguistic knowledge, such as phonology, graphology and grammar, the aim of genre-based pedagogy is to guide students in the authentic application of this knowledge in communication, with a particular focus on literacy (ibid.). The pedagogical approach is integrated in that the scaffolding of micro-level linguistic knowledge is also considered to be important

(Rose, 2012). In Europe, a similar kind of functional approach to the use of (English) language for specific academic contexts has been developed. The kinds of English language required in different subject areas—namely, science, mathematics, history and literature—have been catalogued by the Council of Europe (Dalton-Puffer, 2016). Using this catalogue, Dalton-Puffer (ibid.) discussed the idea of cognitive discourse functions, or academic language functions, considered to be 'the patterns which emerge from the needs humans have when they deal with cognitive content for the purposes of learning, representing and exchanging knowledge' (Ibid., p. 31). This framing of academic discourse in relation to its functions can also be found in EAL literature (see Lin, 2016).

As a result of its functional focus, however, genre-based pedagogy has been critiqued as reductionist and thus as stifling creativity. The more we try to pin down and teach language choices, the more we run 'the risk of over-simplifying complex communicative practices as simple teachable and learnable units' (Lin, 2016, p. 160). We 'kill' language by teaching language choices in specific contexts of use because both contexts and choices are complex and ever-changing. The genre-based response to this critique is an exhortation to conceptualise knowledge of genres as a strategy or a resource for communicating, but in no way as a rule or prescription for what must occur (Martin, 1994). Using genre knowledge can aid creativity by giving more tools for the creation of 'macro-genres', which are considered to be more dynamic than the more elemental components of genre-based pedagogy (Martin & Matthiessen, 2014). An understanding of genre (or language functions) as either a resource or a prescription can thus be considered to lie with the individual teacher.

3.5.3 Language Scaffolding

Cross-curricular language-related pedagogies are not always concerned with the learning of language. Subject-area teachers are required to teach students the subject area, and the learning and displaying of content knowledge may be more of a priority for the teacher than the students' language development. As a result, scaffolding language—as opposed to teaching it explicitly—may be the goal. There is no black-

and-white distinction between this kind of scaffolding and an explicit focus on language; linguistic emphasis certainly acts as a very effective scaffolding technique. However, scaffolding also encompasses the kind of pedagogies that can be useful for all students' understanding of content without a special focus on language learning.

Scaffolding can be conceptualised as contingent, which relates support—both the nature and extent of it—directly to the student (Wood, Wood, & Middleton, 1978). 'It is the *tailored* adaptation to students' existing understanding that determines contingency and, therefore, whether support can be labelled scaffolding' (Van de Pol, Volman, & Beishuizen, 2012, p. 194, italics in original). Tailored adaptation can take place impromptu, at a particular point of need, or it can be planned (Hammond & Gibbons, 2005). Through analysis of EAL student data from action research conducted in six Australian schools, Hammond and Gibbons (2005) developed a 'designed-in' scaffolding framework that incorporated different dimensions of pedagogical practices. These dimensions included linking to students' prior knowledge and experience, considering the selection and sequencing of tasks, participant structures (such as classwork, group work, pair work), semiotic systems and mediational texts (such as wall charts and reading material), and metalinguistic and metacognitive awareness.

Attention to these different aspects of scaffolding allows teachers to plan their teaching by starting with a particular student cohort. Visual scaffolding, simplification of language, a step-by-step breakdown of content and a dialogic approach can all play a role in designed-in scaffolding. In the UK, Liu, Fisher, Forbes, and Evans' (2017) study of EAL learners also led them to devise pedagogical principles that complemented those of Hammond and Gibbons, such as the reduction of language demands, the simplification of tasks, the use of dialogic tasks and cultural sensitivity and inclusion in the mainstream classroom.

Mapping features of effective pedagogy in settings of cross-curricular language exposure and learning has further been conducted in the context of European CLIL. In their research on CLIL programmes, Navés (2002) and de Graaff, Koopman, Anikina, and Westhoff (2007) found that features of effective pedagogy included a focus on the following:

64   M. Turner

1. The clarity and structure of lessons (e.g., describing tasks, pacing the lesson, communicating expectations and maintaining students' attention on tasks)
2. Presentation and communication strategies (e.g., modelling, using visual aids, checking for understanding, using body language, building in redundancy and linking to students' prior knowledge)
3. Monitoring and feedback on content and language (e.g., paraphrasing, clarification requests, elicitation, explicit correction, repetition and metalinguistic feedback)
4. A wide variety of student production (e.g., a range of oral and written work)
5. Compensation strategies (e.g., actively encouraging students to find ways to overcome language difficulties)

These pedagogical features also show overlap with Hammond and Gibbons' (2005) designed-in scaffolding, but focus specifically on more reactive language monitoring. For example, the third feature conceptualises feedback similar to FFI. The fifth feature has an explicit language focus but again does not necessarily have to be designed into the lesson.

In the 4Cs pedagogical framework developed for CLIL (Coyle, 2007), language scaffolding primarily takes place via the 'C' that stands for 'communication'. The communication aspect is conceptualised as a language triptych, with language divided into *of*, *for* and *through* learning. *Language of learning* refers to the language required to understand the content, including any specialised language. *Language for learning* refers to the language required to participate in the classroom activities planned by the teacher to guide the students' learning of particular content. *Language through learning* refers to the language that emerges from the students themselves as they engage in the activities. The language triptych includes the idea of language learning (see Coyle et al., 2010), but it is content-driven. Thus, in a subject-area classroom where students are assessed on their knowledge of content, its primary purpose could be understood by teachers to be the scaffolding of language for the learning of this content, and the linguistic progression of the students may be positioned as a hoped-for benefit rather than a core objective.

3.6 Crosslinguistic Pedagogy

Crosslinguistic pedagogy is the final pedagogy to be discussed in this chapter. Bringing students' linguistic resources to bear holistically on the learning of language in particular and learning in general is the main aim, and this is also broad enough to relate to the two aspects discussed in the previous section: learning language in a developmental way and ensuring understanding of—and ability to produce—the language of the subject area. As mentioned in Chap. 2, crosslinguistic pedagogy is inclusive of translanguaging, and thus also inclusive of the student-centred translanguaging spaces discussed in the section on incorporating heritage languages into English-medium classrooms. These spaces can be understood not only as multilingual but also as multimodal (e.g., Pacheco & Smith, 2015). In the book, the term crosslinguistic pedagogy is used to talk about the planned use and/or facilitation of more than one language in the classroom. Central to the pedagogy is whether or not a teacher shares a language other than the dominant language with her/his students. In the context of heritage-language speakers, it is very common for the only shared language between the teacher and the students to be English. The focus of crosslinguistic pedagogy for teachers who do not share a language is their facilitation of students' language use, whereas for teachers who share a language, it can involve both facilitation and more direct use of the language for communication.

One important factor to consider both for content and language learning is the activation of prior knowledge. As Cummins (2007) maintained, prior knowledge is mediated through the language in which it was encoded and, if this prior knowledge is to be activated in the student's learning, drawing on the language in which it was learned can be significant. Historically, this drawing on more familiar languages has been referred to as code-switching. Empirical support for code-switching when teaching and learning vocabulary has been particularly well established in the literature, including both the use of bilingual dictionaries and the inclusion of a word in a conversation or text in the target language (see Hall & Cook, 2011 for a review). Teachers may also permit students to speak in a more familiar language when collaborating or preparing for some kind of production in the target lan-

66 M. Turner

guage (e.g., Behan, Turnbull, & Spek, 1997; Cummins, 2005; Luk & Lin, 2015). Cummins (2005) further included the development of ideas, communication with an audience and the recording of information.

Strategies that incorporate more than one language can be planned into the lessons. For example, Butzkamm (2003) explored a 'bilingual sandwich' technique where the target language was included after a preview in a more familiar language, and before a summary. García (2009) reported a similar strategy: preview/view/review. The sandwich can also be reversed, and the target language can be the language of the preview and review parts of the lesson. Translanguaging, in its Welsh sense, is conceptually similar to the preview/view/review arrangement. The translanguaging term originated in Welsh–English bilingual education and referred to a teaching approach whereby input and output were designed to be in different languages, both to avoid functional separation and to understand bilingualism as normal (Baker, 2001; Williams, 1996). Reception and production of the two languages are alternated, to give students practice with both listening/reading and speaking/writing in the target language. These bilingual arrangements can be useful in developing competence in the language as well as understanding of content—this is especially true in secondary and tertiary settings given the conceptual and lexical complexity of subject areas and disciplines (ibid., García, 2009). Littlewood and Yu (2011) further linked the role of languages use to different parts of the lesson, which were framed as presentation, practice and production.

Crosslinguistic work and awareness and the benefits of students having their attention drawn to languages in relation to each other can also be considered an important element of crosslinguistic pedagogy, and is an important translanguaging pedagogical goal (see Chap. 2). For example, there is evidence demonstrating that translation involving active crosslinguistic awareness can be an effective language-learning strategy (see Hummel, 2010 for a review), and appears to be common among language learners (O'Malley & Chamot, 1990). Translation refers to mental translation during classroom activities as well as either spoken or written translation (see Hall & Cook, 2011), and the former, which the students do themselves rather than have done for them, can be more effective (Ballinger et al., 2017). In Canadian immersion classrooms,

3 Use of Languages Across the Curriculum   67

there has also been some experimentation with linking French and English language arts classrooms by beginning to read and conduct activities in one language in one classroom and continuing the reading and activities in the other language in another classroom (Ballinger et al., 2017; Lyster, Collins, & Ballinger, 2009). This approach encourages translation as a tool for crosslinguistic work and awareness, as well as the deepening of students' understanding of content. It also protects minority language use in the minority language classroom.

As part of the core goals of language learning and learning in general, crosslinguistic pedagogy can include identity texts (Cummins, 2006; Cummins & Early, 2011). These identity texts are designed to help students access their linguistic and cultural repertoires as a resource for their learning, and help them interpret their own experiences through creatively representing their linguistic and cultural world (e.g., Dagenais & Jacquet, 2008; Prasad, 2015). The 'text' in identity text includes visual representations, such as collage (e.g., Prasad, 2018). In the Australian context, students' linguistic and cultural resources have been leveraged by pedagogically focused identity texts known as language maps, as discussed earlier in the chapter (D'Warte, 2014, 2015; Somerville et al., 2016). Teachers used the maps to help plan lessons and work towards English content goals. The process was found to be successful in that students were engaged and their English improved (Somerville et al., 2016). Students also displayed positive attitudinal change towards their heritage language(s) (ibid.).

As discussed in Chap. 2, crosslinguistic pedagogy is used as an umbrella term to explore different contexts of cross-curricular language learning and use. It is used to refer to planned-in crosslinguistic practices that include translanguaging practices but are not limited to these. García and Li (2014, p. 130) discussed professional learning for teachers, giving examples of what constituted translanguaging and what did not. The following are two examples of translanguaging they used: 'A teacher has students listen to a song in Spanish about the topic of the day. She then has them answer a series of questions about the song in English' and 'a teacher has students look at a series of pictures and asks students to discuss in small groups what they see and what they can infer. They can discuss in any language they wish but are asked to share with the whole class in English'. Two examples that were *not* considered translanguaging were the following: 'a teacher does a word-for-word translation of a text and tells students to either read the English text or the text in their home language; all students choose to read the home language only or the English only text' and 'the teacher speaks in English and then translates what she just said into Spanish after every few sentences'. It is clear here that translation with no follow-up activity that focuses on making meaning is not considered to be translanguaging. I therefore include this kind of translation in the book under crosslinguistic pedagogy rather than under translanguaging pedagogy: I view it as a positive preliminary step towards the encouragement of strategic translanguaging practices. In the study discussed in Chap. 5, this was found to be a way to begin thinking about multilingual classroom language practices for some teachers unaccustomed to the idea that their students' languages could be included in their everyday teaching and learning.

More traditionally, the use of a dominant language when learning (through) a target language has been considered according to the functions it serves (Kim & Elder, 2008; Polio & Duff, 1994). For example, when considering for what purposes another language might be spoken in class, Kim and Elder (2008) distinguished between three dimensions: (1) framework goals (related to classroom management), (2) social goals (related to expression of feelings and concerns) and (3) core goals (related to language teaching). The first two dimensions are relatively self-explanatory: a switch of language can occur to reinforce aspects of desired behaviour and/or to focus on rapport. The third dimension of core goals is not quite so self-explanatory because the learning (and use) of the target language is key to the goal itself. Unlike the first two dimensions, the core goal is directed at increased target language proficiency, rather than the quality of social interaction in the classroom. There is a great deal of overlap between the goals; for example, improving the quality of social interaction can certainly be conducive to language learning. However, attention to core goals through the planning of strategic, structured crosslinguistic scaffolding for language learning is an important point of focus because there is a risk that language proficiency will not increase if a familiar, shared language is used without any strategic planning. Conceptualising translanguaging as much for this context as for English-medium classes with heritage students is important when we think of cross-curricular use and learning of languages in a holistic way in mainstream schools.

3.7 Conclusion

The degree of exposure to the dominant language is an important factor when considering how to incorporate languages across the curriculum—both in bilingual programmes and when embedding students' languages in everyday teaching and learning in English-medium classrooms. Language-based pedagogies have originated in various contexts and with differing emphases, and can be used across different language distributions. The cross-curricular ideas and pedagogies covered in this chapter were explained in order to contextualise and situate the discussion on the four settings that will be explored in Part Two of the book. These discussions take translanguaging pedagogical goals as a frame of reference (see Chap. 2), but pedagogical choices to use a non-dominant target language in a sustained way have the potential to empower students with a greater range of linguistic resources. Thus, in settings where one objective is noted improvement in communicative proficiency in a target language, it can be useful to consider crosslinguistic pedagogies alongside other language-related pedagogies.

References

Australian Curriculum, Assessment and Reporting Authority (ACARA). (2018). *Australian curriculum: English.* Retrieved from https://www.australiancurriculum.edu.au/f-10-curriculum/english/

Baker, C. (2001). *Foundations of bilingual education and bilingualism* (3rd ed.). Bristol: Multilingual Matters.

Baker, C., & Wright, W. E. (2017). *Foundations of bilingual education and bilingualism* (6th ed.). Bristol: Multilingual Matters.

Ballinger, S., Lyster, R., Sterzuk, A., & Genesee, F. (2017). Context-appropriate crosslinguistic pedagogy: Considering the role of language status in immersion education. *Journal of Immersion and Content-Based Language Education, 5*(1), 30–57.

Banegas, D. L. (2014). An investigation into CLIL-related sections of EFL coursebooks: Issues of CLIL inclusion in the publishing market. *International Journal of Bilingual Education and Bilingualism, 17*(3), 345–359.

Beatens Beardsmore, H. (2009). Bilingual education: Factors and variables. In O. García (Ed.), *Bilingual education in the 21st century: A global perspective* (pp. 137–158). Malden, MA: Wiley-Blackwell.

Behan, L., Turnbull, M., & Spek, W. (1997). The proficiency gap in late immersion (extended French): Language use in collaborative tasks. *Le journal de l'immersion, 20*, 41–42.

Blair, A., Haneda, M., & Nebus Bose, F. (2018). Reimagining English-medium instructional settings as sites of multilingual and multimodal meaning making. *TESOL Quarterly, 52*(3), 516–538.

Butzkamm, W. (2003). We only learn language once. The role of the mother tongue in FL classrooms: Death of dogma. *Language Learning Journal, 28*, 29–39.

Canagarajah, S. (2011). Translanguaging in the classroom: Emerging issues for research and pedagogy. *Applied Linguistics Review, 2*, 128.

Cenoz, J., Genesee, F., & Gorter, D. (2014). Critical analysis of CLIL: Taking stock and looking forward. *Applied Linguistics, 35*(3), 243–226.

Christie, F. (2005). *Language and education in the primary school*. Sydney: UNSW Press.

Collier, V. P., & Thomas, W. P. (2004). The astounding effectiveness of dual language education for all. *NABE Journal of Research and Practice, 2*(1), 1–20.

Coyle, D. (2007). Content and language integrated learning: Towards a connected research agenda for CLIL pedagogies. *International Journal of Bilingual Education and Bilingualism, 10*(5), 543–562.

Coyle, D., Hood, P., & Marsh, D. (2010). *CLIL: Content and language integrated learning*. Cambridge: Cambridge University Press.

Cross, R. (2015). Defining content and language integrated learning for languages education in Australia. *Babel, 49*(2), 4–15.

Cummins, J. (2005). A proposal for action: Strategies for recognizing heritage language competence as a learning resource within the mainstream classroom. *The Modern Language Journal, 89*(4), 585–592.

Cummins, J. (2006). Identity texts: The imaginative construction of self through multiliteracies pedagogy. In O. Garcia, T. Skutnabb-Kangas, & M. E. Torres-Guzman (Eds.), *Imagining multilingual schools: Language in education and glocalization* (pp. 51–68). Toronto: Multilingual Matters.

Cummins, J. (2007). Rethinking monolingual instructional strategies in multilingual classrooms. *Canadian Journal of Applied Linguistics (CJAL), 10*(2), 221–240.

Cummins, J., & Early, M. (2011). *Identity texts: The collaborative creation of power in multilingual schools*. Staffordshire: Trentham Books.

Cummins, J., & Swain, M. (1986). *Bilingualism in education: Aspects of theory, research and practice*. Harlow: Longman.

D'Warte, J. (2014). Exploring linguistic repertoires: Multiple language use and multimodal literacy activity in five classrooms. *Australian Journal of Language and Literacy, 37*(1), 21–30.

D'Warte, J. (2015). Building knowledge about and with students: Linguistic ethnography in two secondary school classrooms. *English in Australia, 50*(1), 39–48.

Dagenais, D., & Jacquet, M. (2008). Theories of representation in French and English scholarship on multilingualism. *International Journal of Multilingualism, 5*(1), 41–52. https://doi.org/10.2167/ijm019.0

Dalton-Puffer, C. (2016). Cognitive discourse functions: Specifying an integrative interdisciplinary construct. In E. Dafouz & T. Nikula (Eds.), *Conceptualising integration in CLIL and multilingual education* (pp. 29–54). Bristol: Channel View Publications.

Dalton-Puffer, C., Llinares, A., Lorenzo, F., & Nikula, T. (2014). 'You can stand under my umbrella': Immersion, CLIL and bilingual education. A response to Cenoz, Genesee & Gorter (2013). *Applied Linguistics, 35*(2), 213–218.

Dalton-Puffer, C., & Smit, U. (2013). Content and language integrated learning: A research agenda. *Language Teaching, 46*(4), 545–559.

Day, E., & Shapson, S. (1991). Integrating formal and functional approaches to language teaching in French immersion: An experimental study. *Language Learning, 41*, 25–58.

de Graaff, R., Koopman, G. J., Anikina, Y., & Westhoff, G. (2007). An observation tool for effective L2 pedagogy in content and language integrated learning (CLIL). *International Journal of Bilingual Education and Bilingualism, 10*(5), 603–624.

de Jong, E. J. (2011). *Foundations for multilingualism in education: From principles to practice*. Philadelphia, PA: Caslon Publishing.

de Jong, E. J. (2016). Two-way immersion for the next generation: Models, policies, and principles. *International Multilingual Research Journal, 10*(1), 6–16. https://doi.org/10.1080/19313152.2016.1118667

de Jong, E. J., & Howard, E. (2009). Integration in two-way immersion education: Equalising linguistic benefits for all students. *International Journal of Bilingual Education and Bilingualism, 12*, 81–99.

Derewianka, B. (2011). *A new grammar companion for teachers* (2nd ed.). Newtown: Primary English Teaching Association.

Derewianka, B., & Jones, P. (2016). *Teaching language in context* (2nd ed.). Melbourne: Oxford University Press.

Durán, L., & Palmer, D. (2014). Pluralist discourses of bilingualism and translanguaging talk in classrooms. *Journal of Early Childhood Literacy, 14*(3), 367–388.

Ellis, R. (2001). Investigating form-focused instruction. *Language Learning, 51*(Suppl. 1), 1–46.

Ellis, R., & Shintani, N. (2014). *Exploring language pedagogy through second language acquisition research*. London: Routledge.

European Commission. (2002). *CLIL/EMILE the European dimension: Actions, trends and foresight potential*. Brussels: Brussels European Unit, Public Services Contract 2001-3406/001-001.

Eurydice. (2006). *Content and language integrated learning (CLIL) at school in Europe*. Brussels: Eurydice.

Fitts, S. (2006). Reconstructing the status quo: Linguistic interaction in a dual-language school. *Bilingual Research Journal, 30*(2), 337–365.

Fortune, T. W., & Tedick, D. J. (2008). One-way, two-way and indigenous immersion: A call for cross-fertilization. In T. W. Fortune & D. J. Tedick (Eds.), *Pathways to multilingualism: Evolving perspectives on immersion education* (pp. 3–21). Clevedon: Multilingual Matters.

Fortune, T. W., & Tedick, D. J. (2015). Oral proficiency assessment of English-proficient K-8 Spanish immersion students. *Modern Language Journal, 99*(4), 637–655.

French, M. (2016). Students' multilingual resources and policy-in-action: An Australian case study. *Language and Education, 30*, 298–316. https://doi.org/10.1080/09500782.2015.1114628

García, O. (2009). *Bilingual education in the 21st century: A global perspective*. Malden, MA: Wiley-Blackwell.

García, O., Ibarra Johnson, S., & Seltzer, K. (2017). *The translanguaging classroom: Leveraging student bilingualism for learning*. Philadelphia, PA: Caslon.

García, O., & Li, W. (2014). *Translanguaging: Language, bilingualism and education*. New York: Palgrave Macmillan.

Genesee, F. (1981). A comparison of early and late second language learning. *Canadian Journal of Behavioral Science, 13*, 115–127. https://doi.org/10.1037/h0081168

Genesee, F. (1983). Bilingual education of majority-language children: The immersion experiments in review. *Applied Psycholinguistics, 4*(1), 1–46.

Genesee, F. (1987). *Learning through two languages: Studies of immersion and bilingual education*. Cambridge, MA: Newbury House.

Genesee, F. (2015). Canada: Factors that shaped the creation and development of immersion education. In P. Mehisto & F. Genesee (Eds.), *Building bilingual education systems: Forces, mechanisms and counterweights* (pp. 43–56). Cambridge: Cambridge University Press.

Hall, G., & Cook, G. (2011). Own-language use in language teaching and learning. *Language Teaching, 45*(3), 271–308.

Halliday, M. A. K. (1993). Towards a language-based theory of learning. *Linguistics and Education, 5*(2), 93–116.

Hamman, L. (2018). Translanguaging and positioning in two-way dual language classrooms: A case for criticality. *Language and Education, 32*(1), 21–42.

Hammond, J., & Gibbons, P. (2005). Putting scaffolding to work: The contribution of scaffolding in articulating ESL education. *Prospect, 20*(1), 6–30.

Harley, B. (1989). Functional grammar in French immersion: A classroom experiment. *Applied Linguistics, 10,* 331–359.

Harley, B. (1998). The role of form-focused tasks in promoting child L2 acquisition. In C. Doughty & J. Williams (Eds.), *Focus on form in classroom second language acquisition* (pp. 156–174). Cambridge: Cambridge University Press.

Hummel, K. (2010). Translation and short-term L2 vocabulary retention: Hindrance or help? *Language Teaching Research, 14*(1), 61–74.

Kalantzis, M., & Cope, B. (2008). *New learning: Elements of a science of education.* Cambridge: Cambridge University Press.

Kim, S. H., & Elder, C. (2008). Target language use in foreign language classrooms: Practices and perceptions of two native speaker teachers in New Zealand. *Language, Culture and Communication, 21*(2), 167–185.

Kovelman, I., Baker, S., & Petitto, L. (2008). Age of first bilingual language exposure as a new window into bilingual reading development. *Bilingualism: Language and Cognition, 11*(2), 203–223. https://doi.org/10.1017/S1366728908003386

Lapkin, S., Hart, D., & Swain, M. (1991). Early and middle French immersion programs: French language outcomes. *Canadian Modern Language Review, 48*(1), 11–41.

Lin, A. M. Y. (2015). Conceptualizing the potential role of L1 in content and language integrated learning (CLIL). *Language, Culture and Curriculum, 28*(1), 74–89.

Lin, A. M. Y. (2016). *Language across the curriculum and CLIL in English as an additional language contexts: Theory and practice.* Singapore: Springer.

Lindholm-Leary, K., & Genesee, F. (2014). Student outcomes in one-way, two-way, and indigenous language immersion education. *Journal of Immersion and Content-Based Language Education, 2*(2), 165–180.

Lindholm-Leary, K. J. (2005). The rich promise of two-way immersion. *Educational Leadership, 62*(4), 56–59.

Lindholm-Leary, K. J., & Howard, E. R. (2008). Language development and academic achievement in two-way immersion programs. In T. W. Fortune & D. J. Tedick (Eds.), *Pathways to multilingualism: Evolving perspectives on immersion education* (pp. 177–200). Oxford: Blackwell.

Littlewood, W., & Yu, B. H. (2011). First language and target language in the foreign language classroom. *Language Teaching, 44*, 64–77.

Liu, Y., Fisher, L., Forbes, K., & Evans, M. (2017). The knowledge base of teaching linguistically diverse contexts: 10 grounded principles of multilingual classroom pedagogy for EAL. *Language and Intercultural Communication*, 1–18. https://doi.org/10.1080/14708477.2017.1368136

Lucas, T., & Katz, A. (1994). Reframing the debate: The roles of native languages in English-only programs for language minority students. *TESOL Quarterly, 28*, 537–561. https://doi.org/10.2307/3587307

Luk, J., & Lin, A. M. Y. (2015). Voices without words: Doing critical literate talk in English as a second language. *TESOL Quarterly, 49*(1), 67–91.

Lyster, R. (2004). Research on form-focused instruction in immersion classrooms: Implications for theory and practice. *Journal of French Language Studies, 14*(3), 321–341.

Lyster, R. (2007). *Learning and teaching languages through content: A counterbalanced approach*. Amsterdam: John Benjamins.

Lyster, R., Collins, L., & Ballinger, S. (2009). Linking languages through a bilingual read-aloud project. *Language awareness, 18*, 366–383. https://doi.org/10.1080/09658410903197322

Lyster, R., & Ranta, L. (1997). Corrective feedback and learner uptake. *Studies in Second Language Acquisition, 19*(1), 37–66.

Marian, V., Shook, A., & Shroeder, S. R. (2013). Bilingual two-way immersion programs benefit academic achievement. *Bilingual Research Journal, 36*(2), 167–186. https://doi.org/10.1080/15235882.2013.818075

Marsh, D. (Ed.). (2002). *CLIL/EMILE the European Dimension: Actions, trends and foresight potential*. University of Jyväskylä. Retrieved from https://jyx.jyu.fi/handle/123456789/47616

Martin, J. R. (1985). *Factual writing: Exploring and challenging social reality*. Geelong, VIC: Deakin University Press. (Republished by Oxford University Press, 1989).

Martin, J. R. (1991). Types of writing in infants and primary schools. In *Working with genre: Papers from the 1989 LERN conference* (pp. 33–44). Leichhardt: Common Ground.

3 Use of Languages Across the Curriculum   75

Martin, J. R. (1994). Macro-genres: The ecology of the page. *Network, 21*, 29–52.

Martin, J. R. (2009). Genres and language learning: A social semiotic perspective. *Linguistics and Education, 20*, 10–21.

Martin, J. R., & Matthiessen, C. (2014). Modelling and mentoring: Teaching and learning from home to school. In A. Mahboob & L. Barratt (Eds.), *Englishes in multilingual contexts* (pp. 137–163). Dordrecht: Springer.

Martínez-Roldan, C. M. (2015). Translanguaging practices as mobilization of linguistic resources in a Spanish/English bilingual after-school program: An analysis of contradictions. *International Multilingual Research Journal, 9*(1), 43–58. https://doi.org/10.1080/19313152.2014.982442

Mehisto, P., Marsh, D., & Frigols, M. J. (2008). *Uncovering CLIL*. London: Macmillan Education.

Meyer, O., Coyle, D., Halbach, A., Schuck, K., & Ting, T. (2015). A pluriliteracies approach to content and language integrated learning—Mapping learner progressions in knowledge construction and meaning-making. *Language, Culture and Curriculum, 28*(1), 41–57. https://doi.org/10.1080/07908318.2014.1000924

Moll, L., Amanti, C., Neff, D., & Gonzales, N. (1992). Funds of knowledge for teaching: Toward a qualitative approach to connect homes and classrooms. *Theory Into Practice: Qualitative Issues in Educational Research, 3*(2), 132–141.

Moore, P., & Nikula, T. (2016). Translanguaging in CLIL classrooms. In T. Nikula, E. Dafouz, P. Moore, & U. Smit (Eds.), *Conceptualising integration in CLIL and multilingual education* (pp. 211–234). Bristol: Multilingual Matters.

Navés, T. (2002). Successful CLIL programmes. In G. Langé & P. Bertaux (Eds.), *The CLIL professional development course* (pp. 93–102). Milan: Ministero della' Instruzione della' Universitá e della Ricerca.

Nikula, T., Dafouz, E., Moore, P., & Smit, U. (Eds.). (2016). *Conceptualising integration in CLIL and multilingual education*. Bristol: Multilingual Matters.

Nikula, T., Dalton-Puffer, C., Llinares, A., & Lorenzo, F. (2016). More than content and language: The complexity of integration in CLIL and bilingual education. In T. Nikula, E. Dafouz, P. Moore, & U. Smit (Eds.), *Conceptualising integration in CLIL and multilingual education* (pp. 1–25). Bristol: Multilingual Matters.

O'Malley, J., & Chamot, A. (1990). *Learning strategies in second language acquisition*. Cambridge: Cambridge University Press.

Ortega, L. (2009). *Understanding second language acquisition*. London: Hodder Education.

Pacheco, M. (2018). Spanish, Arabic, and 'English-Only': Making meaning across languages in two classroom communities. *TESOL Quarterly, 52*(4), 1–27. https://doi.org/10.1002/tesq.446

Pacheco, M., & Smith, B. E. (2015). Across languages, modes, and identities: Bilingual adolescents' multimodal codemeshing in the literacy classroom. *Bilingual Research Journal, 38*(3), 292–312. https://doi.org/10.1080/152358 82.2015.1091051

Palmer, D. K., Ballinger, S., & Lizette, P. (2014). Classroom interaction in one-way, two-way, and indigenous immersion contexts. *Journal of Immersion and Content-Based Language Education, 2*(2), 225–240.

Polio, C. G., & Duff, P. A. (1994). Teachers' language use in university foreign language classrooms: A qualitative analysis of English and target language alternation. *The Modern Language Journal, 78*(3), 313–326.

Potowski, K. (2004). Student Spanish use and investment in a dual immersion classroom: Implications for second language acquisition and heritage language maintenance. *The Modern Language Journal, 88*(1), 75–101.

Potowski, K. (2007). *Language and identity in a dual immersion school.* Clevedon: Multilingual Matters.

Prasad, G. (2015). Beyond the mirror towards a plurilingual prism: Exploring the creation of plurilingual 'identity texts' in English and French classrooms in Toronto and Montpellier. *Intercultural Education, 26*(6), 497–514.

Prasad, G. (2018). How does it look and feel to be plurilingual? Analyzing children's representations of plurilingualism through collage. *International Journal of Bilingual Education and Bilingualism.*https://doi.org/10.1080/136 70050.2017.1420033

Reid, J. (1996). Recent developments in Australian late immersion education. *Journal of Multilingual and Multicultural Development, 17*(6), 469–484.

Rose, D. (2012). Integrating SFL theory with literacy teaching. In Z. Yan, J. Webster, & F. Yan (Eds.), *Developing systemic functional linguistics: Theory and application.* London: Equinox.

Rose, D. (2015). Building a pedagogical metalanguage II: Knowledge genres. In J. R. Martin (Ed.), *Applicable linguistics and academic discourse* (pp. 29–58). Shanghai: Shanghai Jiao Tong University Press.

Rose, D., & Martin, J. R. (2012). *Learning to write, reading to learn: Genre, knowledge and pedagogy in the Sydney school.* London: Equinox.

Rubinstein-Avila, E. (2002). Problematizing the "dual" in a dual immersion program: A portrait. *Linguistics and Education, 13*(1), 65–87.

Schecter, S., & Cummins, J. (Eds.). (2003). *Multilingual education in practice: Using diversity as a resource.* Portsmouth, NH: Heinemann.

3 Use of Languages Across the Curriculum   77

Schleppegrell, M. J. (2004). *The language of schooling: A functional linguistics perspective*. Mahwah, NJ: Lawrence Erlbaum.

Schmidt, R. (1983). Interaction, acculturation and the acquisition of communication competence. In M. Wolfson & E. Judd (Eds.), *Sociolinguistics and second language acquisition*. Rowley, MA: Newbury House.

Schmidt, R. (1990). The role of consciousness in second language learning. *Applied Linguistics, 11*(2), 129–158.

Seedhouse, P. (1999). Task-based interaction. *ELT Journal, 53*(3), 149–156.

Seedhouse, P. (2005). 'Task' as research construct. *Language Learning, 55*(3), 533–570.

Somerville, M., D'Warte, J., & Sawyer, W. (2016). *Building on children's linguistic repertoires to enrich learning: A project report for the NSW Department of Education*. Retrieved from http://www.uws.edu.au/centre_for_educational_research

Swain, M. (1985). Communicative competence: Some roles of comprehensible input and comprehensible output in its development. In S. Gass & C. Madden (Eds.), *Input in Second Language Acquisition* (pp. 235–253). Rowley, MA: Newbury House.

Swan, M. (2005). Legislation by hypothesis: The case of task-based instruction. *Applied Linguistics, 26*(3), 376–401.

Tarone, E., & Swain, M. (1995). A sociolinguistic perspective on second language use in immersion classrooms. *The Modern Language Journal, 79*, 166–178.

Tedick, D. J., & Young, A. I. (2016). Fifth grade two-way immersion students' responses to form-focused instruction. *Applied Linguistics, 37*(6), 784–807.

Tedick, D. J., & Young, A. I. (2017). Two-way immersion students' home languages, proficiency levels, and responses to form-focused instruction. *International Journal of Bilingual Education and Bilingualism, 21*(3), 1–16. https://doi.org/10.1080/13670050.2017.1383354

Teo, P. (2008). Outside in/inside out: Bridging the gap in literacy education in Singapore classrooms. *Language and Education, 22*(6), 411–431. https://doi.org/10.1080/09500780802152721

The New London Group. (1996). A pedagogy of multiliteracies: Designing social futures. *Harvard Educational Review, 66*(1), 60–92. https://doi.org/10.17763/haer.66.1.17370n67v22j160u

Thomas, W. P., & Collier, V. P. (2002). *A national study of school effectiveness for language minority students' long-term academic achievement*. Santa Cruz, CA: University of California at Santa Cruz, Center for Research on Education, Diversity, and Excellence.

Turnbull, M., Lapkin, S., Hart, D., & Swain, M. (1998). Time on task and immersion graduates' French proficiency. In S. Lapkin (Ed.), *French second language education in Canada: Empirical studies* (pp. 31–55). Toronto: University of Toronto Press.

Valadez, C., MacSwan, J., & Martínez, C. (2002). Toward a new view of low achieving bilinguals: A study of linguistic competence in designated 'semilinguals. *Bilingual Review, 25*(3), 238–248.

Van de Pol, J., Volman, M., & Beishuizen, J. (2012). Promoting teacher scaffolding in small-group work: A contingency perspective. *Teaching and Teacher Education, 28*, 193–205.

Williams, C. (1996). Secondary education: Teaching in the bilingual situation. In C. Williams, G. Lewis, & C. Baker (Eds.), *The language policy: Taking stock* (pp. 39–78). Llangefni: CAI.

Wood, D., Wood, H., & Middleton, D. (1978). An experimental evaluation of four face-to-face teaching strategies. *International Journal of Behavioral Development, 1*, 131–147.

4

Opportunities to Learn (Through) Languages

4.1 Introduction

In this chapter, I discuss a multilingual practices framework developed in order to link traditions that are frequently considered separately: the learning of/through a chosen target language across the curriculum at school and the incorporation of heritage languages into English-medium classrooms in English-speaking countries. In contexts where students come from linguistically diverse backgrounds and languages are taught at school, it can be useful to engage with language practices in a holistic way, or to have a school-based language policy that can accommodate different kinds of practices for different objectives. This is especially important when target languages are not confined to the languages classroom. The main argument for both the benefit and feasibility of an overarching framework is that it is student-centred. It takes students' learning opportunities as a point of departure, and views these opportunities through both a sociocultural and sociopolitical lens. From a sociocultural perspective, the ways in which individuals participate in situated, social practices are informed by cultural norms and experiences (e.g., McCaslin, 2009; Wenger, 1998). Our motives for learning and using particular languages are negotiated in relation to other people (see Nolen,

© The Author(s) 2019
M. Turner, *Multilingualism as a Resource and a Goal,*
https://doi.org/10.1007/978-3-030-21591-0_4

Horn, & Ward, 2015). A sociopolitical perspective includes a focus on the dynamics of power in language use and learning (e.g., Flores & García, 2017; Makoni & Pennycook, 2007; Pennycook, 2001). This chapter highlights the possible motives for stakeholders' (principals, teachers, students, parents) choices and engagement relevant to the learning and using of language.

I address sociocultural perspectives on learning first in order to show the broad theoretical orientation of what is considered to constitute students' opportunities to learn in formal schooling. The three dimensions that are then discussed are directly related to cross-curricular language learning and use, and the first two include sociolinguistic perspectives. Multilingual stance, the first dimension, takes into account expectations around how—and the extent to which—languages should be taught, learned and incorporated into class. These expectations are predominantly institutional but are also related to specific stakeholders, especially teachers, given their influence on classroom teaching and learning. It is multilingual stance that forms the basis for a school (or class) language policy, and is the point of departure for a multilingual orientation to learning. Student engagement, the next dimension, addresses students' attitudes towards—and use of—particular languages both inside and outside school. Working with and guiding what students (want to) do with languages is an important element of this dimension. The third dimension discusses institutional structures and refers to school organisation and factors relating to the implementation of programmes that promote bi/multilingualism. The framework is then summarised in the final section. Language-based pedagogies, discussed in Chap. 3, are considered alongside more general pedagogies in this third dimension.

4.2 Opportunities to Learn from a Sociocultural Perspective

Sociocultural theory is grounded in the work of the Russian psychologist Lev Vygotsky, and sociocultural traditions based on English translations have applied his work to the field of formal education. As Säljö

4 Opportunities to Learn (Through) Languages 81

(2009, p. 207) pointed out, 'a major interest of a sociocultural perspective is […] the study of how human skills […] are appropriated by individuals'. Appropriation and what mediates this appropriation underpin sociocultural understandings of learning. Appropriation occurs through participation in social and material practices (ibid.), and is mediated both explicitly through the use of stimuli and implicitly through the use of inner speech (Wertsch, 1991). Stimuli—scaffolding, for example—are a way to lead students to the appropriation of new content or concepts, and are gradually removed as the student moves towards task autonomy. According to Vygotsky (1978, p. 211), 'what the child is able to do in collaboration today he will be able to do independently tomorrow'. The benefit of viewing learning in this way, or as an essentially social endeavour, is that it positions the (dis)connections between the social (and cultural) experiences of stakeholders and institutional structures as central to the business of education.

One sociocultural approach that is used to investigate formal learning environments and specifically relates to how we learn is known as the situative perspective (e.g., Boaler & Greeno, 2000; Lave, 1988; Lave & Wenger, 1991; Wenger, 1998). Students are considered to take part in a new activity or practice peripherally, and gradually their participation becomes more central as learning takes place (ibid.). According to Greeno and Gresalfi (2015, p. 171), this approach acknowledges that 'the ways that individuals are positioned with respect to others and the content of the activity is inseparable from their engagement with the content itself'. 'A trajectory of learning' is thus understood to be dependent on students' engagement in particular practices, and can differ depending on the positioning of students (ibid.). Nolen, Ward and Horn (2011, p. 111) give an example of a student who texts a friend in a mathematics classroom. Rather than considering the student to be disengaged, they understand her/him to be engaged in a community of practice outside the classroom, and/or 'engaged in positioning [herself/himself] in opposition to teacher-promoted norms'. Such an understanding of engagement is situated in the classroom but acknowledges membership of various communities: the negotiation of communities of practice that compete or conflict with

82   M. Turner

each other is important for engaged participation in a particular activity (Hickey & Granade, 2004).

These studies of students' engagement in class have been conducted in order to 'inform the more effective design or redesign of learning environments' (Nolen et al., 2015, p. 236). Students' motives to learn are considered to be integral to this engagement. Motivated behaviour has principally been studied as the outcome of choices individuals make on the basis of their beliefs, values and goals (e.g., Bandura, 1997; Eccles, 2005; Elliot & Dweck, 2005). There are two issues with this focus that are addressed by the situative approach, as pointed out by McCaslin (2009). First, choice 'can be misleading because so much of what we do and why is not particularly mindful, knowledgeable, and strategic' (p. 138). Second, choice requires opportunity, and this 'seriously restricts the usefulness of choice in understanding the motivation [...] of those who do not enjoy the problem of selecting (let alone optimally) from an array of desired options' (p. 138). Opportunities and the negotiation of these can therefore be considered central to a situated view of individuals' motivation.

From a situative sociocultural perspective, opportunities to learn can thus be conceptualised as affordances (Greeno & Gresalfi, 2015). This means that opportunities do not derive from a particular object or way of doing things, but exist when these are given meaning by people (or other animals) who see in them a particular purpose (Gibson, 1977; Letiche & Lissack, 2009). To emphasise this relational sense, according to Letiche and Lissack, 'affordances are neither *solely* subject driven, nor situationally determined' (2009, p. 62, italics in original). Van Lier explains this concept as '*action potential*' (2004, p. 92, italics in original). Greeno and Gresalfi later apply to the classroom the idea of the importance of both what the individuals carry with them in their heads and what the environment provides: 'When we say that an activity affords some aspect of participation for some individuals, we mean that it makes it relatively easy for those individuals to participate in that way' (2015, p. 172).

This situated view of learner engagement is useful when thinking about effective and sustainable cross-curricular language(s) use because it

4 Opportunities to Learn (Through) Languages

focuses strongly on the improvement of learning environments and also links learning opportunities to affordances. From this perspective, school-based expectations around language learning and use, as well as students' engagement with different languages, are influential in the taking up of any opportunities presented by the structural organisation of teaching and learning at school.

4.3 Multilingual Stance

School-based expectations of language learning and use can be related to beliefs around whether or not—or the extent to which—this learning and use should be institutionally sanctioned, and also around how language is acquired in formal learning environments. Multilingual stance provides a way to understand these expectations from a multilingual perspective. The stance incorporates positions that range from acceptance to the active promotion of languages in formal education and in everyday life, and draws on pro-multilingual ideologies. In Fitzsimmons-Doolan's (2018) research on language ideologies, defined as 'shared beliefs about how language functions in society' (p. 37), she found evidence of pro-multilingual ideologies among stakeholders influential in the development of language policy in Arizona. Some of the defining statements for this ideology were that 'the use of more than one language should be promoted', 'a person's linguistic abilities are assets', 'the use of more than one language is an economic asset', 'the use of native languages other than English is helpful for sharing tradition', and 'the use of language is a human right' (ibid., p. 40). These ideologies could not be assumed, however. Fitzsimmons-Doolan (ibid.) also found evidence of pro-monolingual ideologies in the study. Some of the defining statements for pro-monolingualism were the following: 'In the United States, public communication should occur in English', 'knowing English helps a person to be American', 'the standard or model form of a language is the most appropriate form for school', 'using one language to complete a task is better than using two languages', and stakeholders could have a negative orientation to 'the use of more than one language should be promoted' (ibid., p. 40).

Some kind of multilingual stance is a necessary point of departure when putting languages across the curriculum, and it may therefore be necessary for the stance to be made explicit in contexts where one language, such as English, is institutionally dominant. Because a positive orientation to multilingualism is important, stakeholder language-related assumptions might need to be addressed before implementing bilingual programmes and/or incorporating languages into English-medium classes in English-speaking countries. The pro-monolingual statements evidenced earlier could be considered to fall under Ruiz' (1984) language-as-problem orientation discussed in Chap. 2. Given the strength of the focus on social cohesion, bi/multilinguals could also demonstrate a pro-monolingual ideology by expecting that heritage-language learning and use is not a part of the institutional domain and is to be used at home and in the community. The position might also be informed by an understanding that language is learnt best in contexts of total immersion.

Thus, taking a multilingual stance at school might require explicit communication and evidence of benefits to stakeholders at the school and in the community. It is also useful to understand the stance on a continuum in order to explore the extent to which teachers and other key stakeholders understand that multilingualism should be institutionally sanctioned. In the US, to further the idea of multilingualism as a resource (as discussed in Chap. 2), de Jong (2018) offered three points on a continuum focused on EAL learners: allow, maintain and foster/affirm. For the first point, students are permitted to use their home language in class if they need to and are encouraged to speak their language in the community domain. The second point is more strategic in that teachers actively provide opportunities for EAL learners to use their home languages for different reasons. The third point relates to learning in general and all students: multilingualism is the standard stance at school and in class. Languages are not incorporated into the classroom only because students are not familiar with the dominant language, but because they are a resource for learning (ibid.).

This idea of a multilingual continuum is useful if we consider language learning and use for *all* students, including those who have very limited

4 Opportunities to Learn (Through) Languages   85

exposure to any language other than English outside school. The principal focus for both Fitzsimmons-Doolan (2018) and de Jong (2018) was minority students—EAL learners—who spoke a different language at home, rather than students learning a target (non-dominant) language at school. Language ideologies, or understandings around how language functions in society, however, are likely to inform stakeholders' attitudes towards learning languages in general. Languages with greater prestige or geopolitical relevance are commonly the ones schools choose to teach formally, and the way they are taught might also be influenced by prevalent ideologies. If the school is more pro-monolingual in orientation, then the teaching and learning of languages may not be attributed much importance. For example, languages education as a discrete subject area should not 'interfere' with the rest of the students' socialisation and learning. To give an illustration of the complexity of ideologies, stakeholders might be broadly pro-monolingual in relation to heritage languages of different groups of migrants, but pro-multilingual in relation to the teaching and learning of prestigious languages. Further, this positioning might only relate to school, and heritage languages might be actively promoted in the community domain by the same stakeholders.

As noted by Fitzsimmons-Doolan (2018), pro-monolingualism is also linked to bounded understandings of language that promote a standard form. The idea of a standard form underpins beliefs about language learning as leading to mastery. This can be considered to be a deficit way of understanding language learning because mastery is elusive, especially if it is tied to the 'native' speaker, as discussed in Chap. 2. If we take a Hallidayan view of language as culturally situated and tied to contexts of use, then the expectations of language learning and use at school can be revised to align with these contexts. Nevertheless, from a practical perspective, a standard form can help to maintain clarity around what kind of language to teach at school. This is especially important for learning languages, as opposed to leveraging students' existing linguistic resources for their learning.

Taking a multilingual stance in relation to *all* students, including for students who only speak English at home, then requires consideration of how the cross-curricular use of a chosen target language is conceptualised by stakeholders, such as school leaders and principals. This exposure to language might be the main avenue for students to increase their linguistic repertoire, and school commitment to a target language can be conceptualised in relation to a multilingual stance continuum: the greater the commitment, the greater the multilingual stance. This is complicated, however, because commitment needs to be firmly linked to opportunities for students to expand their linguistic repertoire. Expectations around how language is learned provide teachers with a sense of what it is they are teaching and also how. Beliefs on whether language learning occurs more effectively in formal teaching and learning through implicit or explicit means or what kind of mix might be needed are particularly significant in shaping language instruction. Krashen (1981), who has been an influential figure in second-language acquisition research, took a particularly strong 'non-interface' position to these two kinds of learning. He argued that explicit knowledge (rule-based knowledge) does not become implicit even when extensively practised.

An understanding of the importance of acquiring knowledge implicitly was the basis of the promotion of communicative approaches to language teaching and learning, as opposed to grammar-based (or rule-based) approaches. A number of researchers have argued that there *is* some kind of interface (see Ellis, 1994 for a discussion on this), and drawing students' attention to rules—with controlled practice—can result in the conversion of knowledge from explicit to implicit. It is clear from the number of developmental language textbooks published globally, and the existence of languages curricula and classrooms that the interface position is generally accepted in formal education. Expectations around language learning are institutionalised in these curricula and textbooks, and teaching students the rules, structures and patterns they need to complete assessments and pass exams is understandably a high priority for teachers. Nevertheless, an emphasis on the implicit learning of language has also led to spaces of increased language exposure in meaning-focused settings, such as immersion and CLIL programmes, and also in language classrooms.

The notion of implicit and explicit learning of language in formal settings can thus also be understood on a continuum. Attention to both is particularly clear in Ellis and Shintani's exploration of the relationship between language pedagogy and second-language acquisition research

4 Opportunities to Learn (Through) Languages 87

when they identify 11 principles of instructed language learning (2014, pp. 22–27):

1. Instruction needs to ensure that learners develop both a rich repertoire of formulaic expressions and a rule-based competence.
2. Instruction needs to ensure that learners focus on meaning.
3. Instruction needs to ensure that learners also focus on form.
4. Instruction needs to be predominantly directed at developing implicit knowledge of the L2 while not neglecting explicit knowledge.
5. Instruction needs to take into account the order and sequence of acquisition (although some debate is acknowledged by the authors about this principle).
6. Successful instructed language learning requires extensive L2 input.
7. Successful instructed language learning also requires opportunities for output.
8. The opportunity to interact in the L2 is central to developing L2 proficiency.
9. In assessing learners' L2 proficiency it is important to examine free as well as controlled production.
10. Instruction needs to take account of individual differences in learners.
11. Instruction needs to take account of the fact that there is a subjective aspect to learning a new language.

The first nine of these principles all relate to the interface of implicit and explicit learning through their emphasis on such aspects as form, meaning and the importance of extensive input and free output. The final two principles relate closely to this book's point of departure.

The interface position also clearly exists outside specific instructed language-learning contexts, for example in CLIL classrooms. Morton (2012), working in the European CLIL context, offered a framework to show the significance of an explicit focus on language across the curriculum. He divided the role of language into three: L2 as a tool for learning (the mediation of content-learning goals), L2 as a curriculum concern (an explicit focus on language) and L2 as a matter of competence (communicative proficiency in the L2). L2 as a tool for learning relates to 'interactional and discursive practices' in the classroom (Morton, 2012,

p. 50). Dialogic teaching—to be discussed later in the chapter under institutional structures—is positioned here, as is working with register (see Gibbons, 2003). Morton (ibid.) drew on common issues from EAL settings, such as students' minimal responses in the target language and difficulties in attending to students' language-learning needs in subject-area classrooms.

Language as a curriculum concern then referred to 'whether, and to what extent, specific aspects of L2 knowledge or skills are prespecified at the planning stage and/or acted on in classroom interaction' (p. 70). Morton included both form-focused instruction and functional language discussed in Chap. 3 under this strand. He then related L2 as a matter of competence to plurilingual competences, or Blommaert's (2010) 'truncated repertoires', as mentioned in Chap. 1: the idea of competence is not limited to one language but is viewed across languages, or in terms of a speaker's linguistic abilities as a whole. Nevertheless, in CLIL, decisions around the prioritisation of content-based learning may limit the students' competence 'when it comes to basic conversational skills, for example the ability to talk about their own needs and experiences relating to the world outside the classroom' (2012, p. 83).

In brief, in the multilingual practices framework, a multilingual stance is conceptualised on a continuum and includes the amount of attention paid to the role of language across the curriculum. A stance inclusive of both heritage students and students of a target language that reaches outside the languages classroom cannot be assumed in institutionally monolingual contexts, such as Australian mainstream schools. According to de Jong's (2018) continuum, when a multilingual stance is present, it may be limited to a passive kind of acceptance (see French, 2016 in Chap. 3), it could be used strategically for students who are not so familiar with English (see Pacheco, 2018) or it could be used to foster/affirm heritage languages in general and for all students from an assets-based perspective (see Blair, Haneda, & Nebus Bose, 2018). It might also include the cross-curricular learning and use of a target language at school. In this latter case, language is considered as a resource for learning but there is an additional focus on actively expanding students' linguistic repertoire via the target language.

4.4 Student Engagement with Languages

Like multilingual stance, student engagement with specific languages—either heritage or non-heritage—is considered to be key to their opportunities to learn in the framework. Language use and learning is understood to be significantly influenced by the students' willingness—or unwillingness—to engage with particular languages in different domains. Ideas such as investment (Norton, 2000; Norton Peirce, 1995), language identities (e.g., Creese & Blackledge, 2010; García, 2009), authenticity and legitimacy (e.g., Kramsch, 2012) and desire (e.g., Deleuze & Guattari, 1977; Motha & Lin, 2014) can help to understand student engagement with different languages and language practices. These ideas explore perceptions of value, membership, connection and competence, as well as aspiration to belong to an imagined or real community. Although not discussed in this section, language proficiency, or familiarity with particular languages, can certainly be viewed as a significant influence on student engagement. However, when considering institutionally monolingual settings, students' willingness to use languages to which they have no exposure outside school, or languages that their peers and teachers may not understand, is crucial to whether or not proficiency improves or a well-known language is openly used as a resource at school.

First, investment is one way to understand students' motivation to engage in particular language practices. Norton Peirce (1995) and Norton (2000) proposed the idea of investment as a way to investigate motivation, and drew upon theorists who considered the way we navigate the world to be both discursively constructed, socially and historically situated and subject to power dynamics (e.g., Bourdieu, 1977; Weedon, 1997). Bourdieu (1977) understood power to influence the way in which discourse is structured because the right to speak is not necessarily evenly distributed among speakers. Some speakers are more 'legitimate' than others, and the social and political practice of using language is very much connected to the value attributed to the speaker. Circumstances and contexts differ, and this may result in a variation to the speaker's 'value': discourse 'can receive different values depending on the market on which it is offered' (Bourdieu, 1977, p. 651). Power is thus considered to be a social construction that lies in relationships between people and groups—it is not a physical possession—and exists at the level of everyday interactions as much as it does at the institutional and global levels (Foucault, 1980). Even though power is a symbolic resource, rather than a material one, it is inextricably connected to material resources and their distribution in society; power gives access to a wide range of resources, and this access also serves to reinforce a sense of privilege (West, 1992).

Thus, in Norton's (2000) framing of investment, the relationship between a language learner and a target language hinges on the unequal power dynamics between speakers and the different degrees of legitimacy of different speakers. She considered investment to complement cognitivist and social cognitivist perspectives on motivation which attribute mindful choice to individuals, and which do not foreground sociocultural histories (Norton, 2000; Norton Peirce, 1995). Norton's understanding of investment was most directly based on Bourdieu and Passeron's (1977) theorisation of cultural capital as the value attributed to particular knowledge and the ways of thinking of particular social groups. Forms of cultural capital have an unequal exchange value because some kinds of knowledge and ways of thinking are considered to be more valuable than others (ibid.) Language learners thus invest in the acquisition of 'a wider range of symbolic and material resources', believing that there will be a subsequent increase in their cultural capital (Norton, 2000, p. 10). However, this may not be straightforward because the social histories and complex desires of the language learner need to be taken into account: the learners 'are not only exchanging information with target language speakers, but they are constantly organizing and reorganizing a sense of who they are and how they relate to the social world' (Norton, 2000, p. 11). Therefore, investment in a language is considered to be an element of identity.

Investment is further based on the idea that language identities are not considered to be fixed and unitary—they can be multiple. Other scholars have also considered language identities in this way. For example, García (2009, p. 170) wrote about the complexity of language identities in the US:

4 Opportunities to Learn (Through) Languages 91

> Even if the US federal government refuses to accept that nationhood in a globalized world is much more than one language, one identity, many North Americans, including US Latinos, claim languages and identities in other ways. [...] Spanish and English local and global varieties, and the multiple identities that these produce in their unending combinations, are meant to be and work together for the common good of all.

This attention to the discursive construction of identity in situations where there are uneven degrees of cultural capital attributed by the society to different languages and varieties of languages has been taken up in translanguaging literature on bi/multilinguals' spontaneous use of two or more languages (e.g., Creese & Blackledge, 2010; García & Kleifgen, 2010; Li, 2011). Different degrees of cultural capital related to different languages can also result in an inability to translanguage; for example, when students do not know very much of their heritage language(s) at all. The following quotation by a boy with a Chinese heritage, taken from a study by He (as cited in Norton & Toohey, 2011 p. 431), evidences the complexity of heritage-language learning:

> My home language is Chinese. My parents are from China. They praised me, scolded me, all in Chinese. [...] My Chinese is really bad. I can't read and I can only write my name. But when I think of Chinese, I think of my mom, dad, and home. It is the language of my home, and my heart.

There is a sense of connection here but also a sense of loss: a student feeling emotionally close to a language in which he feels that he cannot participate. Attempting to increase the cultural capital of heritage and additional languages through attention to students' language practices is key to the promotion of multilingualism in this book.

The cultural capital related to languages is linked to power dynamics, but students' motives to speak another language, or the value they attribute to the other language, may also be personal, rather than societal. In other words, what is considered valuable to the students may or may not reflect dominant understandings around 'legitimate' modes of thinking. The extent to which different students feel connected to languages varies (e.g., Duff, 2007; Kanno, 2003), students can be influenced by their self-perception of proficiency in a particular language (e.g., Huang, 1995) and investment in a language can be constrained or enhanced by other identity positions (Norton & Toohey, 2011), such as 'brainy student' or 'cool student'. How the students perceive themselves and the communities to which they feel they belong is thus useful knowledge for a teacher who seeks to develop learning activities in which the students will engage.

The idea of belonging to a community is also significant when considering what Kramsch (2012) called the 'multilingual subject', or 'learners of languages other than their own or users of multiple languages' (p. 483). The problematising of ideas such as the 'native' and 'non-native' speaker (see Chap. 2) and the decentralising of fixed notions of standard forms of language in today's globalised world does not necessarily make people feel more legitimate or authentic as speakers in different language communities. Authenticity can be found in situated practices and norms, or speaking or acting in a way that fits with a particular group (Gill, 2011). This can also be understood as a process—the process of authentication—in which speakers prove their authenticity through engagement in strategies or practices that 'keep it real' (Bucholz, 2003). Authenticity is connected to something that is identifiable and unquestioned (Heller & Duchêne, 2012): for example, a speaker who grew up in a particular region and speaks the dialect of that region. The construct of legitimacy is similar in that 'a legitimate speaker is assumed to be an authentic member of a group' (Kramsch, 2012, p. 490). However, legitimacy is understood to be sanctioned by an institution (ibid.). What an institution such as a school sanctions in relation to language use can be important even for speakers who feel authentic (natural) when using a particular language or language variety.

For Kramsch (ibid.), feelings of inauthenticity and illegitimacy among multilingual subjects can be related to what she termed 'imposture'. She described imposture in this way:

> The poststructuralist notion of posture and its correlate imposture have to do with the fit between an idealized self, whose idealization is legitimized and even promoted by the media, the market, and the community, and the self one really considers oneself to be. (p. 488)

Kramsch argued that this poststructuralist perspective does not attempt to help multilingual subjects attain some sense of belonging, a goal she ascribed to modernist approaches seeking to empower those without power, but rather considers how a transformation might occur when these subjects 'realise the artificial and constructed nature of the categories imposed upon them' (2012, p. 498). For the transformation to happen, the deconstruction of discourses that impose these categories and an understanding of their 'historically contingent' nature are important. This highlights the importance of finding spaces to work towards one of García and Li's (2014) translanguaging pedagogical goals discussed in Chap. 2: that of the interrogation of linguistic inequity and the disruption of linguistic hierarchies. The teacher, whilst undeniably an important agent in a student's sense of belonging in the classroom and at school, can thus also be considered to have the role of questioner and facilitator of critical reflection on the historically constructed discourses surrounding this belonging.

An idea of imposture can also, perhaps paradoxically, be linked to a driving force, or a desire to expand one's linguistic repertoire. Desire can be understood as a lack or a feeling of incompleteness (see Lacan, 1977), and individuals can be socialised into this feeling, especially in relation to a dominant language such as English (Motha & Lin, 2014). An understanding of desire as lack supports the deficit view of language discussed in Chap. 2. However, in some cases, it may be beneficial to promote identification with some imagined group to which one does not (yet) 'belong'. Communities with which students hope to identify can both be real (they know the members) and imagined (they feel unity with a group of people they have never met). The term 'imagined communities' was first proposed by Anderson (1991) to discuss nation states as a community of people that mainly existed in peoples' minds and that has given rise to some sense of unity with strangers. The notion of imagined community can be related to students' desire to belong to a language community—whatever that means to them—and can be a motive for their engagement in particular language practices.

Desire can therefore be conceptualised as an energy because it can help us progress towards our goals (Deleuze & Guattari, 1977): desire as lack and energy are not mutually exclusive (Ahmed, 2010). Although desires can be forgiving of the inequity inherent in language use, and perpetuate this by, for example, moving away from heritage languages and towards the sole use of English, desire can also be a positive force towards other languages. 'A feeling of promise in the form of lack' may help students who identify as monolingual to engage with other languages (Turner & Lin, 2017, p. 7). The desire to belong to either a real or imagined community can underpin students' language practices, and opportunities may exist to ignite or encourage this desire in the imagination, as well as in communities both inside and outside school.

4.5 Institutional Structures

The extent to which a multilingual stance is adopted in a school, and student engagement with particular languages, are therefore understood to be two dimensions that influence opportunities to learn. Another important dimension is institutional structures, or the organisation of teaching and learning at school level. This dimension is conceptualised as an operational one. Spolsky, Green and Read (1974) proposed that the main operational variables in bilingual education were curriculum, subjects, materials, teachers, language strategies, initial literacy, parental involvement, exit criteria and whole-school buy-in. All of these variables have the potential to afford or constrain learning, both in bilingual programmes and in the education of (emergent) bi/multilinguals. Institutional structures addressed in this section are chosen because they were found to be important influences in the empirical studies to be discussed later in Part Two of the book. They include the degree of organisation and commitment to cross-curricular language use, teachers' professional learning and teacher collaboration—variables that relate to Spolsky et al.'s (1974) curriculum, subjects, extent of school buy-in and teachers. They also include human and material language resources, extracurricular activities, inclusion of parents/the community and student-centred learning. Student-centred learning is not a clear fit with Spolsky et al.'s variables, but it was found to be influential in the studies. The language-based pedagogies discussed in Chap. 3 align loosely with the variable of language strategies. In the studies, language scripts were mostly found to be

4 Opportunities to Learn (Through) Languages 95

divergent from English, or the Roman alphabet, and this is an area that still requires research in bilingual education (Beatens Beardsmore, 2009). Literacy will thus be discussed according to study findings later in the book. Exit criteria that deviated from usual English-medium or language classrooms were not conspicuous in the data.

First, there is a great deal of curricular variation amongst schools that have committed to the use of languages across the curriculum. This can be seen in the previous chapter where Canadian early-immersion programmes teach students entirely through the medium of French before incorporating English, whilst CLIL programmes might only teach one or two subjects through a target language. Schools may also have different streams, with the bilingual stream being opt-in or select-entry, or they might run a whole-school bilingual programme. In their discussion of CLIL in the Australian context, Cross and Gearon (2013) further distinguished between school commitment and school acceptance: by school acceptance they referred to the potential for a teacher to start teaching CLIL bottom-up with approval from the principal but with no change in class organisation or staffing. Drawing on the linguistic resources of students can also be achieved bottom-up by teachers in English-medium classes. Further, school choices around teaching language as a subject area, as well as using it as a medium of instruction for other subject areas, can differ. Sometimes students study the language before it becomes the medium of instruction in other classes: for example, in Germany (Mäsch, 1993; Rumlich, 2014). However, in other programmes, such as Canadian immersion, the target language is used as a medium of instruction straightaway. An abrupt transition between languages can also happen. Students move from studying in their home language for the first three years of primary school to studying in a dominant language (such as English) the next. In other cases, a gradual transition can occur, such as the move in Luxembourg from Luxemburgish to German to French (see Beatens Beardsmore, 2009).

Next, teachers' professional learning can be understood as an important operational variable because teachers are very often themselves educated in monolingual schools and may not have received any specific pre-service training on the integration of language and content in their teacher education. Careful thought on how to incorporate teachers' ongoing in-service learning around the cross-curricular use of a target language, or the incorporation of heritage languages in English-medium classes, is beneficial in these cases. As Beatens Beardsmore (2009, p. 150) stated, a 'lack of training may well account for many of the past inadequacies in outcomes, but even in successful [bilingual education] programs, teachers are often left to fend for themselves'. Confidence in the target language is an important consideration (e.g., Lasagabaster & Ruiz de Zarobe, 2010; Pérez-Cañado, 2016a, 2016b; Rubio Mostacero, 2009) but ongoing professional development in the kinds of pedagogies discussed in Chap. 3 is also important, as Pérez-Cañado (2016a) found in her European study on linguistically proficient in-service CLIL teachers' perceptions of their needs. Morton (2018) suggested that common and specialised knowledge of both the content and language that are required in a CLIL classroom could be integrated, and it is this integration that constitutes the knowledge subject-area teachers require in order to engage in CLIL. Subject-area teachers' professional learning on the use and scaffolding of language is a particularly well-established topic in the field of EAL: there has been a marked trend towards integration and the mainstreaming of EAL students in countries such as Australia, the US and the UK (see Harper, de Jong, & Platt, 2008). Leveraging languages that heritage students know as a resource at school is also something with which teachers may be unfamiliar in institutionally monolingual contexts, and professional learning is likely to be beneficial.

Teacher collaboration is a further operational variable. This is a very important aspect of school life in general, but is particularly relevant to the incorporation of a target language across the curriculum because language teachers are generally teaching the language as a subject in its own right. In the field of CLIL, for example, Dalton-Puffer (2018) viewed the role of the language teacher as a research area in urgent need of attention. Across EAL and immersion contexts, issues around collaboration between language teachers and subject-area teachers have included organisational factors, such as time and support (e.g., Newman, Samimy, & Romstedt, 2010), unequal distributions of power and status with the language teacher positioned as lower (e.g., Arkoudis, 2006; Creese, 2002, 2005), subject-area and language teachers' differing views of teaching either as transmissive or negotiated respectively (e.g., Creese, 2010; Lo, 2014), the prioritising of either content or language (e.g., Lyster, 2011) and the lack of either content or language knowledge (e.g., Kong, 2014). Although there is a scarcity of research in the area, teachers who are dually qualified in language and another subject area may be well positioned to address these collaboration issues. This will be discussed in Chap. 7. Another area that does not appear to be a well-established research focus is that of teacher collaboration in the leveraging of students' linguistic repertoires in class. This kind of collaboration will be discussed in relation to the collegial nature of the teachers' professional learning in Chaps. 5 and 6.

Language resources, extracurricular activities and inclusion of parents/the community are additional variables. Language resources can be both human, in the form of teaching assistants, and material. Teaching assistants may help in the classroom or in a behind-the-scenes capacity, assisting in the creation of teaching and learning resources. Parental/community involvement can be more or less challenging depending on the degree to which values are shared between the school and home and whether or not parents can speak easily to stakeholders at school. Speaking easily refers both to minority parents feeling confident in a particular language and also to whether or not parents view their involvement as appropriate (see Beatens Beardsmore, 2009). Extracurricular activities can include parents and the community, and also incorporate a range of activities, from performances, assemblies, planting vegetable gardens and making artwork for public consumption to a homestay in a different country.

Finally, a very important operational variable is the promotion (or not) of students' active engagement in the learning process. As mentioned earlier in the chapter, from a sociocultural perspective, social interaction is considered to be the site of learning, and novice participation can lead to fuller participation in a particular community of practice. This complements the enquiry-based approach common in schooling in countries such as Australia, where students are given some control over the object of their own learning. In her discussion of different participatory structures, Ur (1996) gave five different kinds of interaction: students are receptive, mainly receptive, equally active with the teacher, more active than the teacher and very active while the teacher is receptive. Within the latter three of these structures, different kinds of interactional strategies

98 M. Turner

have been found to lead to positive learning outcomes and can be considered in relation to cross-curricular language use. These strategies include hands-on activities (Murphy, 2007), the guiding of students' understanding through questioning (Rojas-Drummond & Mercer, 2004), the eliciting of reasons and/or explanations (Kyriacou & Issitt, 2008; Vrikki, Wheatley, Howe, Hennessy, & Mercer, 2018) and expecting extended contributions from students (Alexander, 2001; Vrikki et al., 2018). Alexander (2008, p. 38) also offered an empirically based set of essential characteristics of a dialogic approach that comprised the need for teachers and children to undertake tasks together in a supportive environment, listen to each other and share views, as well as the need for students to coherently build on ideas, and the teacher to ensure attention to specific educational goals.

According to Swain's (1985) output hypothesis (cited in Chap. 3), the extent to which students can actively use language is very important in bilingual programmes. This is a significant factor not only for expanding linguistic repertoire, but also for leveraging existing repertoire in English-medium classrooms where heritage students might be leveraging resources that are not shared by the teacher, or by other students in the classroom. Increasing students' agency in the classroom through a co-constructed, negotiated form of teaching, rather than limiting teaching to transmission, can allow students to bring knowledge not shared by the teacher into the classroom as a resource for learning.

4.6 A Multilingual Practices Framework

Multilingual stance, student engagement with languages, and institutional structures and pedagogies are three dimensions that influence both each other and students' opportunities to learn, especially in conditions of diversity. My main objective in this chapter has been to discuss students' learning opportunities from a sociocultural and sociopolitical perspective, as well as from an operational perspective. Learning opportunities are positioned as inclusive of the recognition and celebration of linguistic knowledge, most importantly in relation to heritage-language speakers, and of a critical understanding of language inequity. These will

4 Opportunities to Learn (Through) Languages

be a focus of the teaching and learning objectives discussed in Chap. 9. A principal assumption underlying the multilingual practices framework discussed here is that linking these practices to student learning is an important way for students' knowledge and experiences to be valued at school.

Language-based pedagogies are included in the framework: they were the focus of Chap. 3 and included form-focused instruction, functional language, language scaffolding and crosslinguistic pedagogy. These pedagogies are considered to be a significant influence on students' language learning and use. They are conceptualised alongside institutional structures because the structures can be pedagogical in nature; student-centred learning, for example, can be a whole-school approach. Together, all three dimensions are conceptualised to afford (or constrain) learning opportunities and all three may be dynamic, or subject to change. The arrows between the dimensions in Fig. 4.1 show the mutual influence of the dimensions on each other. For example, if teachers' multilingual stance shifts, the teachers might modify their pedagogical approach and this might influence students' engagement with languages. A change in one dimension has the potential to influence other dimensions, but is not conceptualised to be automatically influential. For example, institutional structures might change, but teachers (and students) might retain a primarily pro-monolingual ideology regarding schoolwork, or stimulating, language-based pedagogies can be used but students still do not see

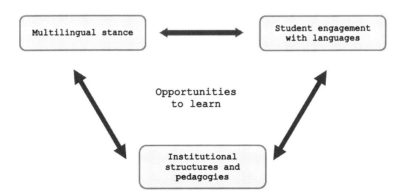

Fig. 4.1 Multilingual practices framework

the point of learning the language they are studying. Also, influence might be exerted within a dimension: for example, teachers' professional learning might lead to greater collaboration or a stronger focus on language scaffolding, even though no changes have occurred across the other two dimensions.

The multilingual practices framework is designed to assist in thinking about how students' linguistic repertoire (language resources) can be leveraged and/or expanded in ways that provide opportunities to achieve different kinds of teaching and learning objectives. Examples of these objectives are discussed in relation to the empirical studies that comprise Part Two and are also collated in Chap. 9. The framework focuses on understanding and working with stakeholder expectations and engagement with languages, as well as the more structural and pedagogical elements of formal education. It takes into account potentially differing institutional expectations around language learning and use, or multilingual stance, as well as variations in students' identification with—and desire to learn—different languages. Changes in institutional structures and pedagogies are likely to go a long way towards the development and implementation of sustainable and effective programmes for (emergent) bi/multilinguals. However, different stakeholders' language-related understandings and practices are influential and are not only the product of experiences at school. Considering what these dimensions might entail in different contexts may be able to assist school leaders and practitioners in formulating an overarching language policy that includes both the incorporation of heritage languages into English-medium classes and the cross-curricular learning and use of a target language.

4.7 Conclusion

The chapter has highlighted important influences on stakeholder participation in cross-curricular language use and learning. A sociocultural perspective is useful for understanding this participation because it promotes engagement with cultural norms and experiences that stakeholders bring with them to school or the classroom. This approach is complementary to sociolinguistic perspectives on language because social interactions can contain an unequal distribution of linguistic power and cultural capital. A focus on this inequity can facilitate its critique. Opportunities for student learning as a result of the leveraging and expanding of linguistic repertoire were discussed in relation to a multilingual practices framework that took into account a multilingual stance, students' engagement with languages and institutional structures and pedagogies. This framework will now be used to discuss the four studies in Part Two of the book.

References

Ahmed, S. (2010). *The promise of happiness*. Durham, NC: Duke University Press.

Alexander, R. J. (2001). *Culture and pedagogy: International comparisons in primary education*. Oxford: Blackwell.

Alexander, R. J. (2008). *Towards dialogic teaching: Rethinking classroom talk*. York: Dialogos.

Anderson, B. (1991). *Imagined communities: Reflections on the origin and spread of nationalism* (revised ed.). New York: Verso.

Arkoudis, S. (2006). Negotiating the rough ground between ESL and mainstream teachers. *International Journal of Bilingual Education and Bilingualism, 9*, 415–433.

Bandura, A. (1997). *Self-efficacy: The exercise of control*. San Francisco: W.H. Freeman.

Beatens Beardsmore, H. (2009). Bilingual education: Factors and variables. In O. García (Ed.), *Bilingual education in the 21st century: A global perspective* (pp. 137–158). Malden, MA: Wiley-Blackwell.

Blair, A., Haneda, M., & Nebus Bose, F. (2018). Reimagining English-medium instructional settings as sites of multilingual and multimodal meaning making. *TESOL Quarterly, 52*(3), 516–538.

Blommaert, J. (2010). *The sociolinguistics of globalization*. Cambridge: Cambridge University Press.

Boaler, J., & Greeno, J. G. (2000). Identity, agency, and knowing in mathematics worlds. In J. Boaler (Ed.), *Multiple perspectives on mathematics teaching and learning* (pp. 171–200). Westport, CT: Ablex Publishing.

Bourdieu, P. (1977). The economics of linguistic exchanges. *Social Science Information, 16*(6), 645–668.

Bourdieu, P., & Passeron, J. (1977). *Reproduction in education, society, and culture*. London and Beverly Hills, CA: Sage Publications.

Bucholz, M. (2003). Sociolinguistic nostalgia and the authentication of identity. *Journal of Sociolinguistics, 7*, 398–416.

Creese, A. (2002). The discursive construction of power in teacher partnerships: Language and subject specialists in mainstream schools. *TESOL Quarterly, 36*(4), 597–616.

Creese, A. (2005). Is this content-based language teaching? *Linguistics and Education, 16*(2), 188–204.

Creese, A. (2010). Content-focused classrooms and learning English: How teachers collaborate. *Theory Into Practice, 49*(2), 99–105.

Creese, A., & Blackledge, A. (2010). Translanguaging in the bilingual classroom: A pedagogy for learning and teaching? *The Modern Language Journal, 94*, 103–115.

Cross, R., & Gearon, M. (2013). *Research and evaluation of the content and language integrated learning (CLIL) approach to teaching and learning languages in Victorian schools*. Melbourne: Melbourne Graduate School of Education, The University of Melbourne.

Dalton-Puffer, C. (2018). Postscriptum: Research pathways in CLIL/immersion instructional practices and teacher development. *International Journal of Bilingual Education and Bilingualism, 21*(3), 384–387.

de Jong, E. J. (2018, Keynote). *Taking a multilingual stance: Quality education for ELLs*. Minneapolis, MN: Minnesota-TESOL.

Deleuze, G., & Guattari, F. (1977). *Anti-Oedipus: Capitalism and schizophrenia*. New York: Viking Press.

Duff, P. (2007). Second language socialization as sociocultural theory: Insights and issues. *Language Teaching, 40*, 309–319.

Eccles, J. S. (2005). Subjective task value and the Eccles et al. model of achievement-related choices. In A. J. Elliott & C. S. Dweck (Eds.), *Handbook of competence and motivation* (pp. 105–121). New York: Guilford.

Elliot, A. J., & Dweck, C. S. (Eds.). (2005). *Handbook of competence and motivation*. New York: Guilford.

Ellis, R. (1994). A theory of instructed second language acquisition. In N. Ellis (Ed.), *Implicit and explicit learning of languages* (pp. 79–114). San Diego, CA: Academic Press.

Ellis, R., & Shintani, N. (2014). *Exploring language pedagogy through second language acquisition research*. London: Routledge.

Fitzsimmons-Doolan, S. (2018). Language ideology change over time: Lessons for language policy in the U.S. state of Arizona and beyond. *TESOL Quarterly, 52*(1), 34–61.

Flores, N., & García, O. (2017). A critical review of bilingual education in the United States: From basements and pride to boutiques and profit. *Annual Review of Applied Linguistics, 37*, 14–29.

Foucault, M. (1980). *Power/knowledge: Selected interviews and other writings 1972–1977* (C. Gordon, Trans.). New York: Pantheon Books.

French, M. (2016). Students' multilingual resources and policy-in-action: An Australian case study. *Language and Education, 30*, 298–316. https://doi.org/10.1080/09500782.2015.1114628

García, O. (2009). Livin' and Teachin' la lengua loca: Glocalizing U.S. Spanish ideologies and practices. In R. Salaberry (Ed.), *Language allegiances and bilingualism in the United States* (pp. 151–171). Clevedon: Multilingual Matters.

García, O., & Kleifgen, J. (2010). *Educating emergent bilinguals: Policies, programs, and practices for English language learners.* New York: Teachers College Press.

García, O., & Li, W. (2014). *Translanguaging: Language, bilingualism and education.* New York: Palgrave Macmillan.

Gibbons, P. (2003). Mediating language learning: Teacher interactions with ESL students in a content-based classroom. *TESOL Quarterly, 37*(2), 247–273.

Gibson, J. (1977). *The ecological approach to visual perception.* Hillsdale, NJ: Lawrence Erlbaum.

Gill, M. (2011). Authenticity. In J. O. Östman & J. Verschueren (Eds.), *Pragmatics in practice* (pp. 46–61). Philadelphia, PA: John Benjamins.

Greeno, J. G., & Gresalfi, M. S. (2015). Opportunities to learn in practice and identity. In P. A. Moss, D. C. Pullin, J. P. Gee, E. H. Haertel, & L. Jones (Eds.), *Assessment, equity and opportunity to learn.* Cambridge: Cambridge University Press.

Harper, C. A., de Jong, E. J., & Platt, E. J. (2008). Marginalizing English as a second language teacher expertise: The exclusionary consequence of *No Child Left* Behind. *Language Policy, 7*, 267–284. https://doi.org/10.1007/s10993-008-9102-y

Heller, M., & Duchêne, A. (2012). Pride and profit. Changing discourses of language, capital and nation-state. In A. Duchêne & M. Heller (Eds.), *Language in Late Capitalism* (pp. 1–21). London: Routledge.

Hickey, D. T., & Granade, J. B. (2004). The influence of sociocultural theory on our theories of engagement and motivation. In D. McInerney & S. Van Etten (Eds.), *Big Theories Revisited* (pp. 223–247). Connecticut: Information Age Publishing.

Huang, G. (1995). Self reported biliteracy and self esteem: a study of Mexican American 8th graders. *Applied Psycholinguistics, 16*(3), 271–291.

Kanno, Y. (2003). *Negotiating bilingual and bicultural identities: Japanese returnees betwixt two worlds*. Mahwah, NJ: Lawrence Erlbaum.

Kong, S. (2014). Collaboration between content and language specialists in late immersion. *The Canadian Modern Language Review/La Revue Canadienne Des Langues Vivantes, 70*(1), 103–122.

Kramsch, C. (2012). Authenticity and legitimacy in multilingual SLA. *Critical Multilingualism Studies, 1*, 107–128.

Krashen, S. (1981). *Second language acquisition and second language learning*. Oxford: Pergamon.

Kyriacou, C., & Issitt, J. (2008). *What characterizes effective teacher-pupil dialogue to promote conceptual understanding in mathematics lessons in England in key stages 2 and 3?* EPPI-centre report no. 1604R, Social Science Research Unit, Institute of Education, University of London.

Lacan, J. (1977). *The mirror stage as formative of the I. écrits: A selection* (A. Sheridan, Trans.). New York: W.W. Norton.

Lasagabaster, D., & Ruiz de Zarobe, Y. (2010). *Spain: Implementation, results and teacher training*. Newcastle-upon-Tyne: Cambridge Scholars Publishing.

Lave, J. (1988). *Cognition in practice: Mind, mathematics and culture in everyday life*. New York: Cambridge University Press.

Lave, J., & Wenger, W. (1991). *Situated learning: Legitimate peripheral participation*. Cambridge: Cambridge University Press.

Letiche, H., & Lissack, M. (2009). Making room for affordances. *Emergence: Complexity and Organization, 11*(3), 61–72.

Li, W. (2011). Moment analysis and translanguaging space. *Journal of Pragmatics, 43*, 1222–1235.

Lo, Y. Y. (2014). A glimpse into the effectiveness of L2-content cross-curricular collaboration in content-based instruction programmes. *International Journal of Bilingual Education and Bilingualism, 16*(3), 375–388.

Lyster, R. (2011). Content-based second language teaching. In E. Hinkel (Ed.), *Handbook of research in second language teaching and learning*. New York: Routledge.

Makoni, S., & Pennycook, A. (2007). Disinventing and reconstituting languages. In S. Makoni & A. Pennycook (Eds.), *Disinventing and reconstituting languages* (pp. 1–41). Clevedon: Multilingual Matters.

Mäsch, N. (1993). The German model of bilingual education: An administrator's perspective. In H. B. Beardsmore (Ed.), *European models of bilingual education* (pp. 155–172). Clevedon: Multilingual Matters.

McCaslin, M. (2009). Co-regulation of student motivation and emergent identity. *Educational Psychologist, 44*(2), 137–146.

Morton, T. (2012). *Teachers' knowledge about language and classroom interaction in content and language integrated learning.* Doctoral thesis, Universidad Autónoma de Madrid.

Morton, T. (2018). Reconceptualizing and describing teachers' knowledge of language for content and language integrated learning (CLIL). *International Journal of Bilingual Education and Bilingualism, 21*(3), 275–286.

Motha, S., & Lin, A. M. Y. (2014). 'Non-coercive rearrangements': Theorizing desire in TESOL. *TESOL Quarterly, 48*(2), 331–359.

Murphy, P. K. (2007). The eye of the beholder: The interplay of social and cognitive components in change. *Educational Psychologist, 42*(1), 41–53.

Newman, K., Samimy, K., & Romstedt, K. (2010). Developing a training program for secondary teachers of English language learners in Ohio. *Theory Into Practice, 49*(2), 152–161.

Nolen, S., Horn, I., & Ward, C. (2015). Situating motivation. *Educational Psychologist, 50*(3), 234–247.

Nolen, S., Ward, C. J., & Horn, I. S. (2011). Motivation, engagement, and identity: Opening a conversation. In D. McInerney, R. A. Walker, & G. A. Liem (Eds.), *Sociocultural theories of learning and motivation: Looking back, looking forward* (Vol. 10, pp. 109–135). Charlotte, NC: Information Age.

Norton, B. (2000). *Identity and language learning: Gender, ethnicity and educational change.* Harlow: Pearson Education/Longman.

Norton, B., & Toohey, K. (2011). Identity, language learning, and social change. *Language Teaching, 44*(4), 412–446.

Norton Peirce, B. (1995). Social identity, investment, and language learning. *TESOL Quarterly, 29*(1), 9–31.

Pacheco, M. (2018). Spanish, Arabic, and 'English-Only': Making meaning across languages in two classroom communities. *TESOL Quarterly, 52*(4), 1–27. https://doi.org/10.1002/tesq.446

Pennycook, A. (2001). Lessons from colonial language policies. In R. D. González (Ed.), *Language ideologies: Critical perspectives on the official English movement* (Vol. 2, pp. 195–219). Urbana, IL: National Council of Teachers of English.

Pérez-Cañado, M. L. (2016a). Teacher training needs for bilingual education: In-service teacher perceptions. *International Journal of Bilingual Education and Bilingualism, 19*(3), 266–295.

Pérez-Cañado, M. L. (2016b). Are teachers ready for CLIL? Evidence from a European study. *European Journal of Teacher Education, 39*(2), 202–221. https://doi.org/10.1080/02619768.2016.1138104

Rojas-Drummond, S., & Mercer, N. (2004). Scaffolding the development of effective collaboration and learning. *International Journal of Educational Research, 39*, 99–111.

Rubio Mostacero, M. D. (2009). Language teacher training for non-language teachers: Meeting the needs of Andalusian teachers for school plurilingualism projects. In *Design of a Targeted Training Course*. Jaén: Universidad de Jaén.

Ruiz, R. (1984). Orientations in language planning. *NABE Journal, 8*(2), 15–34.

Rumlich, D. (2014). Prospective CLIL and non-CLIL students' interest in English (classes): A quasi-experimental study on German sixth-graders. *Utrecht Studies in Language and Communication, 28*, 75–95.

Säljö, R. (2009). Learning, theories of learning, and units of analysis in research. *Educational Psychologist, 44*(3), 202–208.

Spolsky, B., Green, J., & Read, J. (1974). *A model for the description, analysis, and perhaps evaluation of bilingual education*. Navajo Reading Study Progress Report 23. University of New Mexico, Albuquerque, NM.

Swain, M. (1985). Communicative competence: Some roles of comprehensible input and comprehensible output in its development. In S. Gass & C. Madden (Eds.), *Input in Second Language Acquisition* (pp. 235–253). Rowley, MA: Newbury House.

Turner, M., & Lin, A. M. Y. (2017). Translanguaging and named languages: Productive tension and desire. *International Journal of Bilingual Education and Bilingualism.*https://doi.org/10.1080/13670050.2017.1360243

Ur, P. (1996). *A course in language teaching: Practice and theory*. Cambridge: Cambridge University Press.

Vadeboncoeur, J., Vellos, R., & Goessling, K. (2011). Learning as (one part) identity construction: Educational implications of a sociocultural perspective. In D. McInerney, R. Walker, & G. Liem (Eds.), *Sociocultural theories of learning and motivation: Looking back, looking forward* (pp. 223–251). Charlotte, NC: Information Age Publishing.

Van Lier, L. (2004). *The ecology and semiotics of language learning: A sociocultural perspective*. New York: Kluwer Academic.

Vrikki, M., Wheatley, L., Howe, C., Hennessy, S., & Mercer, N. (2018). Dialogic practices in primary classrooms. *Language and Education.*https://doi.org/10.1080/09500782.2018.1509988

Vygotsky, L. S. (1978). *Mind in society: The development of higher psychological processes*. Cambridge, MA: Harvard University Press.

Weedon, C. (1997). *Feminist practice and poststructuralist theory* (2nd ed.). London: Blackwell.

Wenger, E. (1998). *Communities of practice: Learning, meaning, and identity.* Cambridge: Cambridge University Press.

Wertsch, J. V. (1991). *Voices of the mind: A sociocultural approach to mediated action.* Cambridge, MA: Harvard University Press.

West, C. (1992). A matter of life and death. *October, 61*(Summer), 20–23.

Part II

Application

Part II of this book applies the multilingual practices framework to four kinds of mainstream school settings in Australia. Each chapter addresses a particular setting and an associated empirical study. Chapters 5 and 6 relate to studies conducted in primary schools and Chaps. 7 and 8 to secondary schools. In Chap. 5, a study on a generalist primary school setting is discussed. Three schools with a majority of language background other than English (LBOTE) children participated. Chapter 6 covers a government-funded whole-school primary Japanese–English bilingual programme. Chapter 7 focuses on teacher-driven content-and-language-integrated learning (CLIL) initiatives in three lower secondary schools. Finally, Chap. 8 addresses a structured lower secondary CLIL programme with no entry criteria. Although the latter three chapters have an explicit focus on the cross-curricular learning of target languages, heritage languages were conspicuous in the data in all four settings.

Data analysis in the studies was thematic (see Braun & Clarke, 2008), and I returned to the data for each study when writing this book in order to try to understand the sociocultural and sociopolitical dimensions of teaching and learning, and how the way we approach language may help inform decisions around the promotion of multilingualism in mainstream schools. At the beginning of each chapter, I have provided the context of the study, along with details on participants and how I collected data. The studies were all conducted between 2014 and 2017.

110 Part II Application

Each chapter is similarly structured in order to show my thinking in relation to the framework: multilingual stance, student engagement, institutional structures and pedagogies, and—what appears at the centre of the framework—opportunities to learn (through) languages.

Reference

Braun, V., & Clarke, V. (2008). Using thematic analysis in psychology. *Qualitative Research in Psychology, 3*(2), 77–101.

5

Primary Schools with Heritage-Language Students

5.1 Introduction

In 2016 in the Australian state of Victoria, 27 per cent of students identified as coming from a language background other than English (LBOTE) (Department of Education and Training, Victoria, 2017). LBOTE students can be fluent in English with a very wide range of proficiency in their heritage language(s). They may not necessarily be immigrants to Australia themselves, but may speak and/or be exposed to heritage languages as members of successive generations of immigrants. Because TESOL-related government funding is reserved for new arrivals (Oliver, Rochecouste, & Nguyen, 2017), schools are required to make decisions about how to understand and meet the needs of these learners, who can range from having both parents with limited English language proficiency to having at least one parent who is proficient. An important objective of the study reported in this chapter was to assist in guiding teachers' investigation of LBOTE students' linguistic repertoire as an ongoing asset in their schooling. LBOTE students born in the country learn English at school, and may speak (or be exposed to) other languages at home. The study highlighted the 'speaking other languages'

© The Author(s) 2019
M. Turner, *Multilingualism as a Resource and a Goal*,
https://doi.org/10.1007/978-3-030-21591-0_5

111

part of TESOL, and sought to reinforce the value of this by both celebrating it and showing how it might help students learn in English-medium classes.

Three Catholic primary schools participated in the study and, in all the schools, over 80 per cent of students identified as LBOTE (Australian Curriculum, Assessment and Reporting Authority, 2018). The Australian government has a system whereby it measures schools in relation to the socio-educational advantage of communities, and two of the schools were below average on this measure, while the third school was average (ibid.). Students' level of performance in the National Assessment Program: Literacy and Numeracy (NAPLAN) was found to correlate to the socio-educational advantage of the parents (ibid.). In this chapter, the study will be described first, followed by the findings mapped against the multilingual practices framework. A summary of these findings precedes a discussion on each dimension.

5.2 The Study

The study used a design-based research framework (e.g., Anderson & Shattuck, 2012; Cobb, Confrey, diSessa, Lehrer, & Schauble, 2003), which involves collaboration between researchers and practitioners. Design-based research focuses on process, or ways in which particular outcomes are achieved. Instructional hypotheses are generated, trialled and subsequently refined in further iterations. The study was informed by D'Warte's (2013, 2014, 2015) and Somerville, D'Warte, and Sawyer's (2016) research, in which LBOTE students were found to engage positively with the process of mapping their everyday language practices, to show improvement in the quality of their English and to evidence an attitudinal change towards their heritage language.

5.2.1 Aims

The aim of the study was to trial the following instructional hypothesis:

5 Primary Schools with Heritage-Language Students 113

Students' creation of visual representations of their linguistic repertoires—how, where, when and with whom they speak particular languages and how they feel about them—can assist in the leveraging of the students' language practices as a resource for their learning.

5.2.2 Participants and Data Collection

The three Victorian primary schools that took part were given the pseudonyms Madison PS, Hampton PS and Campbell PS. Madison PS (264 students) and Hampton PS (125 students) serviced communities of lower socio-educational advantage than Campbell PS (295 students) (Australian Curriculum, Assessment and Reporting Authority, 2018). Five classes in total participated: two Year 1/2[1] classes and one Year 3/4 class at Madison PS, one Year 3/4 class at Hampton PS, and one Year 3 class at Campbell PS (see Table 5.2). All participating teachers took part in professional learning (see Table 5.1). They had at least 15 years of experience teaching primary, except for one teacher (Jasmine—see Table 5.2) who was in her first year of teaching in Australia. She had taught for

Table 5.1 The three phases of the study

Phase 1	• Classroom observation of each participating teacher's class • *Professional learning day 1* (teachers learn about project and language mapping) • Teachers prepare and teach language-mapping lesson sequence
Phase 2	• *Professional learning day 2* (teachers discuss first lesson sequence as a group[a]) (teachers plan another sequence of lessons leveraging students' language practices) • Teachers prepare, teach and reflect (in written form) on the second lesson sequence
Phase 3	• *Professional learning day 3* (teachers discuss second lesson sequence as a group[a]) • Interviews conducted with teachers, students and school leaders

[a]Discussions were audio-recorded and are referred to in this chapter as Group Reflection 1 (GR1) and Group Reflection 2 (GR2)

---

[1] In Australia, classes in primary schools can often consist of two grades learning as one group.

114   M. Turner

Table 5.2 Participants and data collection

School	Teachers[a]	Class	Students interviewed
Madison PS	Frida	1/2	3
	Sam	1/2	3
	Jasmine	3/4	3
Hampton PS	Sophia	3/4	6
	Cassandra (support)	4	–
Campbell PS	Anne	3	6
	Helen (support)	3	–

[a]Names are pseudonyms. All teachers were interviewed

ten years at a middle school in India and four and a half years at a primary school in Kuwait. She was also the only teacher who identified as speaking other languages: Hindi, Marathi and some Konkani. Anne and Sam had taught in Australian primary schools for over 30 years.

Teachers, students and school leaders were interviewed (see Table 5.1). Questions for teachers focused on the incorporation of students' language practices into their teaching, and also on whether or not their understanding of bilingualism (and how it was recognised at school) had changed over the course of the project. These topics were also the focus of the group reflection (see Table 5.1). Questions for students focused on whether or not the students had enjoyed making the language map in the project (see p. X for some examples of maps), their experience with different languages and whether or not they understood other languages to help them learn. All students interviewed were LBOTE. Work samples in the five classes were also collected. During the project, the two principals at Hampton PS and Campbell PS and the acting deputy principal at Madison PS were interviewed about school structures and student cohort. Thematic analysis (see Braun & Clarke, 2008) was used in the study, and all data were cross-referenced in the identification of themes.

5.3   Lesson Sequences

The teachers in this study designed two lesson sequences. In the first sequence, they investigated students' language practices: this included students' creation of a visual language map. Ideas for this sequence were

5 Primary Schools with Heritage-Language Students   115

adapted from D'Warte's (2013) study. In the second lesson sequence, teachers embedded students' language practices into teaching and learning without deviating from the curriculum content the students were scheduled to learn. This led to far more variation in the second sequence. Where links to the curriculum were explicitly made by teachers, they are included in the tables (Tables 5.3 and 5.4).

Table 5.3 Investigating students' language practices

Links to curriculum	Year	Focus
General—no specific links made	1/2 (Madison PS)	*Frida's and Sam's classes*: • discussed languages spoken by students, when, where and why they were spoken[a] • created language maps and discussed the maps
Understand that languages have different written and visual communication systems, different oral traditions and different ways of constructing meaning	3 and 3/4 (Madison PS, Hampton PS, Campbell PS)	*Jasmine's, Sophia's and Anne's classes*: • discussed language practices, completed worksheets and took language survey home to parents • discussed survey data (not Sophia's class) and did 5 W chart about language practices • created language maps and discussed them with teacher • shared language maps with classmates or presented language maps as a whole class activity • completed a Venn diagram comparing and contrasting language practices (Anne's class)

[a]Frida also created a colourful poster of students' answers for the first three lessons about (1) languages spoken, (2) when/where and (3) why they were spoken

116 M. Turner

Table 5.4 Leveraging students' language practices

Links to curriculum	Year	Focus
Understand that spoken, visual and written forms of language are different modes of communication with different features and their use varies according to the audience, purpose, context and cultural background	1/2	*Sam's class*: • discussed sentences Sam had written out and sent home to parents/ grandparents to write in their heritage language, such as 'I'm going home today' and 'how are you?' Sam collated the responses (from ten families) for the discussion
Understand that spoken, visual and written forms of language are different modes of communication with different features and their use varies according to the audience, purpose, context and cultural background	1/2	*Frida's class*: • shared their language maps with a classmate • listened to a 'Hello' song on YouTube, taught each other how to say 'hello' in their language and, as a class, noted differences between ways to say 'hello' • created puppets with a speech bubble that said 'hello' in different languages • wrote words of their choice in a giant speech bubble and shared the words (and meanings) in a class discussion • orally reflected on their learning
Examine the similarities and differences between individuals and groups based on factors such as sex, age, ability, language, culture and religion Identify personal strengths and select personal qualities that could be further developed	3/4	*Jasmine's class*: • wrote a text (a song, prayer, self-introduction, etc.) in a heritage language at home and translated it into English • made a presentation in their own language and classmates guessed the meaning and thought about the presentation in relation to languages they knew • read the English translation as the final part of the presentation • wrote a reflection on presenting and being part of the audience watching others present

(*continued*)

5 Primary Schools with Heritage-Language Students 117

Table 5.4 (continued)

Links to curriculum	Year	Focus
Understand that languages have different written and visual communication systems, different oral traditions and different ways of constructing meaning	3/4	*Sophia's class:* • gathered information (with parental input) about heritage country, and wrote a scaffolded information report • brainstormed words, as a class, that were going to be used in a geography inquiry unit and took a sheet home with the words to be translated into a heritage language • put the words on a classroom word wall, along with an illustration and definition in English • discussed linguistic similarities and differences • wrote a reflection on their learning
Living things can be grouped on the basis of observable features and can be distinguished from non-living things/ Different living things have different life cycles and depend on each other and the environment to survive	3	*Anne's class*: • interviewed their parents/grandparents (11 families) about an animal in their country of origin: for example, 'where does the animal live?' 'what do they need to survive?' and 'what do they look like?' The activity was scaffolded in class by interviewing a Chaldean-speaking teaching assistant • recorded the parent/grandparent interview, wrote it down, translated it into English, then reflected on the experience of translating

5.4 Summary of Findings

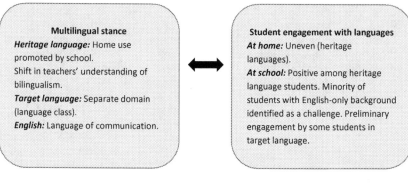

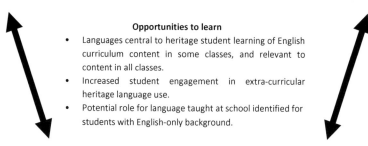

Fig. 5.1 Findings according to multilingual practices framework

5.5 Multilingual Stance

> *Heritage language:* Home use promoted by school.
> Shift in teachers' understanding of bilingualism.
> *Target language:* Separate domain (language class).
> *English:* Language of communication.

In the schools, English appeared to be the taken-for-granted mode of communication outside language classes. However, the teachers' multilingual stance was evident in their encouragement of parents to speak in their own language to the children at home, and their active positioning of other languages as assets. Language separation that was occurring before the study—English at school, heritage languages in the community—appeared to derive from feasibility issues associated with ways of thinking about language. The monolingual teachers' expectations around language use were found to relate to the understanding that bi/multilingualism is an aspect of who people are, rather than what they do. A focus on language practices in the professional learning aspect of the study led to a shift in thinking about bilingualism in general, and to more attention to differences related to speaking/listening and reading/writing practices. It also presented a way for teachers to integrate students' linguistic resources into teaching and learning.

5.5.1 What It Means to Be Bilingual

A shift in thinking related to bilingualism was clear for all the teachers who identified as monolingual. In the professional learning, they demonstrated a focus on what their students did with language, and how it was context-sensitive. Their reflections showed that this was a new way of thinking, and it helped them get to know their students more deeply. It particularly helped the teachers to understand the complexity of their students' language practices. Helen, who was supporting Anne in her Year 3 class at Campbell PS, summed up the shift when asked about whether her view of bilingualism had changed over the course of the study:

> *[Anne] found out to whom the children spoke particular languages and where they spoke [them], and I think that has really added to my understanding of*

120 M. Turner

what bilingualism means. [...] Because I hadn't stopped to think about speaking to a grandparent in one [language] versus a parent in another, versus at school it's different. [...] It's something quite sophisticated that perhaps I'd underrated to a degree. (Helen, interview)

An emphasis on what students were doing with language appeared to facilitate the inclusion of heritage languages into teaching and learning because the teachers' focus was on the students' language practices, rather than their own pedagogical and linguistic knowledge. Instead of the inclusion of different languages as an approach that demands a certain level of expertise from the teacher, a focus on students bringing language to class appeared to be more accessible. For example, Frida, one of the two Year 1/2 teachers at Madison PS, mentioned that she had been exposed to the benefits of students using heritage languages in class previously, but had not included the idea in her lessons:

I did a [Master's] project about the children's funds of knowledge, and [how] the children's language tends to stop at the classroom door. [...] Whilst I was aware of how important the children's languages are, I actually hadn't used it in my teaching in any way. [...] What I implemented in the classroom was a big change compared to what I was doing. (Frida, interview)

When asked why she had not brought children's home languages into her teaching earlier, Frida said:

I wasn't using it because I probably didn't feel I had the expertise to use it. [...] [L]ogistically how do I include everyone's language, even though I had studied it, I wasn't quite sure how to put it into place I suppose. (Frida, interview)

Providing a space for students to share their language practices, rather than thinking that the teacher had to be the one to include the languages in some way, offered a shift of perspective. Sam at Madison PS reinforced Frida's focus on feasibility by reporting that he had believed promoting bilingualism for the children (rather than a transition to English) to be a nice idea but out of reach:

We want [the children] to be bilingual but I think it was all just pie-in-the-sky stuff, now we can probably do something to achieve that goal for them. (Sam, interview)

Incorporating languages into the classroom therefore appeared to relate to an emphasis on students and what they knew and did—and a move away from a more abstract notion of 'being bilingual'—because it helped teachers make classroom connections with their students' lived experiences.

5.5.2 Literacy Practices

Investigating and leveraging students' language practices also highlighted differences in modes of heritage-language use and teachers' expectations around this. Jasmine, the only teacher who did not identify as monolingual, was also initially the only teacher to differentiate between oral communication and literacy. The word 'even' in the following quotation demonstrates Jasmine's emphasis that literacy was a different kind of practice than oracy:

[I was] just trying to tap in to what their language ability was. So, just getting to know if they spoke any language besides English, and how fluent they were. And there were some [...] who said they could even read and write the language. So, just getting to know all that. (Jasmine, interview)

As shown in the lesson sequences in the previous section, all the teachers relied on literacy in the heritage language as a way of leveraging their students' linguistic resources, and the monolingual teachers did not draw an explicit distinction between oracy and literacy in their initial reflections on bilingualism. However, in the planned activities, children could not necessarily read and write their languages, and this highlighted the importance of literacy to the teachers:

Some of [the children] can speak [their language], but none of them could write, so I think if they want to be bilingual it'll be a benefit for them to be able to write. Probably they concentrate on the language more when they're

122 M. Turner

writing it down, probably learn more about the language, and it may have some impact on them learning English as well. (Sam, interview)

For the last few years, we've really pushed [...] every parent that we talk to about speaking their own language at home, and the value of doing that. [...] We find people were speaking English at home, it wasn't very high standard English, and we felt that was holding children back. Whereas if they were speaking their own language the concepts, [...] the language itself is richer [...] so, that would help the child academically. [...] And we've always talked about [...] talking in our own language [...] but we hadn't ever talked about doing the reading and writing. (Helen, GR2)

These quotations indicate the expectation that literacy in a heritage language can be beneficial to both English language learning and academic achievement and thus evidence a growing multilingual stance. Many of the students' heritage languages used a different script, which was an added layer of complexity in reading and writing the language, and different scripts were generally not in evidence in the students' language maps—this will be discussed later in the chapter.

5.6 Student Engagement With Languages

> *At home:* Uneven (heritage languages).
> *At school:* Positive among heritage language students.
> Minority of students with English-only background identified as a challenge.
> Preliminary engagement by some students in target language.

In this study, the incorporation of heritage languages, rather than a target language that all students were learning at school, was the primary focus, and I will discuss student engagement in relation to the capital, or value, attributed to these languages by children and their families. Family investment in heritage languages appeared to be very uneven, with some families committed to their children's learning of the language and others not so committed. Nevertheless, both students and parents/grandparents were found to participate positively in the process of bringing languages into the classroom across all three schools. As heritage-language practices

5 Primary Schools with Heritage-Language Students 123

became a focus in class, family members responded to children's enthusiasm by teaching them some (or more) of the language. Many parents' participation in the activities also caused the teachers to reflect that any lack of previous parental engagement may have been a result of a lack of confidence in English rather than a lack of desire to be involved at the school. The only students who the teachers reported as not being so engaged in the lesson sequences were some of those who identified as monolingual. Activities frequently focused on students learning from each other, and heritage students were more legitimate contributors in that more value was attributed to what they were able to do with language.

5.6.1 Connecting Home and School

Family investment in heritage languages was found to range from a great deal of home exposure and student attendance at community language schools to very limited exposure. In the former case, when parents were less familiar with English and perhaps anxious about interacting with the school community, the inclusion of heritage languages in the classroom provided them with a way to get involved. Anne and Helen reported that parents who participated at Campbell PS were enthusiastic and wanted to engage even more than the activity in the second language sequence allowed, and it was clear in Sam's and Jasmine's classes that parents/grandparents took part (see second lesson sequence in the 'summary of lesson sequences' section earlier in the chapter). Cassandra and Sophia at Hampton PS also emphasised more than once during the course of the study how an emphasis on linguistic resources could increase parental involvement by valuing what they knew:

That element of engagement, community engagement, I think is really, really positive. Because often we want to engage with parents, but it's on our terms, and we can become frustrated, oh, they don't support the chil[dren]—here is a way they're supporting their children, and it's on their terms, and I think they will feel more involved. (Cassandra, GR2)

I think the reason that we don't have a lot of parent involvement is because parents don't feel confident enough, whereas this is something that's, you know,

124   M. Turner

is so natural to them, and they can be a part of without feeling, 'oh, am I doing it right?'. (Sophia, interview)

Through their reflections, the teachers showed an awareness of the unequal nature of language dynamics and how it was an obstacle for parental engagement at school. They viewed the inclusion of heritage languages in students' learning as a way to make richer home–school connections.

In cases where children had very limited exposure to their heritage language(s), increasing the value placed on these in the classroom was found to result in the sharing of language by students' family members at home. Frida's Year 1/2 students evidenced this most clearly in reflections on their learning in the study. Frida asked students to reflect orally and wrote down what they told her. The following two excerpts (emphasis is added) demonstrate a positive familial response to students' interest—the first in relation to oracy and the second, literacy.

Student 1
I learnt how to say different words in different people's languages. I learnt how to say 'hi' in Bari and I learnt how to say 'hi' in Arabic. [Child S] speaks her language at her grandmother's house because her grandmother does not speak English and she wants to talk to her. I learnt that 'Madan' (Bari) is spelt like 'Madan' and I learnt how to count up to 30 in Bari. *I learnt that my uncle speaks Bari and he taught us to say the months and the days.*

Student 2
I loved the language project. I said to my mum we are doing a really fun language project at school. I'm going to learn how to say 'hello' in other people's language. *After the language project, I asked my grandmother to teach me how to write my name in Russian.* I learnt how to say 'hello' in Chinese and that's my friend's language. I learnt that Russian letters have different sounds to English letters. I learnt that [Child A] talks a little bit of Arabic when he plays soccer.

These two reflections show that the children were taking the initiative by talking about language at home, and that they were learning more about a heritage language as a result.

5.6.2 Heritage Languages at School

Inclusion of heritage languages in classroom teaching and learning appeared to be an overwhelmingly positive experience for LBOTE students. All five of the main teachers reported student engagement using superlative language; for example, the students '*absolutely loved it*' (Jasmine), '*it was a really, really positive experience*' (Sophia) and '*I have to say, they loved it*' (Frida). The valuing or affirmation of students' linguistic knowledge as important in their formal learning and being able to share experiences with others appeared to be the main drivers of the students' engagement. This is illustrated by the teachers' following quotations:

[The students] just felt really proud of all the different languages that, you know, they could either read, write, or speak. (Sophia, interview)

When we shared it together, the children were supporting each other by nodding and smiling, and obviously, some of those experiences—they're shared experiences. Just by their positive body language, you could see that they were saying, 'yeah that happens with me'. (Frida, GR1)

I think the kids really liked writing down about themselves, and where they spoke languages, and it made them aware of their own background. But it also made other kids aware of each other's background, and they did a lot of sharing about who spoke what language, and where, also the kids themselves were saying things like, 'oh, I didn't know [student A] spoke three languages'. […] They were looking at similarities and differences, and they were doing a lot of comparing and contrasting between themselves. (Anne, interview)

Different degrees of student investment in heritage languages became clear as a result of the exploring and leveraging of students' language practices; this point links to the teachers' increasing understanding of— and attention to—students' literacy discussed in the previous section. For example, Sam realised that, for at least one of his students, there was some reluctance to speak a heritage language:

One of the Sri Lankan girls said my uncle gives me a prize if I speak Tamil. I thought that's an interesting comment. (Sam, GR1)

126   M. Turner

Anne also reflected on her own assumptions of her students' understanding of their heritage language. She talked about 'first language' but problematised the idea in her reflection:

Well there was one little girl in my room that, English is not her first language, and so I thought she would find the activity of translating quite easy. But she actually found the activity difficult, I'm not really too sure, because I taught her brother when he was in prep and he came just speaking Punjabi. She came speaking more English than him, and I think her brother speaking English influenced her a lot when she was growing up. (Anne, interview)

Teachers thus demonstrated their growing understanding that student investment in their heritage languages was uneven and very much influenced by the languages in which they interacted with important people in their lives. They also discussed ways in which the cultural capital of heritage languages could be reinforced at school through different kinds of positioning. For example, Jasmine, the only bi/multilingual teacher in the study, used herself and a visual representation of her own language practices (her language map) as a way to celebrate and be proud of an extended linguistic repertoire:

[The students] really felt proud of what I was able to do, because they did not know some of the things that were on [my] language map before, so they were quite impressed, and then later on they tried to impress me by doing their language maps. (Jasmine, interview)

In contrast, Anne used her monolingualism to encourage the students:

I'd say to them, you know, if you speak another language you're so lucky, I wish I did, and now they're saying that, like, we're so lucky. […] If we didn't have this opportunity to have done this, they probably wouldn't be speaking like that. (Anne, GR2)

However, along with the apparent increase in cultural capital for heritage-language students and their parents, there appeared to be a subsequent decrease in capital for the minority of students who identified as monolingual: they now lacked something important, as opposed to something that was not previously considered relevant in the school domain. One student at Hampton PS reported to Sophia that the project had been boring because he could only speak English. Finding ways to increase the engagement of monolingual students in the process is likely to be important for the sustainability of the approach, especially in schools where there is a smaller percentage of heritage-language students. As mentioned by the teachers, the sharing of experiences was a source of engagement for the heritage-language children, and the ability to contribute actively to the discussion may be beneficial for monolingual students. This will be addressed later in the chapter.

5.7 Institutional Structures and Pedagogies

Institutional structures: Professional learning, teacher collaboration.
Pedagogies: Student-centred learning, inclusion of the community, and crosslinguistic pedagogy.

The institutional structures that appeared to be relevant to the leveraging of students' linguistic resources included the opportunity for teachers to take part in professional learning and collaboration. Inclusion of the community in activities was also evident in all three schools, particularly in Campbell PS. Although not a direct focus of the study, the schools had language programmes: Italian in Campbell PS and Madison PS and Indonesian in Hampton PS. At Campbell PS, the principal reported a new Year 5/6 initiative whereby parents and grandparents were being engaged as language teachers of their heritage languages to small groups of students with a similar heritage; this was an alternative to learning Italian. The initiative was in its very early stages, and showed a school commitment to assisting with heritage-language maintenance. However, there appeared to be a separation between the generalist classes and the language classes and also, perhaps, between different year groups: Anne and Helen, the Year 3 generalist teachers participating in the study, did not know about the initiative. Finally, in all schools, student-centred approaches to learning provided a space for the leveraging of students' language practices. Crosslinguistic pedagogies used in this space were mainly found to include identity texts and translation.

5.7.1 Professional Learning and Teacher Collaboration

The opportunity for teachers to undertake professional learning was found to be key to the leveraging of students' language resources in class. As discussed in the section on expectations, teachers' understanding of their capacity to incorporate students' linguistic resources changed over the course of the study. Use of English was taken for granted in the different settings, and conceptualising language more as practices in which students engage rather than as bounded entities that make a person bi/multilingual appeared to be a significant part of the process. Collaboration was also an important aspect of this professional learning and was especially evident in the way main teachers were supported in the schools where only one teacher was participating in the professional learning (Anne was supported by Helen at Campbell PS and Sophia by Cassandra at Hampton PS). Working together was not only clear within schools but also between schools: the two Year 3/4 teachers (Sophia and Jasmine) and the Year 3 teacher (Anne) took the initiative to create a virtual shared folder on the first professional learning day, so they could share project-related ideas and resources. Although only indirectly related to the study, it appeared that collaboration between teachers of a target language and generalist teachers at the three schools was not a strong focus. However, the principal at Hampton PS reported that he was attempting to change this by encouraging generalist teachers to use the target language of Indonesian—to whatever degree—in their classes. This point will be picked up in the next section on opportunities to learn.

5.7.2 Student-Centred Learning, Inclusion of the Community and Crosslinguistic Pedagogy

Student-centred learning was evident in the three schools, and it was used as a space for leveraging students' linguistic resources. The approach was particularly conspicuous in Frida's class: she gave her Year 1/2 students

5 Primary Schools with Heritage-Language Students 129

the agency to determine the course of the second lesson sequence. The fourth lesson in her sequence (see summary of lesson sequences earlier in the chapter) was requested by the students, and Frida leveraged their enthusiasm as a learning opportunity. In the Year 3/4 and Year 3 classes, Jasmine, Sophia and Anne all incorporated students' linguistic resources into enquiry-based units. Jasmine's enquiry theme was 'values and identity', Sophia's was geography-based and Anne's was based on living things and sustainability. In all the units, students needed to bring something that they had chosen to do back to class: a text in their heritage language, information about their heritage country and features/characteristics of an animal from their heritage country respectively. The inclusion of parents in everyday teaching and learning was evident in the activities the teachers designed for the study. The only teacher who did not deliberately include parents/grandparents in the activities was Frida, and she commented in the second group reflection that this would have been beneficial.

Students in the classes under study were, for the most part, born in Australia and had been learning through the medium of English from the beginning of their schooling. The main language used in class was thus English, and crosslinguistic pedagogies were needed in order to incorporate other languages. The language maps, or identity texts (Cummins, 2006; Cummins & Early, 2011—see Chap. 3), created by the students opened up a space for students to display their linguistic knowledge. Students most commonly wrote in English but, as shown in the examples (see Fig. 5.2), other languages were sometimes used. In the first language map, the student chose to use Bari and then translate it into English, but only included the word 'Arabic' in English. In the second map, the student chose to include Indonesian, the language she was learning at school, with no translation, and also only included 'Arabic' in English. It is unclear whether students' 'choices' around writing were driven by a lack of knowledge of different scripts, or a more deliberate avoidance. The main crosslinguistic pedagogy used in the second lesson sequence (see summary of lesson sequences earlier in the chapter) was translation. All the teachers relied on this as a way of bringing students' language resources into class (see Table 5.4).

Fig. 5.2 Examples of language maps

5.8 Opportunities to Learn (Through) Languages

* Languages central to heritage student learning of English curriculum content in some classes, and relevant to content in all classes.
* Increased heritage student engagement in extra-curricular heritage language use.
* Potential role for language taught at school identified for students with English-only background.

Opportunities to learn in this setting relate to opportunities to use language resources in English-medium classes rather than to use and learn a target language chosen by the school. Students' linguistic repertoire was being leveraged for their general learning, including their learning of English as a subject area. However, there were clear opportunities to increase students' desire to learn heritage languages at home through attributing value to these at school—this was discussed in the section on student engagement. The investigation of how diverse language practices could be made a part of core learning was central to the study. Opportunities to learn were linked to the teachers' willingness to consider language in relation to practices, as well as a majority of students' positive engagement with the incorporation of languages into classroom activities. In all three schools, students' linguistic repertoires were made relevant to their learning of curriculum content, and these repertoires were found to be central to content-related achievement in two classes. Students' ownership of the process also appeared to have a positive influence on their learning of content. However, those who identified as monolingual were positioned differently: they did not appear to have access to the same opportunities to learn.

5.8.1 Heritage Languages as Central to Learning

The incorporation of heritage languages was found to be highly engaging for students, and, in some cases, was also intrinsic to the way teaching and learning goals were met. In these cases, it appeared that the presence of the languages in the class was directly related to the students' understanding of required curriculum content. For example, in the English curriculum, it was important for the students to demonstrate awareness of different kinds of communication. Frida at Madison PS and Sophia at Hampton PS saw this as a strategic curriculum link. Both teachers made a direct connection between the first and second language sequences: Frida did not specify the curriculum objective for her first sequence but the relationship between the sequences was clearly language awareness, and Sophia made the connection explicit by keeping the same curriculum link for both sequences.

Frida's chosen content description for her Year 1/2 students was as follows:

> *Understand that spoken, visual and written forms of language are different modes of communication with different features and their use varies according to the audience, purpose, context and cultural background.*

As evidenced in the two student reflection samples from her class shown in the section on student engagement on page X, students were able to achieve this content objective as a direct result of the inclusion of other languages in the classroom. The samples demonstrated awareness that language use may need to be varied according to the interlocutor, that spoken and written forms of language may be different depending on the language and that the students themselves had some agency over which language family members might use with them.

For her Year 3/4 class, Sophia chose the following curriculum link:

> *Understand that languages have different written and visual communication systems, different oral traditions and different ways of constructing meaning.*

Sophia embedded activities in a geography-based enquiry unit, but chose to spend more time on the English curriculum objective than the Year 3 and Year 3/4 teachers did in the other schools: her students worked on the geography and English content simultaneously. Student reflections in her class demonstrated achievement of the English content objective. The following are two examples:

Student 1
I liked that when my mum wrote the words in Vietnamese she actually taught me how to say them. I learnt that all different countries have different letters and you can actually write Australian words using the different letters from other countries.

Student 2
It was fun working in a small group for matching the meanings to the words and pictures. I liked thinking of sentences about Cambodia and telling my partner. I noticed some words in different languages looked the same but they aren't actually because some of the letters look the same as the letters in other words like [student S's] language and [student V's]. [Student S's] language is Telugu and [student V's] language is Khmer. Some aren't the same because they have Australian letters. Some of them are spelt with Australian letters. [Student S] taught me a bit of letters in her language and we did 'Heads, Shoulders, Knees and Toes' in her language.

The student reflections from both Frida's and Sophia's classes thus appeared to show that a more sustained focus on the same English curriculum objective assisted students' growing crosslinguistic awareness. Frida worked with the students' interest and allowed them agency. Sophia created a situation where content objectives flowed into each other, strategically reinforcing language awareness whilst also paying attention to other learning areas.

5.8.2 Heritage Languages as Relevant to Learning

All of the teachers were found to be successful in making the incorporation of the students' linguistic repertoire relevant to curriculum content, and were thus able to show that the inclusion of different languages did not need to be limited to the English curriculum. In every case, languages were harnessed to specific teaching and learning goals. For Sam, Anne and Jasmine, although it was not as evident from the data whether or not the inclusion of languages in the activities had been central to the students' understanding of the chosen content, the relevance of the lesson sequences was clear. No work samples were sighted from Sam's class, but samples done by Anne's Year 3 students demonstrated that they were achieving the chosen science content goal through use of their heritage languages. Whether or not the use of different languages helped their understanding in any way was not in evidence because students did not directly reflect on their learning of this content.

As part of her lesson sequence, Jasmine asked her Year 3/4 students to write reflections on their learning. Through this process—similar to the reflections completed by Frida's and Sophia's students—her students demonstrated achievement of one of her chosen curriculum links, but they did not refer to linguistic repertoire as being central to this achievement. The curriculum link was the following:

Identify personal strengths and select personal qualities that could be further developed

The students presented a text in their language and later translated it into English, but they all related personal strengths to the act of public speaking rather than their rich linguistic repertoire. The following are two examples:

Student 1
My personal reflection:
At the start of my presentation I was nervous. When I started I was getting more and more confident. When I finished presenting I was proud of my presentation.

Student 2
My personal reflection:
I felt really nervous and oozy. It was really cool and fun presenting. I was really proud that I did it. After my presentation my friends were happy for me.

Jasmine's students did not report seeing their learning as directly linked to their linguistic repertoire, perhaps because their attention was not specifically drawn to language practices and crosslinguistic awareness. The students were found to be very engaged in predicting what their peers were saying, using non-verbal cues if they did not understand the language, and their enthusiasm for the activity—sighted as video-recorded work samples—was evident. It thus appeared that both relevance and positive student engagement helped to provide opportunities to learn.

5.8.3 Monolingual Students

Finally, monolingual students were sometimes found to be disengaged in activities that incorporated the use of heritage languages. Other students shared and discussed their languages, and monolingual students were not excluded from this process. However, these students may have felt that they had little to offer, and this might have been the reason for their relative lack of participation. Sophia and Cassandra at Hampton PS were found to put the most thought into this, perhaps because they had one student who was particularly vocal about being disengaged. An excerpt from Sophia's written reflection on her second lesson sequence evidences the following:

> *Most of the sheets that were sent home were returned and children were happy to see their words on the wall. Some of them were excited to say the words out loud to the rest of the class. Children who were of only English-speaking backgrounds couldn't really participate. If we had more time, those few children could have asked the Indonesian teacher or a teacher who spoke another language.*

The last comment by Sophia addresses the possibility of providing monolingual students with a different kind of linguistic knowledge to share with the class. Participation, in this case, appeared to be linked to being a legitimate member of the group—not only learning from others but having something to offer oneself.

5.9 Discussion

In the study, it was clear that the teachers were shifting along a multilingual stance continuum by actively promoting the use of different languages in the school domain, and this was leading to a richer understanding of their students' home lives. They appeared to be situated somewhere in between de Jong's (2018) multilingual stance dimensions of maintain and foster/affirm, as discussed in Chap. 4. Some teachers were making relevant connections with heritage languages while others were more explicitly using them as a resource for student learning. Student engagement highlighted how the incorporation of home languages in class can have a very positive effect on participation in learning activities, as well as on students' investment in home languages if this investment is not strong.

However, opportunities to learn as central or peripheral to key curriculum objectives appeared to be important to consider in relation to the sustainability of the approach. This may especially be the case when there are monolingual students present who may not feel like legitimate participants in crosslinguistic activities. In the end-of-project group reflection, Anne and Helen from Campbell PS spoke frankly about whether or not they would continue investigating and leveraging students' linguistic repertoire, even though they had found it of great benefit, given that there were so many competing priorities at school. If curriculum objectives are perceived to be just as easily met with English, it may be difficult for teachers to make the choice to continue to engage with heritage languages. However, if linguistic resources are perceived as a way to guide students towards deeper understanding, or as a more effective way to reach teaching and learning objectives than can be achieved by using only English, their inclusion in teaching and learning will potentially carry more weight.

The nature of these teaching and learning objectives can be understood as identity-affirming, instructional and sociopolitical. The objectives can be related to different purposes of translanguaging, as discussed in Chap. 2: the first includes the affirmation of multilingual identities (e.g., Cenoz & Gorter, 2011; García & Li, 2014; Lin & He, 2017); the second, student demonstration and co-construction of knowledge (e.g., Gumperz & Cook-Gumperz, 2005; Martin-Beltrán, 2014) and metalinguistic and crosslinguistic awareness (e.g., García & Kano, 2014; García & Li, 2014; Lewis, Jones, & Baker, 2012; Martin-Beltrán, 2014); and the third, interrogation of language hierarchies and social structures (e.g., Flores & García, 2017; García & Li, 2014).

5 Primary Schools with Heritage-Language Students   137

First, engagement of heritage students through identity affirmation was particularly clear, and was found to be admirably straightforward for the teachers. However, the instructional goals appeared to be more challenging. The incorporation of other languages was new, and translation was found to act as a useful point of entry, which some teachers were then able to develop into crosslinguistic awareness activities. Crosslinguistic pedagogy, used as a broader term than translanguaging pedagogy, can include this kind of translation: García and Li (2014) did not consider activities which only involved direct translation of texts with no analysis or discussion to be examples of translanguaging because they simply substitute one language with another (see Chap. 3). However, translation can be used as a springboard for different kinds of meaning-making activities, once stakeholders are more accustomed to having different languages embedded in everyday activities in the classroom. These activities might target such aspects as students accessing their background knowledge (or developing this knowledge by accessing the linguistic repertoire of their family/community), metalinguistic and crosslinguistic awareness and the creative use of language.

Real adaptation of content instruction depending on whether students were monolingual, bilingual or emergent bilingual, as recommended by García and Li (2014), was not included in the instructional goals. Differentiation can be conceptualised in relation to students rather than instruction, however, and this idea will be discussed in Chap. 10. Certainly, the lack of instructional adaptation for monolingual students appeared to begin to open up a space for the sociopolitical goals of translanguaging because it positioned these students as not knowing something of value. Disrupting linguistic hierarchies in this way can help to start a critical discussion about language. It is important to note that the discomfort this may produce in monolingual students may lead to their disengagement, as demonstrated in the previous section, but any discomfort can be leveraged in a gentle way by the teacher to draw attention to English dominance and language-related inequity—how EAL students who perceive that their English is not 'good enough' might feel about participating in classroom activities, for example. This is an example of what Palmer, Cervantes-Soon, Dorner, and Heiman (2019) referred to as 'a pedagogy of discomfort', or the way feeling uncomfortable can help learning, elicit growth and widen students' perspectives on the world. Guiding students through any feelings of illegitimacy or perceived irrelevance to their own situation can be done in a positive way that affirms the capacity of these students to increase their linguistic repertoire at school. Some of the teachers were already considering how they could do this by enlisting the aid of the teacher of the target language at school.

5.10 Conclusion

The leveraging of students' linguistic resources in generalist primary classrooms has the potential to increase the cultural capital of heritage languages and stimulate the learning of these languages if student investment is not strong. It also has the potential to deepen learning, including in situations where the students speak English fluently. The study discussed in the chapter demonstrated positive student engagement with the inclusion of heritage languages into generalist primary classrooms, and also evidenced learning that relied on the incorporation of these languages. The leveraging of linguistic repertoire was found to lend itself very well to different subject areas and proved relevant to students' learning. However, given that English-medium learning is the norm in mainstream Australian schools, the sustainability of the approach may rely on the positioning of linguistic resources as core to students' opportunities to learn, rather than peripheral. These opportunities relate to identity-affirming and sociopolitical, as well as instructional, teaching and learning objectives.

References

Anderson, T., & Shattuck, J. (2012). Design-based research: A decade of progress in education research? *Educational Researcher, 41*(1), 16–25.
Australian Curriculum, Assessment and Reporting Authority (ACARA). (2018). *My school*. Retrieved from https://www.myschool.edu.au/
Braun, V., & Clarke, V. (2008). Using thematic analysis in psychology. *Qualitative Research in Psychology, 3*(2), 77–101.

5 Primary Schools with Heritage-Language Students   139

Cenoz, J., & Gorter, D. (2011). Focus on multilingualism: A study of trilingual writing. *The Modern Language Journal, 95*, 356–369.

Cobb, P., Confrey, J., diSessa, A., Lehrer, R., & Schauble, L. (2003). Design experiments in educational research. *Educational Researcher, 32*(1), 9–13.

Cummins, J. (2006). Identity texts: The imaginative construction of self through multiliteracies pedagogy. In O. Garcia, T. Skutnabb-Kangas, & M. E. Torres-Guzman (Eds.), *Imagining multilingual schools: Language in education and glocalization* (pp. 51–68). Toronto: Multilingual Matters.

Cummins, J., & Early, M. (2011). *Identity texts: The collaborative creation of power in multilingual schools.* Staffordshire: Trentham Books.

D'Warte, J. (2013). *Pilot project: Reconceptualising English learners' language and literacy skills, practices and experiences. University of Western Sydney.* Retrieved from http://researchdirect.westernsydney.edu.au/islandora/object/uws:23461

D'Warte, J. (2014). Exploring linguistic repertoires: Multiple language use and multimodal literacy activity in five classrooms. *Australian Journal of Language and Literacy, 37*(1), 21–30.

D'Warte, J. (2015). Building knowledge about and with students: Linguistic ethnography in two secondary school classrooms. *English in Australia, 50*(1), 39–48.

de Jong, E. J. (2018, Keynote). *Taking a multilingual stance: Quality education for ELLs.* Minneapolis, MN: Minnesota-TESOL.

Department of Education and Training. (2017). *EAL learners in mainstream schools.* Retrieved from http://www.education.vic.gov.au/school/teachers/support/diversity/eal/Pages/ealschools.aspx

Flores, N., & García, O. (2017). A critical review of bilingual education in the United States: From basements and pride to boutiques and profit. *Annual Review of Applied Linguistics, 37*, 14–29.

García, O., & Kano, N. (2014). Translanguaging as process and pedagogy: Developing the English writing of Japanese students in the U.S. In J. Conteh & G. Meier (Eds.), *The multilingual turn in languages education: Benefits for individuals and societies* (pp. 258–277). Clevedon: Multilingual Matters.

García, O., & Li, W. (2014). *Translanguaging: Language, bilingualism and education.* New York: Palgrave Macmillan.

Gumperz, J. J., & Cook-Gumperz, J. (2005). Making space for bilingual communicative practice. *Intercultural Pragmatics, 2*(1), 1–23.

Lewis, G. W., Jones, B., & Baker, C. (2012). Translanguaging: origins and development from school to street and beyond. *Educational Research & Evaluation, 18*, 641–654.

Lin, A. M. Y., & He, P. (2017). Translanguaging as dynamic activity flows in CLIL classrooms. *Journal of Language, Identity & Education, 16,* 228–244. https://doi.org/10.1080/15348458.2017.1328283

Martin-Beltrán, M. (2014). What do you want to say? How adolescents use translanguaging to expand learning opportunities. *International Multilingual Research Journal, 8,* 208–230.

Oliver, R., Rochecouste, J., & Nguyen, B. (2017). ESL in Australia—A chequered history. *TESOL in Context, 26*(1), 7–26.

Palmer, D. K., Cervantes-Soon, C., Dorner, L., & Heiman, D. (2019). Bilingualism, biliteracy, biculturalism and critical consciousness for all: Proposing a fourth fundamental goal for two-way dual language education. *Theory Into Practice, 58*(2), 121–133. https://doi.org/10.1080/00405841.2019.1569376

Somerville, M., D'Warte, J., & Sawyer, W. (2016). *Building on children's linguistic repertoires to enrich learning: A project report for the NSW Department of Education.* Retrieved from http://www.uws.edu.au/centre_for_educational_research

6

A Whole-School Primary Bilingual Programme

6.1 Introduction

This book explores mainstream schooling, as opposed to select-entry programmes. Whole-school bilingual programmes can be included in the category of mainstream schools if they do not enrol students on the basis of such factors as academic ability or language proficiency. In Australia, state governments fund a small number of whole-school primary bilingual programmes. In 2016, in Victoria, there were 13 designated state-funded programmes in 11 primary schools, one primary/secondary school and one special school (Auslan for hearing-impaired students) that all taught in or through the target language for at least seven and a half hours per week (Department of Education and Training, 2017). Seven and a half hours per school week equates to students learning through the medium of a target language for 30 per cent of class time. The Victorian government provided a funding incentive in 2016 for schools to increase the percentage of target language distribution to 50 per cent of class time per week, and schools began offering 50:50 programmes as a result. Although heritage-language parents can (and do) opt their children into the programmes, schools have no special entry criteria.

© The Author(s) 2019
M. Turner, *Multilingualism as a Resource and a Goal,*
https://doi.org/10.1007/978-3-030-21591-0_6

141

Findings in this chapter are drawn from a study of a government-funded primary bilingual Japanese programme designed to investigate language processes and outcomes at a time when the school was transitioning from the 30:70 programme that had been run at the school for 20 years to a 50:50 programme. The 50:50 programme was designed to begin with incoming Foundation students and follow them up through the years. In 2017, 380 students were enrolled in the school and 82 per cent of these were recorded to be LBOTE (Australian, Curriculum, Assessment and Reporting Authority, 2018). In a 2017 parent survey done by the school, 22 languages were reported to be spoken by the students at home. The school had a relatively high socio-educational advantage for a government school (ibid.). It regularly performed as well as non-bilingual (and non-LBOTE) schools with a similar socio-educational advantage on the National Assessment Programme: Literacy and Numeracy (NAPLAN) (ibid.). In this chapter, the study will be described first, followed by the findings mapped against the multilingual practices framework. A summary of these findings (see Fig. 6.1) precedes a discussion on each dimension.

6.2   The Study

An ethnographic longitudinal study was designed to investigate language practices in both Japanese-medium and English-medium classes using the design-based framework discussed in Chap. 5 (e.g., Anderson & Shattuck, 2012; Cobb, Confrey, diSessa, Lehrer, & Schauble, 2003). In the case of this study, baseline data were first collected in order to investigate current practices and to generate an instructional hypothesis that would be refined in further iterations. Formal data collection was cross-referenced with numerous conversations with the principal, teachers and parents and playground observations—I was the researcher and also a parent of children attending the school.

6.2.1   Aims

The twin aims of the study were to investigate the relationship between teaching and learning practices and Japanese language use and to leverage students' linguistic resources for their learning in English-medium classes. These aims were interconnected: approximately one-third of students attending the school had a Japanese heritage.

6.2.2 Participants and Data Collection

In 2017 the school was in its final year of teaching a language distribution of 30:70 Japanese/English. This was the first year of the study and the year from which the data in this chapter are drawn. An interview was conducted with the principal, who was asked about school structures. Data were then collected on existing practices in Foundation and Year 5/6 across Japanese-medium and English-medium classes. This data collection included the video-recorded observation of eight lessons: four lessons in the Foundation class and four in Year 5/6 (two English lessons and two Japanese lessons in each). Both the English and Japanese lessons observed for Foundation covered an enquiry-based unit on necessity. Necessity was a whole-school enquiry theme and was also the subject of the two English lessons observed for Year 5/6. The two Japanese observations for Year 5/6 during this phase were conducted during Art lessons with Natsuko (see Tables 6.1 and 6.2).

Later in the school year, a design-based instructional hypothesis for the English-medium classes was implemented. The hypothesis was the same as for the study in Chap. 5, but in a context where two languages (rather than one) were the medium of instruction in the school:

Students' creation of visual representations of their linguistic repertoires—how, where, when and with whom they speak particular languages and how they feel about them—can assist in the leveraging of the students' language practices as a resource for their learning.

I presented the idea of language mapping (D'Warte, 2013) at a professional learning day for the whole school and then collaborated with the two English-medium teachers on Phase 2 and Phase 3 of the professional learning process (see Chap. 5). Observations were conducted in classes where heritage languages were incorporated into the lesson—two classes for Foundation and one class for Year 5/6. In the Japanese-medium classes, more baseline data were collected in order to get a richer understanding of existing Japanese language practices. Two more Foundation classes and two

144   M. Turner

Table 6.1 Teacher participants

Year	Teachers[a]	Experience	Background
Foundation	Natsuko[b] (Japanese)	20 years in bilingual programme	Japanese/English (grew up in Japan)
	Nick (English)	3 years	English (learning Japanese)
Year 5/6	Michiko (Japanese)	1 year	Japanese/English (grew up in Japan)
	Rieko (English)	3 years	English/Japanese (both parents Japanese and grew up in Australia)

[a]All names are pseudonyms
[b]Natsuko also taught Art (in Japanese) to Year 5/6

Table 6.2 Observed lessons

Year	Teacher	Focus
Foundation	Natsuko (Japanese)	1. Features of a plant/tree 2. Life cycle of a plant/tree 3. Storytelling (student creation of a story about monsters) 4. Storytelling (student presentation of their story)
Foundation	Nick (English)	1. Keeping healthy by playing sport 2. Students' sport preferences and introduction to bar graphs
Year 5/6	Natsuko (Japanese)	1. Painting a picture 2. Cutting up a painting of 'cool' and 'warm' colour tones to make a collage
Year 5/6	Michiko (Japanese)	1. Discussing preferences and dreams at different ages 2. Using the petals/roots of a plant to talk about preferences and dreams
Year 5/6	Rieko (English)	1. Immunisation and vaccines 2. Researching benefits and problems of access to a variety of services in different countries

Year 5/6 Japanese classes (Michiko) were observed: the four observations occurred during scheduled Japanese language/literacy time.

Supplementing the observations, data were also collected from students' work samples and written/drawn reflections on their learning. A survey was completed by 13 Year 5/6 students about their language practices and this was used as a springboard for discussion in interviews with 6 of these students. Thematic analysis (see Braun & Clarke, 2008) was used in the study, and all data were cross-referenced in the identification of themes.

6.3 Lessons and Lesson Sequences

These summaries provide information about the observed lessons and also the design-based English-medium lesson sequences taught by Nick in Foundation and Rieko in Year 5/6. Table 6.2 shows the lessons that were observed in order to collect baseline data: the Japanese-medium lessons and four of the English-medium lessons. The next two tables show the lesson sequences designed to address the instructional hypothesis in the English-medium classes. Table 6.3 refers to Nick's and Rieko's lesson sequences that focused on the investigation of students' language practices. No explicit links to curriculum content descriptions were made at this stage. Curriculum links became a focus in the second sequence (see Table 6.4).

In the second sequence of lessons (see Table 6.4), Nick made the following curriculum links for his Foundation class:

Recognise—
* Texts are created by authors who tell stories and share experiences that may be similar or different to students' own experiences.
* Texts are made up of words and groups of words that make meaning.
* Some different types of literary texts and identify some characteristic features of literary texts.

Table 6.3 Investigating students' language practices in the English-medium classes

Links to curriculum	Year	Focus
General—no specific links made	Foundation (Nick)	• Discussion of everyone's languages, creation of an anchor chart and further discussion of what kinds of practices students could put on their language map • Creation of language maps and sharing of ideas with classmates
General—no specific links made	Year 5/6 (Rieko)	• Student completion of a language survey at home • Discussion of different, everyday language practices • Student viewing of teachers' language maps (completed on the professional learning day at the school) • Creation of language maps and discussion with classmates

146   M. Turner

Table 6.4 Leveraging students' language practices

Year	Focus
Foundation (Nick)	**Nick's class** • Listened to an Indigenous artist talk about artwork in Indigenous stories • Compared and contrasted Tiddalick (an Indigenous story) with Little Red Riding Hood (a European fairy tale) • Listened to heritage-language parents tell stories (three Japanese stories read)[a] *(observed)* • Created a play in English (in two groups), after reading a storybook in French—Roule Galette—and predicting meaning • Acted out the play *(observed)*
Year 5/6 (Rieko)	**Rieko's class** • Discussed the role of punctuation and when/where it is used • Discussed the purpose of different punctuation marks and colour-coded punctuation in their own narrative writing • Brought a book or another kind of text in a language spoken in their home to class (five stories in Hindi, Korean, Chinese, Russian and Japanese, and one description in Tagalog were brought to class) • Read the text to their group (students who brought text), and compared and contrasted punctuation patterns in English and other languages (everyone in the group) *(observed)*

[a]This activity was designed for the students to listen to different languages, but the three parent volunteers were Japanese

Rieko was teaching a Year 5/6 class and also had students in the class working towards Level 7. These were the curriculum links she made for her second lesson sequence (see Table 6.4):

Understand—

* How the grammatical category of possessives is signalled through apostrophes and how to use apostrophes with common and proper nouns (Level 5)
* The use of commas to separate clauses/different uses of commas in texts (Level 6)
* The use of punctuation to support meaning in complex sentences with prepositional phrases and embedded clauses (Level 7)

6.4 Summary of Findings

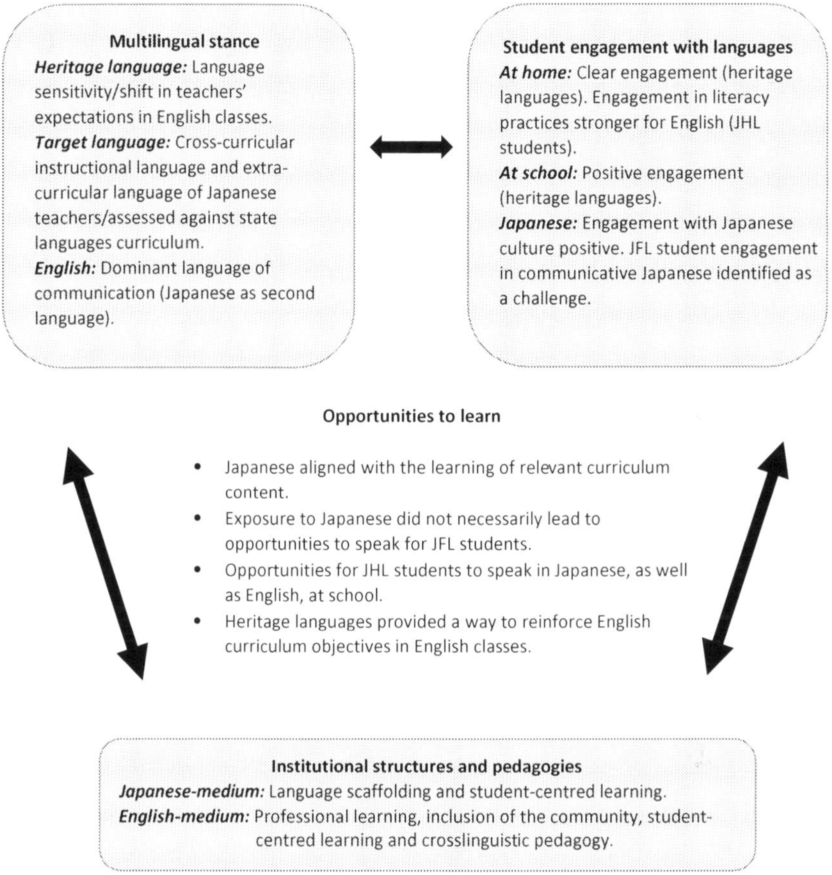

Multilingual stance
Heritage language: Language sensitivity/shift in teachers' expectations in English classes.
Target language: Cross-curricular instructional language and extra-curricular language of Japanese teachers/assessed against state languages curriculum.
English: Dominant language of communication (Japanese as second language).

Student engagement with languages
At home: Clear engagement (heritage languages). Engagement in literacy practices stronger for English (JHL students).
At school: Positive engagement (heritage languages).
Japanese: Engagement with Japanese culture positive. JFL student engagement in communicative Japanese identified as a challenge.

Opportunities to learn
- Japanese aligned with the learning of relevant curriculum content.
- Exposure to Japanese did not necessarily lead to opportunities to speak for JFL students.
- Opportunities for JHL students to speak in Japanese, as well as English, at school.
- Heritage languages provided a way to reinforce English curriculum objectives in English classes.

Institutional structures and pedagogies
Japanese-medium: Language scaffolding and student-centred learning.
English-medium: Professional learning, inclusion of the community, student-centred learning and crosslinguistic pedagogy.

* JHL: Japanese-as-a-heritage-language/JFL: Japanese-as-a-foreign-language
These terms are used to give a very broad sense of whether or not students had communicative exposure to Japanese outside school.

Fig. 6.1 Findings according to multilingual practices framework

148 M. Turner

6.5 Multilingual Stance

> **Heritage language:** Language sensitivity/shift in teachers' expectations in English classes.
> **Target language:** Cross-curricular instructional language and extra-curricular language of Japanese teachers/assessed against state languages curriculum.
> **English:** Dominant language of communication (Japanese as second language).

A multilingual stance was evident among stakeholders—school leaders, teachers, students and parents—in that there was a sensitivity to the use of different languages in the school domain. However, active and strategic incorporation of heritage languages into English-medium classes was new for the teachers. Given the bilingual status of the school, Japanese was clearly visible in the form of signs, posters and artwork. Messages relevant to Japanese activities were sent home to parents in both Japanese and English, there were extracurricular activities where Japanese was spoken, and there was a school-based expectation that Japanese teachers would consistently speak in Japanese with students both inside and outside class. Although English still remained the dominant language of communication, Japanese was a very conspicuous second language. Immersive, or implicit, learning of language was found to be a focus of the school, and expectations of Japanese language use by Japanese as a Foreign Language (JFL) students were linked to the state languages curriculum. More complex Japanese use was informally expected of Japanese as a Heritage Language (JHL) students, but there were no formal differentiated language outcomes for these children.

6.5.1 Heritage Languages

It was clear that different languages were recognised as part of students' and parents' everyday experience and were audible in the school domain. Although languages other than Japanese and English were not visible in written form around the school, they could be heard in the playground. Japanese was the most prominent spoken language other than English because Japanese was the biggest heritage-language group at the school and also because Japanese teachers spoke to children in Japanese. Other languages were endorsed more indirectly by both Japanese and English teachers, however. For example, students danced to songs in different languages at end-of-year concerts and were allowed to use a different lan-

Fig. 6.2 Excerpt from Year 1 student's Father's Day card

guage in class when engaged in an activity that included a parent. An excerpt from a Father's Day card written in a Year 1 class (by my elder son for his Spanish father) is an illustration of this (Fig. 6.2). The presence of other languages showed that there was no *de facto* school-based policy that attempted to limit language use to only Japanese and English.

Heritage languages were thus found to be an accepted part of the school domain, and teachers were interested in the idea that they could be leveraged for learning in English-medium classes. However, some explanation for the parents was found to be needed at Foundation level. For example, Nick invited parents/grandparents to come and read stories in different heritage languages (see section on lessons and lesson sequences) and three Japanese mothers came to read. Nick commented on this in his interview:

> It was really interesting that the parents that were involved, and were engaged were all the Japanese parents for my kids. [...] What I had hoped would happen would be we'd have some variety, a bit of diversity in the languages that were coming. (Nick, interview)

Nick repeated this activity the following year, providing more explanation to parents and changing the time to Friday afternoon (instead of Monday morning), and he was able to secure four different heritage languages (Laotian, Chinese, Russian and Japanese) the second time around. In the first instance, the Japanese mothers may have been the parents who came because they were more accustomed to coming to the school to read to the children in Japanese.

6.5.2 Learning Japanese

The main stance related to the target language was found to be that language is learnt implicitly, or through extensive exposure to Japanese. The expectation that Japanese teachers would speak in Japanese to students both inside and outside class clearly helped students' comprehension. For example, one Year 5/6 JFL student highlighted her receptive abilities in an interview when discussing her visit to Japan. The student was explaining how she thought being a student at the school had helped her Japanese and smoothed her homestay experience:

> *When I went to my homestay, they would ask me questions in Japanese [...] and then they [would] have to get their phones out, and make me speak into the phone, and then it['d] come out in Japanese, so they [could] read it. (Year 5 student, interview)*

The student's focus on comprehension and her avoidance of speaking Japanese was not found to be unusual in the classes observed in the study. Even though Japanese teachers promoted students' use of Japanese in class, JFL students were observed to rely on their JHL friends' linguistic knowledge, and English was found to be the main language spoken by students in both the Foundation and Year 5/6 classes.

Expectations around students' oral language use in class were unclear, perhaps because the Victorian Languages Curriculum was used for assessment and did not have a strong focus on the kind of communicative language teachers and students used daily in class.[1] JHL students spoke in Japanese to teachers and to other JHL students but not commonly to JFL students. This lack of clarity around productive language was also true of written work, which was often content-based, and generally corrected at the individual level of students. To give an idea of the range of Japanese levels, even among the JFL students, two written samples are given in Figs. 6.3 and 6.4—the (uncorrected) excerpts are the complete writing samples for the same work on arguing for and against homework. In the

---

[1] The school was in the process of transitioning to 50:50 language distribution and was moving to a more communicative model of assessing students' Japanese language production. This was still work in progress at the time of writing.

6 A Whole-School Primary Bilingual Programme 151

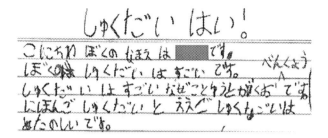

Fig. 6.3 Writing sample 1 (Year 6 student)

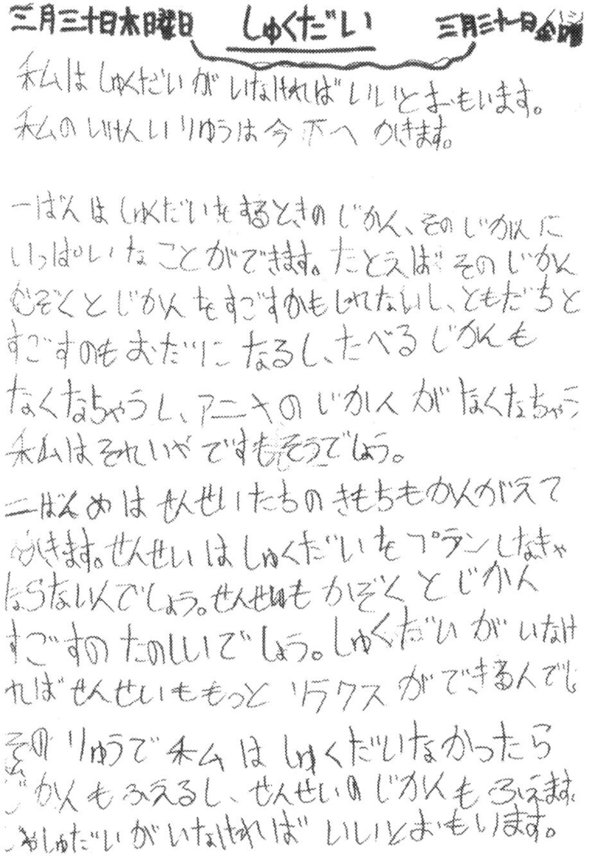

Fig. 6.4 Writing sample 2 (Year 5 student)

152 M. Turner

first excerpt, simple sentences are used, mainly with descriptive adjectives ('homework is great' and 'homework is fun') and, in the second excerpt, there are many examples of compound and complex sentences ('There are so many things you can do in the time you do homework'). Although both excerpts have errors, there is greater fluency evident in the second excerpt. The second student had a Korean heritage. Many of the Japanese-heritage students attended a Japanese community school on Saturdays where there was a strong literacy focus, and this assisted in their writing. The community school followed the Japanese curriculum (from Japan) for writing, and thus had clear expectations around writing levels to be achieved.

Any school-based expectations around children's Japanese language learning other than the level of the Victorian Languages Curriculum relevant to the grade thus did not appear to be clearly defined. This may have been linked to the degree of student and family investment, which will be discussed in the next section. Expectations appeared to be most connected to the understanding, emphasised by both the principal and the teachers, that meaningful exposure to difference and diversity was an asset for all students.

6.6 Student Engagement With Languages

At home:	Clear engagement(heritage languages).
	Engagement in literacy practices stronger for English (JHL students).
At school:	Positive engagement (heritage languages).
Japanese:	Engagement with Japanese culture positive.
	JFL student engagement in communicative Japanese identified as a challenge.

Although student engagement in their heritage languages was evident, engagement in JFL appeared to vary greatly among students, and was brought up by teachers as a challenge. However, JFL students who were not observed to use Japanese in a communicative way in class reported positive engagement with Japanese culture and bilingual education in general. This was also mostly true of the JHL students. Foundation students were observed to participate very actively in their Japanese classes and JHL and JFL students still appeared to be in the process of understanding how they might be positioned differently to each other in the classroom. Student engagement in heritage

6 A Whole-School Primary Bilingual Programme

languages other than Japanese was evidenced by an ability to read and write different scripts, and also in the pride taken in sharing linguistic repertoire with classmates. Only one student—a JHL student—was found to be actively disengaged with his heritage language.

6.6.1 Japanese

Even though students were attending a whole-school Japanese bilingual programme, English was still the dominant language. The principal's and teachers' understanding that exposure to diversity was a benefit of the programme was echoed anecdotally by the parents, and students' investment in speaking Japanese varied widely, especially as children went into middle and upper primary. The need to increase this investment underpinned what teachers understood to be a challenge at the school. In the following excerpts from interviews, teachers spoke of engaging students more fully with Japanese; Nick focused on his role as co-learner, Natsuko on building students' confidence, and Rieko on fun aspects of Japanese culture:

> A big reason why I started to learn Japanese is because when I started using the language every now and again in [the English-medium] class, the kids would look at me and go, 'ooh, if [Nick] is doing it, maybe this is fun, maybe we should be involved as well'. (Nick, interview)

> [A challenge for bilingual education is], especially from Grade 3 onwards, or even [...] earlier too, to keep the students' motivation going. [...] [The students] hesitate, and they don't want to make a mistake. That's very understandable. [...] But it's ok to make a mistake, and creating that sort of learning environment in both languages I think is very important. (Natsuko, interview)

> If [the students] want to speak Japanese they will. You know, whether that be a Japanese anime, because that's like a hot topic in my class. They would talk about Naruto all the time, and that would be in Japanese. That's amazing—for them to have that language to talk about an anime they like. (Rieko, interview)

Even given their enthusiasm for *anime*, in the Year 5/6 classroom observations, JFL students were found to avoid the use of Japanese and they reported in the survey that they generally did not speak Japanese outside classroom activities. Despite lacking sufficient investment in Japanese for active communication, the students were very positive about Japanese culture: food as well as *anime/manga* were the main cultural items cited. They also reported that they liked the Japanese language and enjoyed such aspects as feeling special or smart, and being able to communicate in another language. Of the 13 Year 5/6 students who completed the survey for the study, 12 reported that they enjoyed reading in English and only 1 of these (a JHL student) reported that she also enjoyed reading in Japanese. Japanese as a spoken medium of instruction was found to do better: when asked what they would like to learn and in what language, 7 students had no preference for the language of instruction, 1 wanted to study more in Japanese, 1 wanted to learn more languages and 4 chose English. Many JFL students' lack of preference for English as a medium of instruction for their choice of topic was an interesting finding, and may have been related to such observed factors as teacher scaffolding (discussed in the next section), assistance from JHL peers and the opportunity to speak in English.

In the Foundation class, students reflected very generally that they liked both English and Japanese, and JHL and JFL students still appeared to be negotiating their different positioning. For example, the following exchange is taken from an observation in a Japanese class. It took place between a JHL student (S1) and a JFL student (S2):

> S1: *Speak in Japanese when you're in Japanese.*
> S2: *Why?*
> S1: *Because we're in Japanese.*
> S2: *I'm in Victoria so I can talk in Japanese or Victorian.*
> S1: *Talk Japanese.*
> (*Foundation Classroom observation*)

The dialogue indicates that the JHL student had not completely grasped that his friend did not share his linguistic repertoire, appearing to think that his friend's avoidance of Japanese was a deliberate choice. His friend, in turn, was attempting to give his lack of Japanese language use more geographical legitimacy by calling English 'Victorian'. After the exchange, the JHL student was observed to speak in English to his friend, thus indicating that communication took precedence over language 'choice'.

6.6.2 (Other) Heritage Languages

Investment in heritage languages was clear in the school because different languages were used by both parents and students to communicate. The leveraging of students' linguistic repertoire in Year 5/6 also revealed engagement with different scripts: four of the five languages that were brought into class (excluding Japanese) were written with different scripts—Hindi, Russian, Korean and Chinese—and the heritage students were all able to read the texts they had brought.[2] There was also written evidence of heritage-language scripts in the students' work samples and language maps (examples of language maps appear in the next section). Two of the Venn diagrams students completed in groups as part of Rieko's second lesson sequence are shown in Figs. 6.5 and 6.6. Engagement with Japanese at the bottom of the first diagram evidenced the group's desire to demonstrate an expanded linguistic repertoire—comparing and contrasting one heritage language with English was the instruction for the activity, but they also chose to add Japanese.

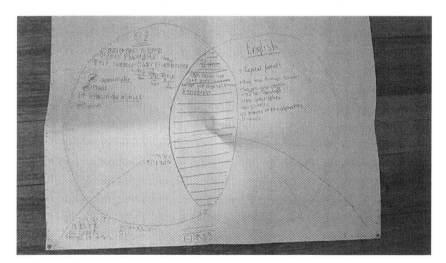

Fig. 6.5 Year 5/6 classroom activity: Venn diagram 1

---

[2] Data on whether or not speakers of other heritage languages (not Japanese) liked to read in their heritage language were not collected in the study.

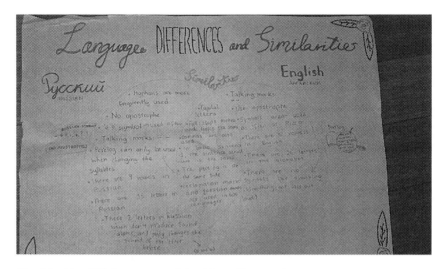

Fig. 6.6 Year 5/6 classroom activity: Venn diagram 2

Students' enjoyment of sharing their heritage languages and learning about the linguistic background of their classmates was also evident in the classroom observation. The lesson focused on punctuation, but the conversations between students included broader discussion on language in general as they became interested in different aspects of the texts their classmates had brought. There was a significant amount of student engagement during the lesson, and one group of students in particular was visibly disappointed when the lesson ended.

6.7 Institutional Structures and Pedagogies

Japanese-medium classrooms:	Language scaffolding and student-centred learning.
English-medium classrooms:	Professional learning, inclusion of the community, student-centred learning and crosslinguistic pedagogy.

In the study, institutional structures that were found to be relevant to English–Japanese language distribution and practices, as well as language practices associated with other heritage languages, included a focus on student-centred learning. As with the Chap. 5 study, it was this

6 A Whole-School Primary Bilingual Programme

learning approach in particular that facilitated the incorporation of heritage languages into the English-medium classroom. However, it appeared to be harder to navigate in the Japanese-medium classroom. Crosslinguistic pedagogies were an aspect of the design-based part of the study, again similar to Chap. 5, but were not found to be a strategic aspect of Japanese language teaching. The main language-focused pedagogy in evidence in the Japanese-medium classroom was the scaffolding of language through attention to such aspects as task selection, semiotic systems, mediational texts and participant structures (Hammond & Gibbons, 2005—see Chap. 3). An emphasis on form-focused instruction was also sighted in lesson plans, and aspects of genre-based pedagogy were found to be incorporated into written activities across English- and Japanese-medium classes.

6.7.1 Consistency and Student-Centred Learning

Consistency across the English and Japanese classes was found to be clear in the themes for the enquiry-based units and also in the approach to writing. Each school term, the Japanese and English teachers worked towards the same theme: for example, identity, necessity and change. Text types (genres), such as narratives and information reports, were also explained in a similar way across the languages. This consistency in practices overall was noted by the principal in an interview:

> *We have good pedagogy in our classrooms, we have consistent practices, [...] particularly in our literacy practices and our enquiry practices which at the moment are done in both languages. (Principal, interview)*

Although the way learning was structured was consistent, the way teaching took place in the classroom could be different. Rieko discussed the point in an interview, expressing her concern about differences in approach in the two languages. Alongside teaching classes in English to the Year 5/6 students, she was responsible for teaching the Foundation students once a week. She was the only teacher in the school to teach in English and Japanese and was well positioned to see any differences:

158   M. Turner

I feel like student behaviour management is a struggle. I think it's not a coincidence that some students misbehave in certain languages and not in others, whether that be a relationship with the teacher, and it's difficult because Japanese teachers spend less time with students, and I struggle with Foundation students, because I only see them once [a] week. (Reiko, interview)

The school was in the process of changing to a 50:50 language distribution model, so the issue of Japanese teachers spending less time with the students was in the process of being resolved. However, the idea of students misbehaving in certain languages is an interesting, and important, consistency-related issue in bilingual education. Understanding and working with student engagement with a target language from a student-centred perspective will be discussed at the end of the chapter.

As evident from the focus on enquiry, student-centred learning was endorsed by the school. The principal commented on this when asked about how she understood the students' role:

Our latest wave is really centring the student at the middle of the learning process rather than being teacher done to student. [...] We want [the students] to be pushing boundaries. And we want them to be pursuing their areas of interest. [...] I love seeing the hum and the chatter with their learning in their classrooms, because they're actively engaged in it. And that I guess is their role—to be drivers of their learning. (Principal, interview)

This kind of student-centred learning was observed in the English-medium classes. In Foundation, Nick drew on students' background knowledge, relating what they knew to their learning. In the Year 5/6 English classes, students were observed to be using group work actively to discuss issues and work out problems together. Even when students became distracted from the questions they were supposed to be answering, they were often still discussing points of interest deriving from the activity. An example of this was mentioned in the previous section: the punctuation activity was extended by students to other aspects of language.

Student–student interaction in Japanese was found to be more challenging, and the issues involved appeared to influence the nature of learning. Children had, to a significant degree, gained background knowledge through the medium of English. This included the Japanese-heritage children, who were observed to be conversationally fluent in English. By Year 5/6, the gap in English–Japanese conversational fluency remained considerable for most JFL students. In class, students were observed to use communicative Japanese (1) to give and respond to simple classroom instructions (Foundation), (2) to read stories that they had created out loud (Foundation), (3) to respond to simple teacher-directed activities (Foundation and Year 5/6), and to take part in a controlled information-gap activity with a familiar structure (Year 5/6). In Year 5/6, pair work was observed to be a way to practise language, but the constructing and sharing of knowledge was observed to occur through teacher–student interaction.

6.7.2   Language-Related Pedagogies

The reliance on teacher–student interaction (rather than student–student interaction) in the Japanese-medium classrooms appeared to be connected to the issue of language scaffolding. Pedagogy in the Japanese classes was found principally to be meaning-focused: securing understanding of content or how to participate in a particular activity. For example, in the Foundation classroom, Natsuko used a lot of visuals and realia with the students, translating any English responses into Japanese, and she further aimed to increase the students' confidence in speaking Japanese through singing and chanting. A focus on form, or particular language structures, was evident in her lesson plans; these were vocabulary and sentence structures relevant to content that were to be emphasised for the children's oral language production (see Table 6.5). Michiko also scaffolded language for Year 5/6 through such methods as using visuals, demonstrating to students how to complete activities and writing questions on the whiteboard. Singing was found to be highlighted in her classes, and most of the students had memorised the song they were observed to sing, along with the movements. A structured focus on form was evident in Michiko's classroom in that she also identified, and wrote on the board, relevant language structures for the students to practise in pairs and groups.

160   M. Turner

Table 6.5 Foundation lesson plan—Japanese

Lesson: Students will start to write their own stories using their created monster

Learning intentions:
WALT: **We are learning to understand how the story forms.** There is a beginning, middle and ending in the story. Students will be able to write the beginning sentence of むかしばなし
WILF: **What I am looking for—students to create their own story using their creativity.** They will be able to introduce their monster. They need to decide which emotions they are going to use to tell their story and give their monster a special name

Activities:	Communication:
1. Game to practice self-introduction in the group.	こわい、かなしい、うれしい、おこる、
2. Same game, but this time they are using their own monster puppet to introduce their monster.	がっかり、たのしい、おもしろい、おばけ
3. Ask students how they feel after playing game.	どの"きもち"を使いますか。
4. Using their own monster puppet, they will start their story sentences with むかしむかし あるところに、＿＿＿が すんでいました。	おばけのなまえは、なんですか。
(Worksheet)	おばけのなまえは、＿＿で
1. Name the monster.	す。
なまえは、＿＿でした。	
2. Practise reading using the emotion.	
3. Shared Time.	

Students were observed to be able to participate in classroom activities without having to use Japanese outside structured, scaffolded activities: they had recourse to many different non-linguistic cues, as well as English from their classmates, if they did not understand. Although crosslinguistic pedagogy was not planned into the lesson, students appeared to be constructing meaning through the use of English as well as Japanese.

Planned crosslinguistic pedagogy was evident in the English-medium classrooms as a result of the design-based part of the study. Similar to the study in Chap. 5, identity texts and translation were the two main pedagogical strategies used. Nick chose to structure the identity text of his Foundation students into four parts in order to help them with the activity, and Rieko's Year 5/6 students chose their own structure (see the language map samples in Figs. 6.7 and 6.8). Students' desire to show their linguistic repertoire by writing their heritage language in its script was

Fig. 6.7 Language map—foundation student

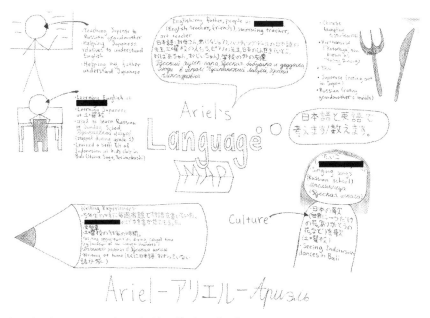

* Redactions were made to de-identify the school.

Fig. 6.8 Language map—Year 5 student*

common on the language maps, as evidenced in the samples. Both Nick and Rieko chose to use texts in the second lesson sequence, reflecting a similar literacy focus to the teachers in the study in Chap. 5. For the Foundation students, translation was a meaning-making activity and focused on students' ability to 'read' the storybook pictures and textual clues. For the Year 5/6 students, crosslinguistic awareness was a planned objective of the translation. This can be seen in the previous section in the Year 5/6 Venn diagram examples, as well as in the earlier summary of the lesson sequences for both classes. Venn diagrams were also used by teachers in the study discussed in Chap. 5, but to compare and contrast language practices rather than elements of different languages.

6.8 Opportunities to Learn (Through) Languages

* Japanese aligned with the learning of relevant curriculum content.
* Exposure to Japanese did not necessarily lead to opportunities to speak for JFL students.
* Opportunities for JHL students to speak in Japanese, as well as English, at school.
* Heritage languages provided a way to reinforce English curriculum objectives in English classes.

Opportunities to learn in the context of this study included learning a target language as well as leveraging heritage languages. Content from subject areas taught in Japanese-medium classes was aligned to the relevant subject-area curriculum documents. Expectations appeared to be driven by a multilingual stance, and by an understanding that exposure to diversity—both cultural and linguistic—and the kinds of rich learning experiences that happen as a result of this exposure are beneficial for children. School structures and pedagogies drew on the immersion characteristic of language separation in the language of instruction, but uneven investment in learning Japanese appeared to contribute to different opportunities for students' language production. Opportunities to learn as a result of incorporating heritage languages into the English classroom were clear in student engagement but not as clear in their reflections on what helped them learn content objectives. Learning opportunities could also be different according to whether the heritage language entering the English-medium classroom was Japanese or a different language.

6.8.1 The Japanese-Medium Classroom

Opportunities to learn content through the medium of Japanese were aided by crosslinguistic consistency/scaffolding in enquiry-based themes and also through a similar way of thinking about genres (see Chap. 3). There were a number of non-linguistic cues that students could use in order to understand content and complete activities, and this was important for students' learning. With the focus on content, opportunities to learn how to engage in everyday communication in Japanese appeared to be significantly dependent on students' (and parents') existing investment in the language. Given that the bilingual programme in the school had run for 20 years, parents' expectations around the extent to which students would learn Japanese (and their commitment to this) were also likely to have helped shape teachers' expectations and the kinds of pedagogies implemented at the school.

In the study, all stakeholders were found to have a multilingual stance and were very supportive of different cultures and diversity. However, expectations of how much Japanese the students would be able to use by the end of Year 6 appeared to be diluted by the dominance of English: students could reach Year 6 still struggling to speak. One way that the school was seeking to increase all students' opportunity to learn the language was through greater exposure: a transition to a 50:50 language distribution model. In 2017, the school was also in the process of moving away from the Victorian languages curriculum to a framework that offered an increased expectation of Japanese language use.

6.8.2 Heritage Languages in the English-Medium Classroom

Opportunities to learn through the incorporation of heritage languages in the English classroom were clear given the relevance of the language use to curriculum-directed learning activities and very positive student engagement, especially in the Year 5/6 classroom. Over the course of the second

164   M. Turner

design-based lesson sequence, it also became evident in both Foundation and Year 5/6 that Japanese as a heritage language could scaffold learning differently from other heritage languages given its position as a target language for everyone in the school. The use of Japanese in class could reinforce the learning of Japanese as well as serve as a resource for other content objectives. For example, the inclusion of storybooks written in Japanese in the English-medium Foundation classroom, as a way to investigate the structure of (English) narratives through crosslinguistic analysis, led to a space for discussion of how narrative genres may be structured differently in the two languages. This helped the children understand both English and Japanese structure more deeply. In his reflection on this lesson, Nick commented:

> *I think it was really engaging for the kids and they were able to pull out similarities and differences between the Japanese and the English texts, which was really good. [...] One particular example that I remember was [name of student] saying there is no resolution here because in a traditional Japanese story there isn't a resolution, it's just a problem. (Nick, oral reflection on first observed lesson of the second lesson sequence)*

As mentioned in the previous section, one of the ways consistency was conceptualised in the school was through an approach to genre. In the Japanese classes, narrative genres thus appeared to be generally framed around the structure of narratives appropriate to Australian schools, where there is an orientation, problem, resolution and (optional) coda. In Japanese, this had been translated to はじめ (introduction), つみあげ (laying the bricks), もんだい (problem), かいけつ (solution) and おわり (end). It was therefore an interesting observation that traditional Japanese stories may not necessarily have a resolution. Crosslinguistic analysis appeared to offer an opportunity to learn about Japanese in the English classroom whilst still working towards English curriculum objectives.

In the Year 5/6 classroom, the incorporation of other heritage languages was also harnessed for the purpose of crosslinguistic analysis and a deeper understanding of the way the structure of language—English as well as other languages—is linked to particular ways of thinking. Although students demonstrated very positive engagement with the process of bringing heritage languages into the classroom, no one mentioned this aspect as integral to their learning about punctuation in written reflections on what helped them learn. This may have been because they initially learnt about punctuation in English and the heritage languages were brought in as a way to consolidate their learning. The unit was also mainly taught in English with heritage languages being the focus of only one lesson, and this may have further contributed to the absence of students' explicit association between crosslinguistic analysis and their understanding of content.

6.9 Discussion

The sensitivity towards language in this setting normalised a fostering and affirming multilingual stance (see de Jong, 2018), and the presence of so many children from families who spoke a heritage language at home indicated that the school was a haven for multilingualism. Similar to the Chap. 5 study, although heritage languages were not being incorporated into English-medium classes in a planned, strategic way, their introduction was quickly embraced by the teachers. The affirmation of multilingual identities (see Cenoz & Gorter, 2011; García & Li, 2014; Lin & He, 2017) was clear: positioning the students' heritage languages as something important in the English-medium classroom was met with positive student engagement.

In this setting, as with the Chap. 5 study, working with different languages in the classroom as a resource for the co-construction and demonstration of knowledge (e.g., Gumperz & Cook-Gumperz, 2005; Martin-Beltrán, 2014) was not necessarily found to be intuitive. Here, there was also the added dimension of a prominent target language in the school. Careful explanation that heritage languages were being incorporated into everyday teaching as a way to deepen and progress the learning of different content, rather than as a way for everyone to formally learn the language in question, was found to be important. However, even though the leveraging—rather than the learning—of languages in the English-medium classroom might have needed some explanation, their inclusion did not appear to lead to disengagement on the part of students who only spoke English at home, as it did in the study in Chap. 5. The sociopolitical goal of disrupting linguistic hierarchies (e.g., García & Li, 2014) was already happening to a certain extent: Japanese was valued in the school and being able to speak other languages was more actively positioned as an asset in school life. The students thus appeared to be more accustomed to a multilingual mindset in this formal learning domain, and those who only had exposure to English at home seemed to accept that value was attached to resources that they did not share; they were observed to be enthusiastic about their peers' heritage languages in English-medium classrooms.

Finally, the expectation of implicit language learning through a Japanese medium of instruction and language separation—traditionally associated with North American immersion programmes (Ballinger, 2015; de Jong, Yilmaz, & Marichal, 2019)—was met with an uneven degree of student engagement with Japanese, and this appeared to have an effect on JFL students' opportunities to produce language. Attention was thus being paid to explicit instruction of relatively simple language forms, but this tended to lead to Japanese language production only in very controlled activities, and did not cater to students who were speaking Japanese at home. Encouraging students to speak in the target language when their exposure is mostly limited to school interactions is well established as a challenging issue in bilingual education (see Chap. 3), and it follows that extending the linguistic knowledge of heritage speakers when so many students in the class are not particularly engaged with the language is part of the challenge.

One way to encourage language use from a translanguaging perspective may be to implement more student-centred communicative activities. Translanguaging begins from the students' own language practices (García & Sylvan, 2011) and allows for the fact that they may not know enough of the Japanese language they need to express themselves fully. Maintaining an expectation that the teacher speaks in Japanese all (or most) of the time, in order not to dilute the amount of student exposure to the language, whilst encouraging the students to employ all their linguistic resources, in student–student as well as student–teacher interaction, as they move towards more Japanese language production, can be a way to work with student engagement, and also actively guide students' crosslinguistic awareness. Students can begin with what they want to say using their linguistic repertoire in a more holistic way, rather than be constrained by a limited ability to make meaning in Japanese. Identity-focused activities, storytelling and performances based on *anime* are examples of where students might have fun with communicative language, and creative self-expression may flow. The teacher's role in the embedding of activities in weekly teaching and learning is important in order to ensure the recycling of certain kinds of language. Recycling is likely to give students a chance to expand their linguistic repertoire by becoming comfortable with the new language. Considering students' investment in Japanese, and the kinds of language expectations, structures and pedagogies that may support this focus, is an ongoing point of investigation in the school.

6.10 Conclusion

A whole-school bilingual primary programme can be considered to be mainstream if students are not selected according to any predetermined criteria. Absence of selection is an important factor because commitment to a chosen language cannot be assumed, and the uneven nature of student (and parent) engagement was found to influence students' opportunities to learn. Working with this engagement from a translanguaging perspective may be a way to increase the language production of all students in this kind of setting. Also, at the school, a multilingual stance was very much in evidence, and it was clearly related to the recognition, valuing and celebration of linguistic diversity. Students (and parents) were found to be invested in their heritage languages and, similar to the study discussed in Chap. 5, teachers were able to incorporate the use of these languages into classroom activities as the students worked towards English curriculum objectives. In the context of the bilingual programme, the presence of Japanese allowed for an extra dimension. Heritage languages that were not shared by everyone in the class and Japanese—a heritage language that everyone knew to varying degrees of proficiency—could both be leveraged for learning.

References

Anderson, T., & Shattuck, J. (2012). Design-based research: A decade of progress in education research? *Educational Researcher, 41*(1), 16–25.

Australian Curriculum, Assessment and Reporting Authority (ACARA). (2018). *My school.* Retrieved from https://www.myschool.edu.au/

Ballinger, S. (2015). Linking content, linking students: A cross linguistic pedagogical intervention. In J. Cenoz & D. Gorter (Eds.), *Multilingual education: New perspectives* (pp. 35–60). Cambridge: Cambridge University Press.

Braun, V., & Clarke, V. (2008). Using thematic analysis in psychology. *Qualitative Research in Psychology, 3*(2), 77–101.

Cenoz, J., & Gorter, D. (2011). Focus on multilingualism: A study of trilingual writing. *The Modern Language Journal, 95*, 356–369.

Cobb, P., Confrey, J., diSessa, A., Lehrer, R., & Schauble, L. (2003). Design experiments in educational research. *Educational Researcher, 32*(1), 9–13.

D'Warte, J. (2013). *Pilot project: Reconceptualising English learners' language and literacy skills, practices and experiences. University of Western Sydney.* Retrieved from http://researchdirect.westernsydney.edu.au/islandora/object/uws:23461

de Jong, E. J. (2018, Keynote). *Taking a multilingual stance: Quality education for ELLs.* Minneapolis, MN: Minnesota-TESOL.

de Jong, E. J., Yilmaz, T., & Marichal, N. (2019). A multilingualism as a resource orientation in dual language education. *Theory Into Practice.* https://doi.org/10.1080/00405841.2019.1569375

Department of Education and Training. (2017). *EAL learners in mainstream schools.* Retrieved from http://www.education.vic.gov.au/school/teachers/support/diversity/eal/Pages/ealschools.aspx

García, O., & Li, W. (2014). *Translanguaging: Language, bilingualism and education.* New York: Palgrave Macmillan.

García, O., & Sylvan, C. (2011). Pedagogies and practices in multilingual classrooms: Singularities in pluralities. *The Modern Language Journal, 95*, 385–400.

Gumperz, J. J., & Cook-Gumperz, J. (2005). Making space for bilingual communicative practice. *Intercultural Pragmatics, 2*(1), 1–23.

Hammond, J., & Gibbons, P. (2005). Putting scaffolding to work: The contribution of scaffolding in articulating ESL education. *Prospect, 20*(1), 6–30.

Lin, A. M. Y., & He, P. (2017). Translanguaging as dynamic activity flows in CLIL classrooms. *Journal of Language, Identity & Education, 16*, 228–244. https://doi.org/10.1080/15348458.2017.1328283

Martin-Beltrán, M. (2014). What do you want to say? How adolescents use translanguaging to expand learning opportunities. *International Multilingual Research Journal, 8*, 208–230.

7

Teacher-Driven CLIL Initiatives in Secondary Schools

7.1 Introduction

CLIL in Victoria has been conceptualised as a pedagogical approach that focuses on the integration of content and language (see Cross, 2015), and a CLIL training course for in-service teachers has been endorsed by the Victorian government. Official bilingual programmes, such as the primary setting discussed in Chap. 6, are in the minority, and teachers attending the in-service course are most commonly employed by schools with no special focus on learning a target language. This can mean that CLIL pedagogy is adapted to the language classroom, to subject-area classrooms or to both. In the course, teachers design a CLIL unit of work tailored to their particular teaching context, and are encouraged to teach it. Although there is some concern that 'CLIL programs are being implemented in rather minimal (and probably ineffective) ways, covering perhaps a single unit or term, rather than the much more extensive programs envisaged by CLIL advocates' (Spence-Brown, 2014, p. 190), there is evidence that teachers are using aspects of CLIL pedagogy to innovate their teaching. The study discussed in this chapter aimed to investigate teachers' adaptations and explore different ways in which Japanese and French could be used across the curriculum in mainstream schools where language learning is not a particular priority.

© The Author(s) 2019
M. Turner, *Multilingualism as a Resource and a Goal,*
https://doi.org/10.1007/978-3-030-21591-0_7

Findings are drawn from three government secondary schools, given the pseudonyms Acacia, Banksia and Cassia. In 2014, the year the study began, Acacia had 839 student enrolments, a lower-than-average socio-educational advantage and 9 per cent of students reported as LBOTE (Australian, Curriculum, Assessment and Reporting Authority, 2018). Banksia and Cassia were both listed as having a higher-than-average socio-educational advantage, but Banksia had a much smaller number of students (503) than Cassia (1804). The percentage of LBOTE students in each school was 40 per cent and 56 per cent respectively (ibid.). In the study, at least one participant teacher in each school had completed the CLIL training course. These teachers were language teachers, and they were the main drivers of the CLIL-related innovations under investigation. The approach to CLIL could therefore be considered to be bottom-up, as opposed to the top-down approach (a school-driven commitment) discussed in Chaps. 6 and 8. In this chapter, the study will be described first, followed by the findings mapped against the multilingual practices framework. A summary of these findings (see Fig. 7.1) precedes a discussion on each dimension.

7.2 The Study

The study was designed to investigate collaboration between language teachers who had completed the CLIL training course and subject-area teachers. In 2014, a seminar day was organised for 12 teachers from six different schools in order to give language teachers and subject-area teachers ideas and space to collaborate on the design of a Japan-related unit of work in history or geography. Five teachers (from three schools) who participated in this seminar day agreed to participate further in the study by teaching a Japan-related unit of work. As an offshoot of this project, the Japanese teacher at Banksia along with a French language colleague participated in a 2015 design-based study (see Chap. 5 for an explanation of this kind of research) with three iterations.

7.2.1 Aims

The aim of the 2014 study was to investigate how Japanese could be used to teach history or geography units in secondary settings where there was

7 Teacher-Driven CLIL Initiatives in Secondary Schools 171

no structured CLIL programme. The subsequent 2015 design-based study at Banksia then had this overarching instructional hypothesis: *An explicit, planned-in focus on students' oral production of the target language can increase their language use in CLIL-inspired units.* The driver for this hypothesis was the 2014 observation at Banksia that students' oral Japanese production in class was limited despite language scaffolding and an immersive experience in the Japanese classroom.

7.2.2 Participants and Data Collection

Table 7.1 gives an overview of teacher participants (all names are pseudonyms) and number of students involved in the 2014 and 2015 studies. In 2014, at Cassia, Kathy was a history teacher and did not speak Japanese

Table 7.1 Summary of participants and data collection

School	Teachers	Year	Students	Observation	Teacher interview	Student surveys
Acacia	Anne[a]	7	52 (combined class) Japanese heritage (1)	×2 (combined geography/ Japanese class)	Yes	26
	Ting	7			No	
Cassia	John[a]	8	28 Japanese heritage (2) Chinese heritage[b] (23)	×2 advanced Japanese language class	Yes	10
	Kathy	8	24 From John's class (6): Japanese heritage (2) Chinese heritage (4)	×2 history class	Yes	16
Banksia	Akio[a]	10	20 Japanese heritage (0)	×6 Japanese language class	Yes (×4)	18 (×3)
	Michel	10	19 French heritage (0)	×6 French language class	Yes (×4)	16 (×3)

[a]Teachers who had received CLIL training
[b]Information included because of the strong pedagogical focus on *kanji*/Chinese characters in this context

172   M. Turner

and John was a dually-qualified Japanese and history teacher. The other participating teachers were qualified language teachers. Data from the 2015 study were drawn from three content-based units of work delivered at Banksia in Year 10 Japanese language classes (with Akio) and French language classes (with Michel).

Data were collected to investigate teachers' pedagogical decisions, the basis for these decisions and student engagement with the CLIL-inspired innovation. In both the 2014 and 2015 studies, all the participating teachers' classes were observed twice for every unit of work delivered. In Acacia and Cassia, the teachers were observed delivering one unit of work. In Banksia three units of work were part of the design-based study, which equated to six observations of each of the Year 10 Japanese and French language classes in this setting. The teachers were interviewed after each unit of work about the experience of planning and teaching it. Kathy and John at Cassia chose to conduct the interview as a dialogue between them. A joint interview was also conducted with Akio and Michel at the end of the 2015 study. Students in all five classes completed surveys after each unit of work observed (three surveys each for Akio and Michel's students). Surveys were short, focusing on the students' linguistic background, experience with/interest in the target language, whether or not they liked the unit of work and why/why not. At Banksia, there was an additional question on each survey about whether or not the students were planning to study Japanese or French in Year 11. (In most Australian schools, language study is compulsory up until Year 10, and then becomes an elective subject in senior secondary.) Thematic analysis was used (see Braun & Clarke, 2008) and data were cross-referenced to identify themes.

7.3   Units of Work

Units of work are shown here to give an overview of the teachers' approach to CLIL (see Table 7.2). The Year 7 group at Acacia consisted of three separate classes combined into one. Anne—as the teacher trained in CLIL—led the teaching of the combined group and Ting and one other teacher played a supporting role. A Japanese teaching assistant was also present in the lessons.

7 Teacher-Driven CLIL Initiatives in Secondary Schools 173

Table 7.2 Summary of units of work

School	Year	Subject area	Focus
Acacia	7	Geography/ Japanese (combined class)	The study of compass points using Japanese language. Students were assessed on their geography knowledge using Japanese
Cassia	8	History/Advanced Japanese language (separate classes)	The study of the *shogun* (a mandated part of the history curriculum for Year 8). Students in an advanced Japanese language class learned *shogun*-associated Japanese *kanji* and vocabulary. The students then shared this knowledge with other students and had it reinforced in their (otherwise monolingual) history class. Students were able to complete their history assessment in Japanese (optional). This unit was co-written by John and Kathy
Banksia	10	Japanese/French language (separate classes)	Enquiry-based units inspired by what students were studying in humanities classes were delivered with a Japanese/ French theme in Japanese/French language classes 1. Me, my career and Japan/France 2. Community project—animals 3. Geographical features (Japanese) and job interview (French)

At Cassia, a connection was made between the history class and advanced Japanese language class. All the Year 8 history teachers in the school were teaching the same *shogun* unit of work, and *shogun*-related Japanese language had been written into the unit. This language was taught in Japanese classes and then brought to the various history classes by the advanced Japanese language students. Six advanced Japanese language students were in the history class observed in the study (see Table 7.1). At Banksia, Akio and Michel identified history and geography enquiry-based units where the students were required to investigate a topic of choice, and tailored these units to Japanese and French. Akio was found to have a stronger focus on Japan than Michel had on France in his materials: Akio had been trialling a CLIL approach for around three years and had developed a variety of Japan-related resources. Michel was new to the approach. For each unit of work, Akio, Michel and I (the researcher) discussed how a combination of group work and a humanities-driven focus on cognitive skills, such as comparison/contrast and analysis, might be leveraged to facilitate more production of Japanese/French language.

7.4 Summary of Findings

Multilingual stance
Heritage languages: Mostly invisible in the classroom, but knowledge of Chinese leveraged in Japanese use in one school.
Target languages: Advocacy conspicuous in teacher-driven cross-curricular use/ languages mostly considered a separate domain.
English: Language of communication (with target language in language classrooms).

Student engagement with languages
At home: Clear (for Chinese and Japanese).
At school: Engagement mostly positive from both heritage and non-heritage students in different subject areas, but investment in learning a target language could be low.

Opportunities to learn
- Linguistic repertoire found to assist in the learning of content and/or be relevant to content objectives.
- CLIL in language classes could be harnessed for developmental language learning, but could also be viewed as an obstacle to this kind of learning.
- Immersive experience in target language rare but observed in one language classroom.

Institutional structures and pedagogies
Professional learning, collaboration, cross-curricular Asian content focus, student and/or instructional differentiation, crosslinguistic pedagogy, language scaffolding and form-focused instruction.

Fig. 7.1 Findings according to multilingual practices framework

7.5 Multilingual Stance

> *Heritage languages*: Mostly invisible in the classroom, but knowledge of Chinese leveraged in Japanese use in one school.
> *Target languages*: Advocacy conspicuous in teacher-driven cross-curricular use. Languages mostly considered a separate domain.
> **English**: Language of communication (with target language in language classrooms).

In the studies, stakeholders generally had a multilingual stance in that no one was found to question the need to learn other languages. However, there appeared to be no expectation at the schools that the use or learning of any language other than English would be prioritised except in its specific domain. English was taken for granted as the main medium of instruction at schools, and there was no policing of its use as a medium of instruction in language classes. In the observed language classes, teachers used a mix of English and the target language, and the kind of sustained target language use by teachers in the Japanese classes discussed in Chap. 6 was only found in Akio's Japanese language classroom at Banksia. Drivers of CLIL-related innovations were found mainly to be language advocacy, and the related expectation that making language learning relevant to other learning was key. Except in Akio's class, advocacy appeared to be linked to explicit, more than implicit, learning of language. Although the studies focused on learning a language at school rather than using a heritage language, heritage language was found to be relevant in the Cassia context in particular, and John and Kathy positioned students' linguistic repertoire as an asset relevant to classroom learning.

7.5.1 Advocacy and Relevance

At the three schools, there was found to be a general expectation that languages belonged in the language classroom where, guided by curriculum-based achievement standards, they were mostly to be taught explicitly. There was no clear, school-based incentive for the teaching and learning of communicative language in different contexts. It was the (optional) role of language teachers to take the initiative and find ways to advocate any cross-curricular, meaning-focused use of Japanese or French to students, and also to other teachers in the school in the case of Acacia and Cassia. Identifying ways in which a CLIL approach could add value to different subject areas was the common thread in the language teachers' initiatives.

At Acacia, it appeared to be the need to advocate for Japanese that helped Anne's process of thinking through CLIL—an approach that she did not perceive to be straightforward:

> *I did the CLIL course [...] and that was all very theoretical, and then when you've got to teach it, it's 'OK, this is quite challenging'. (Anne, interview)*

At the time of the study, Acacia had undergone some structural changes—this will be discussed later in the chapter—and Anne had successfully negotiated retaining Japanese language hours by combining these hours with the teaching of some humanities units. For Anne, combining geography and Japanese offered an opportunity to recycle previous learning about compass points for the students and cover interesting aspects of Japanese culture:

> *We found that Japanese [people] would actually use compass points more for direction than, you know, saying 'left' and 'right' [...] so we kept finding things that we can build in that are really interesting. [...] A lot of the feedback we get from Japanese is [the students will] say 'I find the language hard, I find the characters hard', but they really like the culture because it's so different. (Anne, interview)*

Using Japanese concepts and vocabulary to assist geography content learning, and building on students' interest in Japanese culture was thus a strong focus of CLIL-inspired classes at Acacia.

At Banksia and Cassia, Japanese culture was also leveraged as a way to engage students. With the aim of infusing relevant content into his language teaching, Akio chose to tailor units of work from history and geography to include Japanese themes. At the time of the study, he was working towards establishing different Japanese foci in all his language classes, his aim being students' well-rounded understanding of Japan by the end of school. John and Kathy chose to link Japanese to a *shogun* unit that was in the general Year 8 history curriculum, thereby ensuring that

7 Teacher-Driven CLIL Initiatives in Secondary Schools   177

the relevance of the innovative use of Japanese in the history classroom was clear to stakeholders.

7.5.2   Japanese/French Language Use

Expectations around Japanese and French language use varied widely, but the use was generally regarded to be difficult by students of both languages. This may have guided teachers' choices around focusing on explicit language teaching, as evidenced by Anne's earlier quotation. In the observed lessons, she was found mainly to use common expressions in Japanese and relevant vocabulary, and students were observed to use Japanese words to complete activities but otherwise speak in English (see Turner, 2017). Akio also reported in an interview that students' beliefs about the learning of Japanese language did not appear to be realistic, and this could result in the idea of challenge:

> Kids often assume that they can speak the language well after learning it for one year, or they think that's something they can never learn [...] there's a huge gap in between. We believe that if they spend a lot of time, if they, you know, make an effort, they can speak. [...] There is always the gap or the discrepancy of their understanding. (Akio, end-of-project interview)

Akio's comment can be linked to the teachers in the study discussed in Chap. 5, and their shift of understanding of 'bilingual' to encompass practices. The way Akio reported students' perceptions of speaking other languages appeared to indicate their understanding of bilingualism as a state of being rather than a process of engagement. By giving his students an immersive experience in Japanese, Akio demonstrated an underlying expectation that a combined implicit–explicit approach could help the students learn. This will be discussed later in the chapter under school structures and pedagogies.

Teachers' expectations around language use might also need careful management. At Cassia, John showed that he understood the importance of this management—both his own disappointment in not being able to offer the unit himself and the potential anxiety of monolingual history teachers. He also needed to consider the enthusiasm of the advanced

178 M. Turner

language students. In the following quotation, the teachers were discussing John's plan to teach the CLIL unit himself:

> *Last year when we [were] talking about [CLIL], I think we were talking more about you taking a class, as in [...] they'd be learning history in history but it'll be in Japanese. (Kathy, interview)*

> *That was the initial proposal [...] but it just proved to be a bridge too far to have that [...] in our school. (John, interview)*

This then seeded the idea of John and Kathy's collaboration in writing the Year 8 *shogun* unit. In order to alleviate any teacher anxiety, John ensured that the advanced language students scattered amongst the History classes would have the *kanji* and vocabulary knowledge the class would need to help guide the Japanese language aspects of the unit. He also let teachers know that he would assess any work in Japanese. In the interview, he commented:

> *There would have been only two [out of eight history teachers] who genuinely had some resistance or some concerns about it, who genuinely felt uncomfortable to the point where [...] their levels of distress and anxiety doing the unit might have impacted on how their classes went. (John, interview)*

Given the importance of making it acceptable to all stakeholders, the approach did not necessarily fulfil the expectations of the advanced language students, and this will be discussed further in the next section. In an interview John spoke of his students' enthusiasm for the initiative and the way he needed to dampen this a little in order for the unit to go ahead:

> *Some of the [Japanese and Chinese] background speakers got really excited about this [history] unit, and we tried to keep them in the realms of what we could satisfactorily deliver, because it [had to] hit the majority of the students. (John, interview)*

Even though the language use needed to be more diluted than if the advanced language students had been able to study history in Japanese, using language in existing subject-area classes showed a positive move towards the encouragement of a multilingual orientation across the curriculum.

7.6 Student Engagement With Languages

> *At home*: Clear (for Chinese and Japanese).
> *At school*: Engagement mostly positive from both heritage and non-heritage students in different subject areas, but investment in learning a target language could be low.

It appeared that general student investment in Japanese and French was quite low across the schools, and language teachers thus positioned themselves as language advocates, as discussed in the previous section. Heritage languages were not visible at Acacia and Banksia, but linguistic knowledge of Japanese and Chinese (via *kanji*/Chinese characters) was leveraged to learn content at Cassia. The findings at Cassia were different from the other two schools because it was clear that many of the Chinese-heritage students in particular appeared to be committed to their heritage language, and also indicated a desire to engage in more extensive Japanese language learning than was offered in the language classes. At Acacia, making Japanese relevant and/or culturally appealing appeared to have a positive influence on some student engagement, but this depended on the profile of the student. At Banksia, student lack of engagement was found to be particularly challenging for Michel—students studying Japanese appeared to be more engaged with the language than those studying French.

7.6.1 Increasing the Capital of Linguistic and Cultural Knowledge

The leveraging and valuing of linguistic knowledge was especially reported as a positive outcome of the initiative at Cassia. The advanced language students were positioned as knowers of something of value—some of this knowledge they had gained in their Japanese language class in the form of *shogun*-related *kanji* and vocabulary and some they knew as a result of being able to read/write either Japanese or a logographically similar language (Chinese). As John pointed out,

> *[We] probably inflated the egos of you know half of the students [...] because they got to be the big shot. And they might not necessarily have been. A lot of*

180 M. Turner

these kids that are here are quiet kids [...] all of a sudden, they are the 'go-to' person in the classroom because they've got the answers. (John, interview)

These students were found to engage positively with being the 'go-to' person in the history classes by actively volunteering what they knew. In the interview, Kathy also explained what the advanced language students did if they could not remember some of the relevant *kanji* they had learned, and her explanation showed that the students had a level of knowledge about *kanji*/Chinese characters that indicated a certain degree of exposure:

We're getting [the kanji] off the Internet, just trying to figure it out [...] because a lot of the boys, quite a few of them were native speakers, [said] 'well, it looks right', if that makes sense. I think there's kind of a story. (Kathy, interview)

The leveraging of relevant linguistic knowledge was prominent in this quotation in that the knowledge was shared by Chinese- and Japanese-heritage language speakers, and Kathy attributed the term 'native speaker' to students who participated knowledgeably in *kanji*- related activities. Four of her six advanced language students were Chinese-heritage students. The two other students were of Japanese heritage, and it appeared that their heritage became more visible when there was more cultural capital attached to it:

It was interesting because there were students that I didn't know had a Japanese background. They had kept that very on the down-low until we did this. (Kathy, interview)

Another indication of investment in Japanese language in particular was the decision of four advanced language students to complete the *shogun* assessment—a *manga* poster—in Japanese. The inclusion of *manga* as an assessment was particularly noted on the survey as positive by the two Japanese-heritage students, who mentioned this aspect when asked what they had liked about the unit.

7.6.2 Japanese/French

The CLIL approaches were different at Acacia and Banksia, and engagement was not so connected to the leveraging and valuing of linguistic knowledge. As at Cassia, there was an advanced Japanese class at Acacia, but this class was joined with the other two classes for the CLIL initiative. It appeared that the combined class may have had the unwitting effect of decreasing the advanced students' engagement—Anne noted that 'the mainstream kids' were 'coping with [the CLIL approach] a lot better than some of the top students'. At Acacia, 13 out of 26 students stated on the survey that they liked the unit but, for a variety of reasons, with only five students mentioning Japanese culture. One student who said she was interested in Japanese because she had a Japanese heritage reported the class to be too easy. This particular student may have benefitted from the approach at Cassia—she was very much in the minority at Acacia where differentiation between Japanese language proficiencies was not observed to occur in the combined class.

At Banksia, there was also no instructional differentiation observed in the CLIL-inspired classes, and it appeared that the students in the Year 10 Japanese class were more engaged in their language learning than in the Year 10 French class. This was clear in classroom observations, where the Japanese language students as a group appeared to take their study seriously. In the French class, a conspicuous number of students appeared to be indifferent. In the Japanese class, there was a critical mass of Japanese students who planned to continue their Japanese studies into Year 11 (9 compared with 12 who were planning to stop). In contrast, only 1 out of 18 students in the French class planned to continue her French studies. Students were asked about continuing their language studies on each of the three surveys over the course of the 2015 study, but it appeared that they had already made up their mind at the beginning of the year because no one's response was found to change. Michel noted the challenge in the end-of-project interview at the end of the school year:

We need to keep in mind that these students do not want to do French. They are one week away from never doing French again. […] I had a few of them coming to me last month telling me […] 'I would like to apologise because I didn't learn—I wasn't very involved', and I'm thinking, 'no, the year is not over'. That was a month ago. […] When you put it in those terms, yeah, it's quite incredible that they actually did something. (Michel, third interview)

182 M. Turner

Given these circumstances, as Michel pointed out, it is perhaps more realistic to measure any kind of achievement as hard-won rather than think about the students' lack of engagement as a complete pedagogical failure. Indeed, Michel demonstrated an innovative approach to engagement when trialling group work in the design-based study. He prioritised engagement above ability and found the approach was an efficient one in this context:

I started [...] sorting out students per abilities, and that didn't really work. Then I started [...] to mix students of different abilities, and that didn't work [given] that the students with low abilities weren't doing anything, and were relying on the others to do everything. So, in the end, I thought OK [...] I will let them sort [themselves] by motivation. If they are very motivated to work [...] they will group together, and they will improve their French. [...] And if they are not motivated at all, they will stick together. [...] But at the end of the day, they still need to produce something. [...] The thing is, they group themselves. But what [the less motivated students] do not understand is that if they had been in a group with some students who are working, they would not have to do anything. [...] I use three groups [...] and this way I can get through [...] so much more. (Michel, second interview)

A focus on student engagement, rather than ability, was a very interesting one, and a creative way to teach a class in which many students' disengagement with French was a significant obstacle to teaching and learning.

7.7 Institutional Structures and Pedagogies

Institutional structures: Professional learning, collaboration and cross-curricular Asian content focus (for Japanese).
Pedagogies: Student and/or instructional differentiation, crosslinguistic pedagogy, scaffolding and form-focused instruction.

Institutional structures that allowed the CLIL initiatives to take place included professional learning in the form of both collaboration and the CLIL training course and, for Japanese, a cross-curricular focus of the newly adopted national curriculum which promoted more Asia-related content in different subject areas (Australian Curriculum Assessment and

Reporting Authority, 2015). Pedagogically, settings were found to differ and this was linked to whether or not the class was a language class, a subject-area class or a mixture of both. Genre-based pedagogy was not in evidence but other kinds of language scaffolding were being used. Crosslinguistic pedagogy as deliberate and strategic was observed in the classes that had a focus on content. In the language classroom, as in the setting in the previous chapter, crosslinguistic pedagogy tended to be less strategic and more driven by students' incomprehension of a particular language or habitual tendency to communicate in English. In the subject-area classes, the default language was English and other languages were mainly used to assist in the learning of content.

7.7.1 Collaboration, Professional Learning and Cross-curricular Priorities

In Cassia, the school structures that most conspicuously influenced the CLIL initiative were the presence of a *shogun* unit in the Year 8 history curriculum, John's CLIL training and John and Kathy's opportunity to collaborate on writing the unit of work. Kathy's willingness to be a part of the initiative, as a monolingual teacher, may have acted as a calming influence on the other history teachers; the fact that it was permitted to happen in the first place when there was uncertainty around the novel approach was a big step. Kathy's part in the collaboration effectively demonstrated that it did not need to be John, the dually-qualified Japanese/history teacher, teaching the unit.

In Acacia, there was a restructure happening at the school, and it was during this process that CLIL became a course of action, a way forward viewed as possible on account of Anne's CLIL training. She explained the negotiated restructure in an interview:

When we changed to four period days, there was a big slicing up of time between KLAs [Key Learning Areas] and one thing all the other KLA coordinators were pushing for was that language had less time. [...] So we stood and fought our ground, but one thing that happened was that we were given parts of the humanities course to teach in Japanese or German [the two languages taught in the school]/So it was really a structural thing. (Anne, interview)

184   M. Turner

Collaboration in this case occurred among the language teachers, rather than between the language teachers and humanities teachers, and Anne spoke of the language teacher collaboration in positive terms:

> *I've enjoyed the opportunity to team teach and collaborate on a unit. […] We had this really cool group of people who had different skills and we all worked together using those skills. (Anne, interview)*

In Banksia, Akio's CLIL training also appeared to be the main school structure driving the initiative. For him, collaboration with other Japanese language teachers appeared to be more challenging. He reported that he enjoyed talking to subject-area teachers in order to align his units of work with work in the curriculum by either taking a particular Japan-related focus in a more general enquiry-based unit or aligning with an elective unit that the humanities teachers had decided not to teach. He found the history teachers in particular had been interested in hearing about CLIL. However, he was not in a leadership position and he found this to be a challenge with regard to the mentoring of other teachers, stating in his 2014 interview:

> *Sometimes you share the same year level with other Japanese teachers and the biggest challenge is to, you know, support them so they can run it. […] We obviously have to share curriculum […] and that's the challenging part of it. […] We don't have time on our own and I'm not coordinator or anything, so I'm not given time to, say, support them. (Akio, interview)*

Akio demonstrated his desire to collaborate by finding a like-minded teacher in Michel in 2015. In the study, they attempted to align what they were doing with each other, as can be seen in the unit summary earlier in the chapter.

7.7.2   Language-Related Pedagogies

Crosslinguistic pedagogy was in evidence in all three schools. In the language classroom at Cassia, translation was found to be a deliberate teaching tool in assessments, and in the combined language-and-content class

7 Teacher-Driven CLIL Initiatives in Secondary Schools　185

at Acacia, English was used in instructions, followed by the translation in Japanese (see Figs. 7.2 and 7.3). At Cassia, the attention to vocabulary and *kanji* across the language and history classrooms allowed for crosslinguistic work and awareness, not only between Japanese and English, but between Chinese and Japanese. Although the *kanji* and vocabulary introduced into the history classroom were not explicitly found to help students' conceptual understanding of the *shogun* content, there was a chance for deeper understanding to occur through the meanings of the *kanji* (e.g., *sho* refers to 'commander' and *gun* to 'army' or 'troops'). Finally, at Banksia, translation was mainly used by students as they searched for and translated words they needed to complete content-based activities. Assessments were project-based and explanations for these were written entirely in English, but more sustained use of the target language was observed in

Reading (24 Marks):

1) のうみんはおみやげをかいました。ちいさかったです。 4 Marks

2) 大名はじんじゃに行きました。おもしろかったです。 4 Marks

3) ひまな時に 将 はすしをつくります。 4 Marks

4) あとで、けんどうのれんしゅうをしましょう。 4 Marks

5) 金曜日のよる、将軍はローラーコースターにのりました。こわくてたのしかったです。 8 Marks

Writing: Translate the following sentences into Japanese (39 Marks):

1) Afterwards, I will drink water with the Farmers (Noumin). 7 Marks

2) On Friday night I will go the temple with the Samurai. 8 Marks

3) In my spare time I will read a book. 5 Marks

4) Before school the Shogun bought a Military hat (Kabuto). It was expensive. 11 Marks

Fig. 7.2 Excerpt from advanced Year 8 students' language assessment at Cassia

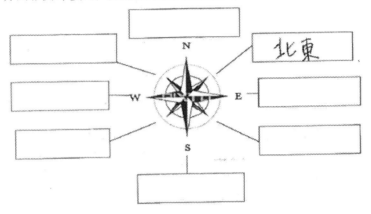

Fig. 7.3 Excerpt from Year 7 assessment at Acacia

teaching and learning activities, especially in Akio's class, for reading as well as in teachers' oral language use (see Fig. 7.5). Akio was observed to employ scaffolding techniques similar to those used by the Japanese teachers in the study discussed in Chap. 6: for example, establishing routines in class, repetition, showing students how they might answer, and visuals (Fig. 7.4).

In the design-based study, the objective was to experiment with Akio's existing focus on group work—observed in 2014—in order to try to increase students' language production. Akio and Michel focused on trying to assist students in communicating meaningfully in analytic and creative tasks. Michel reported challenges with this approach and these

7 Teacher-Driven CLIL Initiatives in Secondary Schools   187

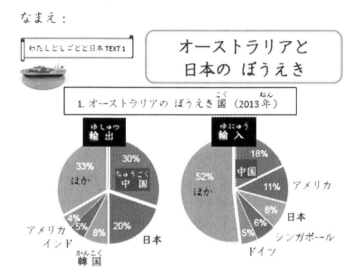

Fig. 7.4 Excerpt from Year 10 'Me, my career and Japan' unit at Banksia

will be discussed in the next section. In the third iteration, Akio chose to change the unit structure he had been using in order to encourage students to produce language. He had been basing his units on key readings in Japanese to give his students a point of reference (see Fig. 7.5). However, in the final iteration, he prepared a series of PowerPoint slides (also given to the students as reference) through which he gradually introduced vocabulary and structures all related to Mount Fuji (see Fig. 7.6), and the students were then required to create and present a text for Japanese speakers about an Australian geographical feature. Ten out of 21 students responded on the third survey that the approach was better than the former approach when asked very generally if they had liked the unit and 19 students in total responded positively to the question. They thus appeared to appreciate a type of bottom-up approach of discrete structures, later leading to language production, more than a top-down approach of receiving texts, which could then be used as a springboard for language use and activities. The structured language input provided on the PowerPoint slides can be related to form-focused instruction (see Chap. 3) because it invited the students to notice important content-related language in a structured way.

Fig. 7.5 A reading text used for the Japanese community project unit at Banksia

Nouns					Verbs		また
	人	まわり	かんこう きゃく		き 来ます		
ふじさん 富士山	てん 点	しぜん	Adjectives	あります	のぼります	そして	
にんき 人気	くるま 車	ぶんか	いい	いります	こまります	…から	
がいこく 外国	ごみ	きょうみ	おお 大きい	なります	Others		
せかい 世界いさん	バス	もんだい	うるさい	もちます	たくさん		
やまご 山小や	エコ	トイレ	しずか	ふえます	もっと		

Fig. 7.6 Excerpt from PowerPoint slides used for the Japanese geographical features unit at Banksia

In the language class at Cassia and the combined class at Acacia, communicative language scaffolding was not so apparent because what was observed was mostly based on the learning of vocabulary and *kanji*. In Cassia, this coincided with the linguistic knowledge the students would be taking into the history unit on the *shogun*. In the combined class in Acacia, the students were learning geography-related words (Fig. 7.3).

7.8 Opportunities to Learn

* Linguistic repertoire found to assist in the learning of content and/or be relevant to content objectives.
* CLIL in language classes could be harnessed for developmental language learning, but could also be viewed as an obstacle to this kind of learning.
* Immersive experience in target language rare but observed in one language classroom.

Similar to the previous chapter, opportunities to learn in the three schools under study were related to different kinds of objectives. Languages were primarily considered to 'belong' to a particular domain at school (the language classroom), and a conspicuous number of students were not particularly engaged with Japanese or French at Banksia. However, there was one group, the advanced language group at Cassia, who did appear to be more engaged in Japanese and a number of students also invested in their heritage language of Japanese or Chinese. Leveraging students' linguistic repertoire at Cassia was found to provide greater opportunities for everyone to learn Japan-related content across the curriculum. Teaching and learning about the cultural dimension of target languages was found to be prioritised in all three schools, which appeared to increase language-learning opportunities. This was more the case in Acacia and Banksia, however; in Cassia, the focus was clearly more on content than on language. Institutional structures and pedagogies also appeared to facilitate opportunities to learn, albeit unevenly, across different student profiles and classes.

7.8.1 Leveraging Language to Learn Content

Opportunities to learn content appeared to be very different, and could depend on whether or not the class was a content class, a content-and-language class or a language class. In the classes at Cassia, content objectives were the primary focus of the history class, and language objectives were very much the domain of the language class. The leveraging of advanced language students' linguistic knowledge, as well as the opportunity to complete the assessment in Japanese, was found to increase the cultural capital of these students' linguistic repertoire in the history classroom; students were found to respond positively to their 'expert' positioning. Engagement with Japanese language in the *shogun* unit was found to be not limited to the advanced language students. Six of the 16 students who completed the survey in Kathy's class wrote about the use of Japanese language when asked generally what they had liked about the unit of work. Three of these students did not study Japanese and three studied Japanese but were not in the advanced class. Opportunities to learn for these students thus appeared to be connected to their interest in the way the unit was delivered.

In the combined class at Acacia, the Japanese language teachers focused on revising geography concepts by presenting the material in a different, innovative way—through a mixed medium of Japanese and English. As Anne commented in the interview:

> *I think humanities teachers expect [the students] to know [compass points] from primary school. [...] I was mentoring a teacher and she was teaching this unit in humanities, a lot of the kids didn't know it, and she just walked in expecting that students would know it. [...] So we sort of took a quiet gentle opportunity to go, it's OK if you don't know that. Just sort of do some revision of that. (Anne, interview)*

Opportunities to learn thus appeared to be geared towards the students who needed revision of geography content. Language-learning opportunities were also driven by content vocabulary in that the language focus in the combined class was more on vocabulary and *kanji* rather than on communicative language structures. An emphasis on

7 Teacher-Driven CLIL Initiatives in Secondary Schools 191

language structures may have been occurring in other, more language-focused classes. However, in the combined classes, students who already knew the geography content and/or were comparatively more engaged in Japanese were perhaps not benefitting from the same opportunities to learn.

7.8.2 Leveraging Content to Learn Language

At Banksia, the CLIL-inspired lessons took place completely in the language classes, and they also appeared to provide differing opportunities for the students to learn. Whilst content was being used to drive the lessons, the learning was related more to language than content objectives. Michel in particular found it difficult to juggle the content and language in his French class. In the interview after the third iteration he put this down to being a novice teacher, but also expressed his concerns about the use of content to guide language learning. As he reported, humanities content objectives could require more sophisticated language constructions:

I'm struggling a bit there [with the approach of content driving the lesson] because being able to answer higher order thinking questions, well, you need the high order thinking grammar. You need to have all that certainty and be able to include conditionals or subjunctive in French. You know, assumptions, when you make assumptions, you need to use specific tenses, which are very complicated. [...] Year 7, I would expect French descriptive, cette, c'est un chien? It's a white dog. [...] In Year 8, I expect more, it's a white dog. I like him because he's white. (Michel, third interview)

Given his students' very low proficiency level, coupled with their lack of engagement with French, Michel found it challenging to provide year-level-appropriate content and scaffold the language so the students would learn French in a systematic way. John at Cassia supported Michel's view in that he considered the Cassia initiative to be suitable only for the advanced-level class:

I think if I tried to do this [initiative] with the mainstream Japanese class, it would have been a subtractive process. They needed to have basic verb forms,

192 M. Turner

basic particles, and it would be remiss of me not to prepare them, you know, in that respect. (John, interview)

In these cases, the inclusion of content in language learning was perceived to hinder students' opportunities to achieve language objectives—or rule-based, developmental language learning—in the language classroom. Different challenges could also be attributed to different languages—the subjunctive in French, for example. Akio at Banksia was found to address the issue of complexity in his Japanese class by adapting the content to language structures that were at or close to the students' level. All the texts and resources observed in the study were created by him. Even so, as mentioned in the previous section, the students demonstrated via the surveys that they preferred the bottom-up approach of receiving language structures and then creating a text than starting with reading a text and slowly deconstructing it in different activities. The main approach Akio was observed to take was a focus on information texts and description, with some opinion and comparison/contrast.

7.9 Discussion

The focus of the study discussed in this chapter was on the learning of target languages at school (Japanese and French), rather than the incorporation of heritage languages into English-medium classrooms. However, the importance of viewing cross-curricular language use holistically was clear in the study, especially for Cassia, where so many Chinese-heritage students and some Japanese-heritage students were studying Japanese. A multilingual stance of fostering/affirming students' linguistic repertoire (see de Jong, 2018) outside the language classroom was in evidence for the advanced language students. Generally, where a target language was being used to teach a subject area, rather than a subject area being an additional bonus in the language classroom, crosslinguistic pedagogy was found to be used strategically, and often had a positive effect on students' engagement. In cases where the effect was more neutral or negative, it appeared to be more related to students' desire for more, rather than less, use of the target language. The amount of target language

7 Teacher-Driven CLIL Initiatives in Secondary Schools   193

used in the content classes was not extensive, and the medium of communication was predominantly English.

Crosslinguistic pedagogy frequently relied on direct translation and did not necessarily incorporate students' language practices as a way of making meaning in class. However, the inclusion of *kanji* in history classes at Cassia laid the foundations for a greater conceptual understanding of content. This will be explained further in the next chapter, where a deeper understanding of content was explicitly related by stakeholders to the presence of *kanji* in the classroom. The use of Japanese in the geography class at Acacia was also found to be leveraged as a novel way to make content revision more interesting for students. These aspects align with the opportunity translanguaging provides for the co-construction of knowledge (cf. Gumperz & Cook-Gumperz, 2005; Martin-Beltrán, 2014); content instruction was adapted for students based on their knowledge of Japanese, as well as on an objective to expand this linguistic knowledge. Instruction tended to be delivered in the same way, however, regardless of students' linguistic proficiency, and either the resources and/or needs of particular groups of students in the classes drove the innovations at Cassia and Acacia. At Cassia, this appeared to be identity-affirming for the advanced language students (cf. Cenoz & Gorter, 2011; Lin & He, 2017). At Acacia, heritage speakers of Japanese, or a language with important similarities, were not an explicit focus of the CLIL initiative.

From a sociopolitical perspective, linguistic hierarchies were beginning to be disrupted in Cassia in particular because Kathy and the other history teachers were allowing a language that some students knew much better than they did into the classroom. This instigated a teacher-as-co-learner model in which Kathy was found to ask questions of the advanced students and learn from them with the other students. The metalinguistic awareness that she gained, that 'the *kanji* tell a story', was something she wanted to explore with students in future classes. Thus, although there was no clear encouragement of flexible language practices and interrogating linguistic inequity (see García & Li, 2014), like in Chap. 6, this appeared to be a step towards becoming more comfortable with different ways of teaching and learning. It involved thinking about the kinds of linguistic repertoires that students were bringing to class, albeit in relation to similarities with a target language (Japanese).

Finally, expectations around implicit and explicit learning of language in formal settings appeared to be complex, and meaningful communication in the language classroom seemed to be challenged by an institutional need to focus primarily on language-as-subject-area or a rule-based competence (see Ellis & Shintani, 2014). The language teachers needed to ensure the teaching and recycling of language through content in the language classroom happened in a way expected by the (language-driven) curriculum. The challenge was exacerbated by students' uneven engagement in the target language, especially in the French classroom. Understanding and expanding students' language practices from an engagement perspective in a content-and-language-driven classroom is therefore important, as is careful resourcing and planning of activities. This is especially the case in secondary settings, where the increased complexity of content may call for more sophisticated language. Although more challenging than a sole focus on developmental language learning, the endeavour of promoting an equal emphasis on stimulating (and often cultural) content has the potential to increase students' linguistic repertoire in a far more meaningful way.

7.10 Conclusion

The bottom-up approach of providing CLIL training to teachers, who then decided how to adapt CLIL for their particular context, was found to lead to different kinds of innovations. At the heart of these innovations lay the notion of advocacy, or the need to nurture and protect the learning of languages in Australian schools. At the three schools in the study, a multilingual stance was evident amongst stakeholders, but associated expectations of language learning and use in the school domain appeared to be diluted. Engagement was found to vary widely. A conspicuous number of students across the three schools were only invested in the target language insofar as pedagogies, content and assessment engaged them. At one school, the heritage languages were taken into account in the CLIL initiative, alongside the target language of Japanese. Institutional structures conducive to cross-curricular use of other languages were also found to vary widely, but the initiatives mainly relied on teachers' CLIL training—one teacher at each school in the study—and structures that allowed collaboration. Working with students' linguistic repertoires in both language and subject-area classrooms, as well as encouraging teachers to be co-learners of language, may be a way to move students towards deeper and more critical knowledge of language and content.

References

Australian Curriculum Assessment and Reporting Authority (ACARA). (2015). *Asia and Australia's engagement with Asia.* Retrieved from http://www.acara.edu.au/curriculum/cross_curriculum_priorities.html

Australian Curriculum, Assessment and Reporting Authority (ACARA). (2018). *My school.* Retrieved from https://www.myschool.edu.au/

Braun, V., & Clarke, V. (2008). Using thematic analysis in psychology. *Qualitative Research in Psychology, 3*(2), 77–101.

Cenoz, J., & Gorter, D. (2011). Focus on multilingualism: A study of trilingual writing. *The Modern Language Journal, 95,* 356–369.

Cross, R. (2015). Defining content and language integrated learning for languages education in Australia. *Babel, 49*(2), 4–15.

de Jong, E. J. (2018, Keynote). *Taking a multilingual stance: Quality education for ELLs.* Minneapolis, MN: Minnesota-TESOL.

Ellis, R., & Shintani, N. (2014). *Exploring language pedagogy through second language acquisition research.* London: Routledge.

García, O., & Li, W. (2014). *Translanguaging: Language, bilingualism and education.* New York: Palgrave Macmillan.

Gumperz, J. J., & Cook-Gumperz, J. (2005). Making space for bilingual communicative practice. *Intercultural Pragmatics, 2*(1), 1–23.

Lin, A. M. Y., & He, P. (2017). Translanguaging as dynamic activity flows in CLIL classrooms. *Journal of Language, Identity & Education, 16,* 228–244. https://doi.org/10.1080/15348458.2017.1328283

Martin-Beltrán, M. (2014). What do you want to say? How adolescents use translanguaging to expand learning opportunities. *International Multilingual Research Journal, 8,* 208–230.

Spence-Brown, R. (2014). On rocky ground: Monolingual educational structures and Japanese language education in Australia. In N. Murray & A. Scarino (Eds.), *Dynamic ecologies, Multilingual education* (pp. 183–198). Dordrecht: Springer.

Turner, M. (2017). Integrating content and language in institutionally monolingual settings: Teacher positioning and differentiation. *Bilingual Research Journal, 40*(1), 70–80.

8

A Structured, Opt-In Secondary CLIL Programme

8.1 Introduction

In Chap. 7, CLIL was discussed in relation to teacher-driven initiatives. In Australia, structured programmes follow the prototypical characteristics identified by Dalton-Puffer, Llinares, Lorenzo, and Nikula (2014): CLIL does not take the place of the language classroom, and content is delivered (and assessed) by teachers qualified in that subject area. Although the target language may not be a *lingua franca*—the third characteristic—languages are commonly chosen because they are considered prestigious and/or relevant to the learners in some way. Structured CLIL programmes are most conspicuous in the state of Queensland where ten junior secondary school programmes were established over a decade ago, and one (French) programme has been offered for over three decades (Smala, 2016). These programmes have traditionally been called immersion, but tend to be similar to many secondary CLIL programmes in Europe (ibid.). Although the teaching time can vary, three subjects, such as science, mathematics and humanities, are usually taught using the CLIL language. Students study, and are assessed on, the curriculum of the relevant subject area. Teachers are qualified in the subject under study,

© The Author(s) 2019
M. Turner, *Multilingualism as a Resource and a Goal*,
https://doi.org/10.1007/978-3-030-21591-0_8

and are not necessarily dually qualified as language teachers. CLIL languages include French, German, Italian, Japanese and Chinese (ibid.). Even though they are funded by the government, most of the programmes are interested in attracting academic high achievers (Read, 1996; Smala, 2011).

Findings discussed in this chapter were drawn from a similarly structured CLIL programme operating in a large co-education Catholic secondary school in Victoria. The programme was opt-in—the school did not have any criteria the students had to meet to enter the programme. The establishment of CLIL grew out of a 2010–11 idea of Japanese immersion. At the time, CLIL was starting to be discussed in Victoria as a viable way to include more language learning across the curriculum, and schools were beginning to trial the approach. The CLIL programme at the school was also extended to Italian. In 2017, the school had 1929 student enrolments and was listed as having a slightly higher socio-educational advantage than average. Amongst the students 64 per cent came from a language background other than English—a conspicuous number of these had an Italian heritage—and 1 per cent of the students had an Indigenous background (Australian Curriculum and Reporting Authority, 2018). Students studied a language class in addition to CLIL, and CLIL classes were humanities and religious education (both Italian and Japanese) and science and visual arts (only Japanese). The structured programme ran from Year 7 to Year 9, but students were able to (and advised to) enter in Year 8 if they showed an interest in the language in Year 7. For Italian CLIL students, there was a post-Italian CLIL advanced language initiative available to the students in Year 10. In this chapter, the study will be described first, followed by the findings mapped against the multilingual practices framework. A summary of these findings (see Fig. 8.1) precedes a discussion on each dimension.

8.2 The Study

The study, conducted in 2017, was designed to research opportunities, student (and teacher) engagement and student outcomes in the Italian and Japanese CLIL programmes at the participating school. Structured opt-in secondary CLIL programmes were uncommon in the Australian context and literature around choosing CLIL, structuring CLIL into the curriculum, pedagogy, language use and assessment in this setting was scarce. The qualitative study was conducted in order to help the school identify what was going well and also as a way to make recommendations. The number of students who had opted into the CLIL programme was small and appeared to be decreasing. In 2017, 7 students had elected to study Italian CLIL and were grouped together in a bigger class of 27 students. The 20 students in the class who had not elected to study in the CLIL programme were studying Italian as a subject. No Year 7 Japanese CLIL programme was running due to a lack of students (see Table 8.1).

8.2.1 Aims

The aim of the study was to investigate opportunities available to different stakeholders—principal, teachers, students, parents—associated with CLIL, organisational features, the structure of units, perspectives on teaching and learning, language use, and content and language outcomes.

8.2.2 Participants and Data Collection

Participants included the principal, five teachers, their students and parents of the students. The principal had been working in the position since 1991 and was very supportive of languages education. He was initially interviewed about the context of the school and the way CLIL was implemented. The five participating teachers (see Table 8.2—all names are pseudonyms) were also interviewed about their perspectives on—and experiences with—CLIL. Yvonne had been teaching visual arts in the

Table 8.1 Number of students at each year level studying CLIL

Year level	Japanese CLIL	Italian CLIL
Year 7	0	7
Year 8	13	15
Year 9	8	12

Table 8.2 Summary of participants and data collection

CLIL	Teachers (all interviewed)	Subject area and teaching arrangement	Class observations	Student interviews	Student surveys	Parent surveys
Year 7 Italian	Angela + Sophia (Italian coordinator)	*Humanities* Co-teaching: experienced humanities teacher new to CLIL + experienced CLIL/ humanities teacher	×2	3	21[a]	26[a]
Year 9 Italian	Sophia	*Humanities* Sole CLIL/humanities teacher	×2	3	11	–
Year 8 Japanese[b]	Audrey (non-Japanese-speaking science teacher) Louise (Japanese language teacher)	*Science* Co-teaching: both teachers new to CLIL. Science teacher with a Japanese language teacher in supporting role	×2	6	8	8
	Yvonne (Japanese coordinator)	*Visual Arts* Sole CLIL/visual arts teacher	×2	–	–	–

[a]Non-CLIL students and parents also filled out the surveys
[b]The same students attended both Japanese CLIL subject areas

8 A Structured, Opt-In Secondary CLIL Programme 201

Japanese CLIL programme for six years and Sophia had been teaching humanities in the Italian programme for four years. They both had eight years of teaching experience. The other teachers were new to CLIL, and their experience varied: Louise had been teaching one year, Audrey six years and Angela over 30 years.

Given that the teachers did not all approach CLIL in the same way, the study attempted to capture the breadth of what was happening at the school. This was done by including humanities classes at different year levels (Year 7 and Year 9) in Italian CLIL, and two subject areas (visual arts and science) at Year 8 level in Japanese CLIL. These classes included a co-teaching arrangement in which two teachers taught a mix of CLIL and non-CLIL students studying in the same class (Year 7 Italian CLIL humanities), another co-teaching arrangement between a monolingual (in English) science teacher and a Japanese language teacher in a supporting role (Year 8 Japanese CLIL science) and two classes in which the teachers were solely responsible for their CLIL class (Year 9 Italian CLIL humanities and Year 8 Japanese CLIL visual arts). All classes were observed and video-recorded twice. After each observation, the teachers were audio-recorded reflecting on the lesson. Twelve students were interviewed about their linguistic and cultural background and their attitudes towards CLIL, and documents such as work samples and unit planners were collected. A parent survey was also conducted on perceptions about the CLIL programme (see Table 8.2). Thematic analysis was used (see Braun & Clarke, 2008) and data were cross-referenced to identify themes.

8.3 Lessons

Two lessons were observed for each class. The Italian CLIL Year 7 class was a co-teaching arrangement in which Angela was the main teacher and Sophia supported her. The teachers spoke in Italian to both the CLIL and non-CLIL students in this class and invited the non-CLIL students (rather than expected them) to complete activities in Italian. In the other classes, all the students had opted into the CLIL programme.

202 M. Turner

Table 8.3 Observed lessons

CLIL	Focus
Year 7 Italian	*Humanities (geography)*
	1. How water supports life
	2. The water cycle and pollution
Year 9 Italian	*Humanities (geography)*
	1. Palm oil production
	2. Tourism
Year 8 Japanese	*Science (physical and chemical change)*
	1. Properties of solids, liquids and gases
	2. Simple chemical reactions
	Visual arts (digital print)
	1. Manipulating Photoshop tools
	2. Producing and describing a Photoshop image (humanity vs. nature)

Sophia was the sole teacher for the Italian Year 9 humanities class. The students were studying a larger topic on ecosystems, and an extract from the end-of-unit ecosystem assessment was sighted for the study. The Japanese Year 8 science class was a co-teaching arrangement differed from the Italian CLIL Year 7 class in that Audrey, a science teacher for the Year 8 cohort in the large school, did not speak Japanese. She worked alongside Louise, who was responsible for the Japanese language use in the lessons. Finally, Yvonne was the sole teacher for the Japanese Year 8 visual arts class. In all the CLIL classes, the students were expected to complete the same assessments as their non-CLIL peers (Table 8.3).

8.4 Summary of Findings

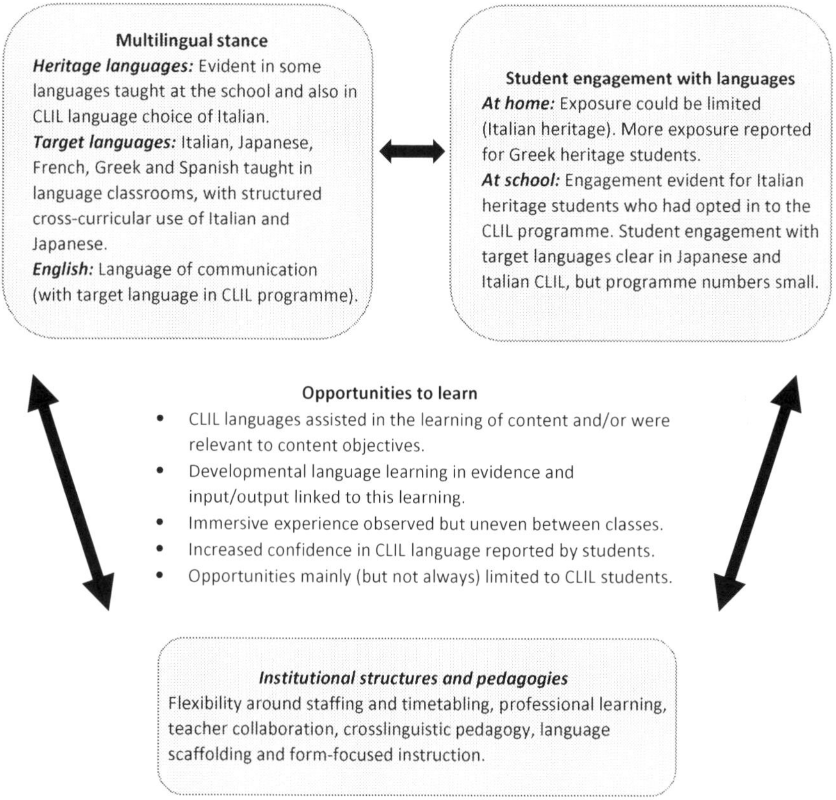

Multilingual stance
Heritage languages: Evident in some languages taught at the school and also in CLIL language choice of Italian.
Target languages: Italian, Japanese, French, Greek and Spanish taught in language classrooms, with structured cross-curricular use of Italian and Japanese.
English: Language of communication (with target language in CLIL programme).

Student engagement with languages
At home: Exposure could be limited (Italian heritage). More exposure reported for Greek heritage students.
At school: Engagement evident for Italian heritage students who had opted in to the CLIL programme. Student engagement with target languages clear in Japanese and Italian CLIL, but programme numbers small.

Opportunities to learn
- CLIL languages assisted in the learning of content and/or were relevant to content objectives.
- Developmental language learning in evidence and input/output linked to this learning.
- Immersive experience observed but uneven between classes.
- Increased confidence in CLIL language reported by students.
- Opportunities mainly (but not always) limited to CLIL students.

Institutional structures and pedagogies
Flexibility around staffing and timetabling, professional learning, teacher collaboration, crosslinguistic pedagogy, language scaffolding and form-focused instruction.

Fig. 8.1 Findings according to multilingual practices framework

8.5 Multilingual Stance

> *Heritage languages:* Evident in some languages taught at the school and also in CLIL choice of Italian.
> *Target languages:* Italian, Japanese, French, Greek and Spanish taught in language classrooms, with structured cross-curricular use of Italian and Japanese.
> *English:* Language of communication (with target language in CLIL programme).

A multilingual stance was evident in the structured CLIL programme at the school through the value attributed to learning and using languages, including heritage languages. It was clear that expectations around the use of target CLIL languages were higher in this context than in the schools discussed in Chap. 7, and this could be linked to the structured nature of the programme and the increased exposure this gave the students to their chosen language. Although immersion was considered to be ideal in the CLIL classes, the expectations of both teachers and students were found to be content-driven, or to align first with content and then with exposure to—and use of—Japanese or Italian. The institutional expectation of developmental language learning was leveraged to help structure language use and this may have helped to alleviate the perception of challenge evidenced around the incorporation of a target language in content-driven classrooms. Challenge was positioned as a benefit by participants in the study, but the principal and teachers also spoke of it as a reason for many students not opting into the programme; for these students, languages were still confined to language classrooms and/or the community domain.

8.5.1 Challenge

The idea that cross-curricular language use and learning was challenging was conspicuous in the data among all stakeholders, and feasibility appeared to be an important element of multilingual stance, as with the other settings. Challenge was positioned both as a benefit and a disadvantage but, however it was considered, management of it was a priority, especially given the opt-in nature of the programme and the small numbers of students who were choosing CLIL in such a large school. Four of the 12 students interviewed understood challenge to be a benefit, and considered it as one reason for studying in the programme—see the following two interview excerpts:

I like that there are challenges within CLIL. [...] I chose CLIL [be]cause I knew that there was [going to] be a challenge. (Student, Year 8)

I thought it would be a nice challenge to do some other subjects in Italian as well. (Student, Year 7)

In the survey, five parents also cited the idea of challenge as a reason for choosing CLIL; for example, one parent reported that 'mainstream would have been too easy' and another that '[my son] wanted to learn a language in a challenging setting'.

However, during the interview, four of the teachers discussed how students and their parents could be anxious about the challenge of CLIL. From a student perspective, it appeared that the feeling could change if they opted into the programme, but they needed to have the experience to know that any sense of confusion or incomprehension was likely to ease. Two of the students reported this to be the case:

At the beginning in Year 7 I was, like, completely shook [...] [be]cause our teachers would like speak in Japanese and it was a bit hard [...] it was a rocky start because I did speak Japanese in primary school but not as much as we spoke over here [...] it was like hard at the beginning, but then I was able to come through. (Student, Year 8)

I really like how in depth they go with the Japanese, like, we can really understand [...] for the first couple of months everything will be so confusing, then one day it'll just click and you can fully understand what the teachers are saying. (Student, Year 8)

These students opted in despite the difficulties at the beginning, but the idea of challenge may have been an obstacle to others. For example, in the interview, the principal discussed an attempt to begin a Greek CLIL programme, in recognition of the number of students who were electing to study Greek at the school. In the end, he did not have a sufficient number of students for the CLIL programme to go ahead, and one of the reasons he thought some parents had not chosen CLIL was scepticism:

I think some parents were sceptical [...] of doing humanities in Greek. They won't learn as much [after doing] seven years of study in primary school in English. (Principal, interview)

The institutional expectation, which was larger than the school's, that language could be contained within the language classroom, and that the rest of the school day would only be taught through the medium of English, was the norm. Thus, management of the way the CLIL programme was perceived by students and parents appeared to be an important factor in its sustainability.

8.5.2 Japanese/Italian Language Use

The main language expectations on the part of the teachers appeared to be that this challenge could be managed through a flexible approach to language use and explicit language teaching. Both of these will be discussed further in the section on institutional structures and pedagogies, but it is important to note influences on the strength of the teachers' multilingual stance. Students' understanding of content was prioritised, as was their ability to demonstrate this understanding in English; they would later be studying the subject areas in English in senior high school. Louise in particular reported the complexity involved in decision-making when teaching content through the medium of a target language with recourse to a dominant language that everyone understands:

If I'm asking questions about reproduction in Japanese, and [the students] get some of those questions wrong on the test, can I assume that that's because they don't know the content? Or was that a language barrier? I know that I taught them those words, but it doesn't mean that they picked up those words. [...] I don't know, should I test those words first? I sort of have that slight worry of assessing fully in the language. (Louise, interview)

Louise's concerns were reinforced by students' comments in interviews, where they all clearly demonstrated their appreciation of having English in the assessments. Two excerpts from student interviews, the first from Japanese CLIL and the second from Italian CLIL, are provided here:

8 A Structured, Opt-In Secondary CLIL Programme

Say we're doing a science test, we'd have the normal English test and then attached would be an extra Japanese sheet. So we could look at—we'd learn it—take the Japanese that we've learnt from the class and then answer on the test, and I like that way of being assessed. (Student, Year 8)

I think the way we're assessed is very good because we're not expected to do an entire assessment completely in Italian, so they give us certain sections or certain paragraphs that they'll say write this part in Italian, and then try and work on your grammar. So, for example, when I did the palm oil task, we weren't expected to write everything in Italian, just certain parts. (Student, Year 9)

Even in sections where students were encouraged to write in the target language, they were not found to lose marks if they used English. The extracts in Fig. 8.2 are taken from a Year 9 assessment on ecosystems. In the first extract, it is clear that the student attempted to write in Italian but reverted to English and did not lose any marks. In the second, only Italian was used but the student lost marks. By correcting but then ticking language mistakes, Sophia demonstrated attention to language but also her focus on content. This flexible approach to the use of the target language, as well as a focus on explicit language structures that could be

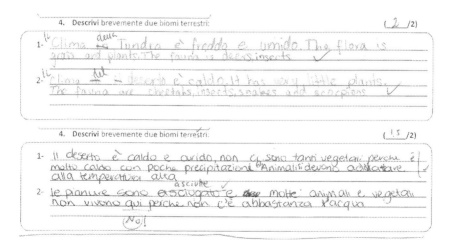

Fig. 8.2 Extracts from the Italian CLIL Year 9 assessment (two different students)

used by students in the assessment (to be discussed later in the chapter) was a pragmatic way to manage challenges associated with use of the CLIL language. The approach was found to give rise to opportunities to learn: this will also be discussed later in the chapter.

8.6 Student Engagement With Languages

> *At home:* Exposure could be limited (Italian heritage). More exposure reported for Greek heritage students.
>
> *At school:* Engagement evident for Italian heritage students who had opted in to the CLIL programme. Student engagement with target languages clear in Japanese and Italian CLIL, but programme numbers small.

Engagement in most of the classes was different from the studies reported in Chaps. 6 and 7 because the CLIL programme was not whole-school or related to language classes and general class initiatives where engagement could not be assumed. Students were at an age where they were likely to have a say in opting in to the programme, and were demonstrating some degree of investment in the CLIL language. Reasons behind this investment were found to differ between Italian and Japanese CLIL because a large proportion of students in the Italian CLIL groups had an Italian heritage, whereas none of the students in the Japanese CLIL group had a Japanese heritage. Additionally, in the Italian CLIL Year 7 class—the one class where CLIL students were studying alongside their non-CLIL peers—non-CLIL students were found to engage very positively with Italian, but this did not appear to lead a desire to enter the CLIL programme in Year 8. Finally, the cultural capital attributed by the school to the CLIL languages was high compared with Australian mainstream schools generally. However, there was an accelerated programme running in the school for high-achieving students, and this operated parallel to the CLIL programme. Thus, if students and parents attributed more cultural capital to academic recognition and accelerated advancement, they were less likely to opt into CLIL. This positioned CLIL differently from programmes in Queensland, which historically have had an explicit focus on high-achieving students.

8.6.1 Exposure to CLIL Language Outside School

Students with an Italian heritage were conspicuous in the Italian programme. In the interviews, four of the six Italian CLIL students cited speaking to family members as a reason for choosing Italian CLIL. A big focus for these students appeared to be everyday communication. They reported that they spoke basic Italian at home and they were enjoying being able to speak more as a result of the programme. In 'Italian CLIL' parent surveys, 12 out of 26 parents wrote that Italian was a home language, and the question of home language may have hidden a greater number of parents who had an Italian heritage but did not speak Italian at home. Sofia, the coordinator for the Italian CLIL programme and the Year 9 humanities teacher, referred to the importance of heritage during interview when asked about the kind of students she thought accessed the CLIL programmes:

A kid who actually has a connection with the [language], with an Italian background in this case. (Sofia, interview)

Having a background in the language did not automatically mean that students would choose to study in a CLIL programme, however. When discussing students'/parents' lack of interest in Greek CLIL, the principal wondered whether Greek-heritage students' exposure to Greek outside school may have been discouraging them from participating because they were already communicating—and learning in—Greek:

A lot of the Greek children—more than any of the other languages at the moment, I think, at the school—speak Greek at home a lot. Then they go to Saturday school. (Principal, interview)

This comment relates to the issue of whether or not the degree of investment in a heritage language may influence students (and parents) opting in to a CLIL programme. In the primary bilingual setting in Chap. 6, Japanese-heritage parents, who spoke Japanese to their children and also sent them to Saturday school, were choosing to send their children to the bilingual programme. Possible similarities and differences between the two settings will be discussed in Chap. 9.

In contrast to Italian- (and Greek-) heritage students, the connection students in the Japanese CLIL programme had with Japanese was not at all related to heritage. Three of the six students interviewed cited interest in Japanese culture as a reason for choosing CLIL. Two of these students also spoke of the benefits of learning a language in general. Another liked the fact that she could talk to her sister, who had also studied Japanese CLIL, and her parents would not understand. The final two students said that it was the challenge that attracted them to CLIL. Students were observed to be trying to say what they knew in class, and Yvonne mentioned that they greeted her outside class in Japanese. Engagement with Japanese may have also been facilitated by a sense of belonging to a class community—the Year 8 Japanese CLIL class was a small group and they reported that they felt as if they were learning with their friends.

8.6.2 Non-CLIL Students

In the Italian Year 7 class, the seven students who had opted into the CLIL programme had one lesson a week apart from their peers where their exposure to Italian was increased. The rest of the time CLIL and non-CLIL students studied together in a combined class and Angela, the lead teacher for this class, reflected on motivating the non-CLIL students:

We are teaching a majority of students who are not doing CLIL. [...] We need to make them individually interested. We want them to experience something different where they can have fun. (Angela, first after-class reflection)

It was clear from observations that Angela was using fun as a motivational tool and reported that students engaged with the approach:

I start the class in English [...] to tell [the students] that there is going to be some kind of a new thing now, sort of a switch, but I don't want them to be scared about it. It's going to be exciting actually to be able to go in and be able to get clues. [...] I want them to pay attention to language that might seem like English to them. So I want them to get into a game of spying. [...] OK, what is [it] that you are going to look for to be able to understand what is happening? [...] Afterwards, I go to the students who are not part of CLIL, just students

8   A Structured, Opt-In Secondary CLIL Programme   211

who are in the geography class, to see what they've got, and they're willing to play the game. (Angela, second after-class reflection)

In this Year 7 class, 20 out of 21 students completing the survey said that they enjoyed learning languages and 13 out of 21 enjoyed learning CLIL (six students mentioned that they did not choose it and two said it was too hard). This was a much larger number of students enjoying CLIL than the seven students who were part of the CLIL programme. As will be discussed in the next section, it was also clear from the work samples that the non-CLIL students were using Italian on their geography work-sheets. However, Sophia reported that non-CLIL students were still not opting into CLIL in Year 8 even though she was actively trying to recruit more students. The students appeared to be happy to engage with Italian but were not ready to commit to a structured programme.

8.6.3   CLIL Versus Acceleration

Investing in the target/heritage language at school via participation in the CLIL programmes was found to compete with investing in struc-tured academic acceleration in the case of high-achieving students. This did not mean that students automatically chose the accelerated pro-gramme, but the choice did appear to indicate that more students may have accessed CLIL, given the choice. In the interview, the principal commented on this:

A lot of students who do CLIL would have got into the [accelerated] program had they sat it. [But] CLIL loses out for some who in the end really [want to] do the accelerated, and who could do CLIL. (Principal, interview)

Given that the CLIL programme and the accelerated learning programme were the two 'special' programmes offered by the school, Yvonne also pointed out that a relative lack of knowledge about CLIL might have been an obstacle to choosing the programme:

There are a lot of schools around here that offer enhancement, enrichment, acceleration, and I think that's really easy to understand. But I think CLIL is

[...] not quite as common. [...] I conducted a survey of the Year 7 students and parents as well, and the information that I got back from that suggested that, 'no we don't really know much about this'. [...] So they don't understand what it is, but they're not keen to find out what it is, if it doesn't directly affect them. (Yvonne, interview)

Yvonne was attempting to change this by planning such initiatives as taking Japanese CLIL students to feeder primary schools to help mentor the Year 5/6 students as she taught them (using Japanese) how to prepare props for a play. Given the very low number of students in the Italian CLIL class and the lack of uptake for Year 7 Japanese CLIL, student engagement was a concern and was being actively targeted by both Sophia and Yvonne.

8.7 Institutional Structures and Pedagogies

Institutional structures: Flexibility around staffing and timetabling, professional learning, teacher collaboration.
Pedagogies: Crosslinguistic pedagogy, language scaffolding and form-focused instruction.

The main institutional structures that appeared to influence the CLIL programme related to timetabling, staffing, professional learning and an emphasis on collaboration. The principal demonstrated his commitment to CLIL through the provision of classes for relatively small groups of students opting into CLIL, and also through the co-teaching staffing arrangements in the Italian Year 7 geography class and the Japanese Year 8 science class. The co-teaching served a different purpose in each case—in the former, Sophia was supporting Angela as she taught CLIL for the first time, and in the latter, Louise was responsible for bringing Japanese into Audrey's Year 8 science class. In interview, the principal commented that he would 'like to get to a stage where CLIL is how we deliver our [languages] program', and he was working towards that goal by addressing logistical challenges as they arose. Form-focused instruction (see Chap. 3) was evident in the Japanese Year 8 visual arts and Italian humanities classes and Louise discussed the way a focus on Japanese language structures helped her plan lessons for the Japanese Year 8 science

8 A Structured, Opt-In Secondary CLIL Programme

class. Language scaffolding was also in evidence and crosslinguistic pedagogy was used in different ways in different classes, mainly through translation and allowing students the space to express their knowledge of content in English. Connections between language and content classrooms were beginning to emerge, as were overviews of language foci in different content classes.

8.7.1 Logistics and Professional Learning

The principal was found to address logistical issues such as staffing and timetabling in creative ways. The Japanese CLIL programme had two more subjects than the Italian CLIL programme (science and visual arts, as well as humanities and religious education), and this was mainly related to staffing. The principal noted that 'if I can find a CLIL trained Italian science teacher, I'll extend that as well'. There was an initial opportunity to teach science in Japanese because there was a Japanese-speaking science teacher at the school. When this teacher left the school, the principal was able to leverage the skills and knowledge of Louise, who was initially hired in a Japanese language–supporting role for the Japanese CLIL teachers. She had a Japanese language–teaching qualification and a Bachelor's degree in science, and the principal placed her in a co-teaching role with Audrey, with the eventual aim of appointing her as the sole CLIL science teacher. The principal spoke of this pragmatic approach to CLIL subject areas in interview:

> I'm always on the lookout for new subjects where I can introduce CLIL. I [need to] have the teacher who can speak the language and then be CLIL trained, [...] and then I [need to] have the number of students as well. And each time I do this I complicate things for the timetable of course. (Principal, interview)

Both CLIL training and timetabling challenges are clear in this quotation, and these were also mentioned by Yvonne when discussing the challenges around CLIL for teachers. She further added preparation to these challenges. As Angela put it in her interview, 'Honestly, many times I

214   M. Turner

thought I wish I never ever [got] into CLIL because it's a lot of [...] work'. However, this extra work led to a significant advantage in that the principal and the teachers, including Angela, reported that it reinvigorated the teachers' approach to their teaching:

> *The way the content is presented is more varied. [...] I think that's an absolute benefit to all. [...] I changed my teaching. Since I started teaching CLIL, it's so true, that actually has reflected in all my other mainstream classes as well. (Angela, interview)*

Sophia mentioned in her interview that CLIL had 'taught her a lot' and Yvonne that 'being a CLIL teacher makes you a really good teacher'. The reasons cited were an increased attention to language, a focus on varied activities and a reduced reliance on textbook teaching.

8.7.2   Language-Related Pedagogies

Attention to language in the CLIL classes could be considered under the umbrella of form-focused instruction because the lessons were content-driven, or primarily focused on meaning. Teachers were found to actively search for language structures conducive to particular content that they could reinforce and recycle. In the Year 8 visual arts class and the Year 9 geography class, Yvonne and Sophia stated the language goals on their planners (see Fig. 8.3 for an example). This was the language that was observed to be encouraged and practised orally with the students in class, through question-and-answer activities and in written form. In addition to co-teaching in the science class, Louise supported teachers across the Japanese classes and, in this role, attempted to share and recycle language structures:

> *I'm trying to bring [language] continuity across all the CLIL classes. [...] I've set up a [...] Google classroom [...] so that we can make connections between the classes and support each other. [...] I'm lucky because I get to go round to all the classes so I'm probably the person who posts on there the most. (Louise, interview)*

8 A Structured, Opt-In Secondary CLIL Programme

Year 8 CLIL Japanese Visual Art Unit Planner

Semester	Topic & Assessment	Class Activities	Language Goals	Homework Tasks	Japanese Content and Culture
Semester One	Digital Print – Humanity Vs Nature Week Four	• Lesson objectives • Review of classroom language • Review of language to describe experiences within an artwork/virtual world. • Sentence structure activity with Giacomo Costa's "Aqua no. 10" – pair activity. Students examine the artwork and use the words provided as prompts to describe what they imagine being able to see, smell, hear and feel within the work. (TIMED TASK – 10 Minutes + discussion) • Students continue with Humanity vs Nature (『人間性と自然』task sheet) – plan, sketch annotate in English and Japanese. • Kahoot! Quiz – sentence ordering quiz on prepositions of place (context: Photoshop Tools)	• Use prepositions 上、下 and となり in a full sentence when locating Photoshop Tools. • Complete sentences in Japanese that describe what can be seen, heard, smelt and felt within the world of an artwork (creative responses). • Use language to seek help and clarify meanings of Japanese words.	• Complete any unfinished work by next week's class in preparation for working in Photoshop.	Classroom Language – EG: Greetings/formalities/responding to the roll おはつ、れい、ちゃく せき Seeking teacher assistance/attention: • 先生、すみません。Excuse me • 先生、しつもんです。I have a question • 先生、これはいいですか？Is this ok? • 先生、たすけてください。Please help me • 手を上げて下さい。Raise your hand, please. • 日本語で何ですか？What's that in Japanese? Asking for meanings/clarification of Kanji readings: • 先生、すみません。この漢字は何ですか？Excuse me, what's this Kanji? • 先生、すみません。＿＿＿は英語でなんですか？Excuse me, what's (＿) in English? Prepositions : 上、下、となり Grammar/Sentence Structures: （Tool）は＿＿の上・下・となりにあります。 Theme : 人間性と自然（Humanity VS Nature） Describing experiences within an artwork /virtual world : 何が見えますか？　　　＿＿が見えます。 何が聞こえますか？　　＿＿が聞こえます。 何をしていますか？　　＿＿＿＿＿＿＿＿。 気分はどうですか？　　＿＿＿＿＿＿＿。 何のにおいをしますか？＿＿のにおいをします。 一人ですか？

Fig. 8.3 Weekly planner—Japanese CLIL Year 8 visual arts

Sophia had also begun putting subject areas and Italian language classes side by side on a unit planner for Year 7 in order to compare and contrast language goals. This was a useful exercise in that it was clear what students would have reinforced or would be learning for the first time. For example, 'describing people' was a language goal of the language class, humanities and religious education units during the same time frame, but students were learning how to ask questions in humanities before they were learning how to ask questions in their Italian language class. By cataloguing form-focused instruction in this holistic way, issues of sequencing could be addressed.

Language scaffolding was further found to take place through such strategies as the use of visuals, repetition and the explicit teaching of the kinds of structures students would need for activities. Crosslinguistic pedagogy as a planned-in strategy was also used to scaffold language. Yvonne and Sophia both targeted sections of assessment to be completed in Japanese or Italian, ensuring that the students had practised the relevant language in class. An example from one of Yvonne's assessments appears in (Fig. 8.4), and an Italian excerpt from a Year 9 geography assessment was shown earlier in the chapter (see Fig. 8.2).

In the Year 8 Japanese CLIL science class, Louise attached a page of assessment in Japanese—sentences the students had to decide were true or false. She also led warm-up activities in Japanese and quizzes at the end. Audrey and Louise prepared the presentations together, and Louise's main crosslinguistic strategy was translation (see Fig. 8.5). She and Audrey both encouraged the students to use the Japanese they knew while doing group work. In Angela's combined CLIL/non-CLIL Year 7 class, translation was also a clear strategy, both on presentation slides and in oral work. For example, Angela would check understanding by asking students for the meaning in English: '*Non sono in ordine*. What did I just say?' In this class, students were assessed in English.

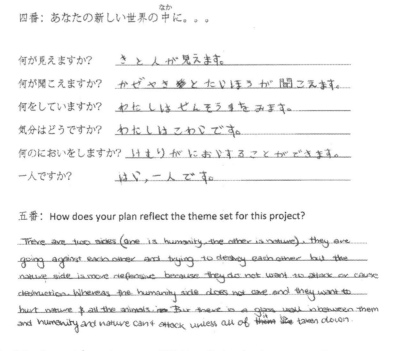

Fig. 8.4 Excerpt from Japanese CLIL Year 8 visual arts assessment

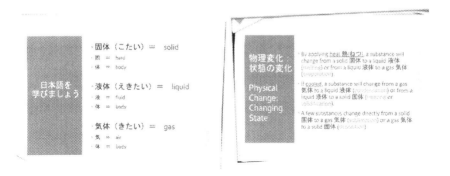

Fig. 8.5 Excerpts from Japanese CLIL Year 8 science presentation

8.8 Opportunities to Learn

- CLIL languages assisted in the learning of content and/or was relevant to content objectives.
- Developmental language learning in evidence and input/output linked to this learning.
- Immersive experience observed but uneven between classes.
- Increased confidence in CLIL language reported by students.
- Opportunities mainly (but not always) limited to CLIL students.

Opportunities to learn were found mainly—but not always—to be significantly influenced by student engagement because the CLIL programmes were opt-in and students who were more committed to learning either Italian or Japanese in an enhanced way were the students who received this opportunity. The opportunity also related to the teachers' management of the perception of challenge in light of the common Australian institutional expectation that other languages are only spoken in the language classroom. Non-CLIL students in the Italian Year 7 class were receiving an unsolicited opportunity, which many took advantage of by attempting to understand and write in Italian. All the CLIL teachers were found to link the language they used in the classes to the kinds of structures the students were learning in their language classes as a way to anchor and reinforce what the students were learning and to encourage output. The students' opportunities to learn content were considered to be the priority, given that the classes were content classes and the students were studying the same work as their non-CLIL peers. Seven of the 12 CLIL students interviewed reported that the presence of the target language led to either increased engagement and/or understanding of different subject areas, and one of the teachers—Louise—deliberately leveraged classroom use of Japanese in a way that enhanced the students' understanding of content. Opportunities to learn language were also in evidence, especially in relation to students' increased confidence in the CLIL language.

8.8.1 Opportunities for Non-CLIL Students

In the Italian Year 7 CLIL/non-CLIL combined geography class, there were some activities, such as matching vocabulary and images, that required the use of Italian, and other activities where students were free to use either English or Italian (see Fig. 8.6). Non-CLIL as well as CLIL students were found to complete the Italian activities in Italian, and sometimes to attempt more Italian on the activities that required a longer response. The non-CLIL students were all studying Italian language as a subject area, and thus the relevance of making an effort with the Italian was likely to be clear. Angela and Sophia also had a focus on engaging these students, who were the majority in the class, through fun activities and through being careful with how much

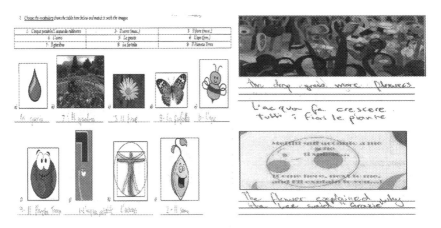

Fig. 8.6 Excerpts from Year 7 Italian non-CLIL students' humanities worksheets

Italian was used, or expected of the students. The way that the teachers needed to consider the needs of the non-CLIL students made it more difficult for some of the CLIL students, however, because it resulted in one separate lesson a week where a lot more Italian was expected of them. The intensity of this separate lesson could be overwhelming—when asked what she thought could be improved, one Year 7 CLIL student replied:

> *I feel like if [the lesson we do in Italian] was maybe broken up into, like, smaller areas, so over the three lessons in the week you learn more things, so it's not just a full bit of information coming at you, and you get overwhelmed. So maybe if they separated it so that it's not just one day of learning all Italian. (Student, Year 7)*

However, it is important to note that, given the small numbers of students opting into Year 7 CLIL, this solution of a combined class did allow the programme to go ahead: the existence of the opportunity for CLIL students appeared to demand a compromise.

8.8.2 Leveraging Language to Learn Content

Although CLIL was considered to be challenging, there was evidence that opportunities to learn content were enhanced by the approach. For example, two students in Japanese CLIL Year 8 reported that it made subject areas they did not enjoy more interesting (one mentioned humanities and the other science). Two Italian CLIL Year 9 students reported that learning Italian in subject-area classrooms was fun, and one of the students further said that it helped him understand humanities. An Italian CLIL Year 7 student articulated how Italian helped him learn a subject area:

> *I guess you just get a better understanding once you go through it, especially in English and then you go back in a different language. […] And then you can really say, oh I understand this because you read it in a different language and you try to put the pieces together and then you go, oh that's why this happens then. (Student, Year 7)*

220   M. Turner

Teachers' commitment to teaching via CLIL also appeared to provide opportunities to learn content through their focus on language. This appeared to be happening in a general way; for example, an Italian CLIL Year 9 student mentioned that he liked 'the way that the teachers approach us, instead of getting us the content, they give us the content and they talk to us about it because we need to try and understand it as well as learn it'. Here, the student was indicating how a focus on language ensured that teachers did not assume students' understanding of content just because they had read about it. The opportunity to learn content was also found to be language-specific in that Louise found a way to help students' conceptual understanding of science through the use of *kanji* (see Turner, forthcoming). As Louise explained:

> *I tend to use a lot of kanji because they're characters that contain meaning, like they're not just phonetic, they have the meaning as well. And so often it can make a meaning clearer. [...] I've noticed that benefit, and so I do try to teach the words and the kanji, you know put a lot of kanji on the slide shows, or well just, you know, the key words on the slide shows, mixed in with the English. (Louise, interview)*

One student in particular talked about this as an example of why she thought the Japanese CLIL programme was helping her learn different content, and Audrey, the non-Japanese-speaking science teacher in the class, understood the *kanji* to be a beneficial conceptual tool in that it translated back into English in different ways, and this could help students understand. When asked if she thought the use of Japanese was slowing down the students' learning of science, she disagreed, saying 'I think, if anything, it's actually helping them understand in a deeper way'.

8.8.3   Leveraging Content to Learn Language

Opportunities to learn language were evident in the students' work and also in their reports of increased confidence and proficiency. It was clear from the Italian CLIL Year 9 students' work, in particular, that they were using Italian to take notes (see Fig. 8.7). Sofia mentioned in her interview that her students 'love to take notes, they love to translate'. The transla-

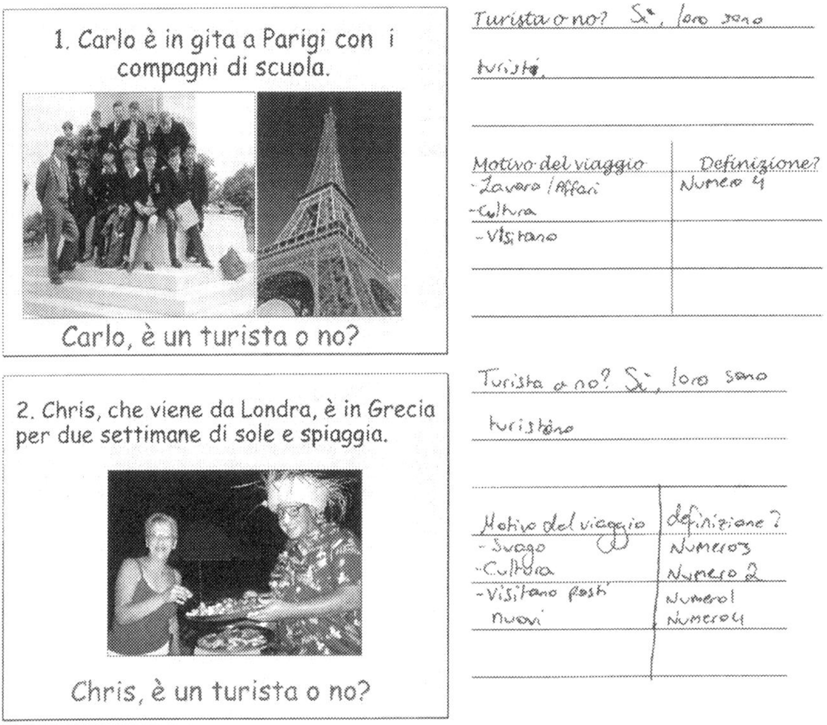

8 A Structured, Opt-In Secondary CLIL Programme

1. Carlo è in gita a Parigi con i compagni di scuola.

Carlo, è un turista o no?

2. Chris, che viene da Londra, è in Grecia per due settimane di sole e spiaggia.

Chris, è un turista o no?

Fig. 8.7 Example of students' note-taking in the Year 9 Italian CLIL humanities class

tion appeared to also be popular amongst Italian CLIL Year 7 students. Crosslinguistic pedagogy was an accepted aspect of CLIL, and one that students appreciated (as mentioned earlier in the chapter). Increased confidence and ability to communicate was also very conspicuous in the reported data. Two Japanese CLIL Year 8 students mentioned that they felt that their confidence was growing and one student in this group liked his increasing ability to understand *anime*. The Italian CLIL Year 7 students had not been in the CLIL programme for long, but the Year 9 students reported that they enjoyed their increasing linguistic knowledge. Two of these students specifically referred to being able to speak to their grandparents and attributed this to CLIL.

The CLIL teachers were found to search for ways that content could lend itself to language learning, and sometimes took responsibility for

222 M. Turner

providing resources to language teachers. Sofia in particular reported that she shared articles and related questions with the Italian language teacher so that language she was using in humanities was reinforced in the language class. Angela also showed that she was thinking as a language teacher as well as a subject-area teacher when engaging in the CLIL approach:

> *For me a language class CLIL would be ideal. [...] I have my language class where I teach math, science, where my course outline is divided into subjects, into topics, that I can immerse into my language class, geography, history. I can talk to my math colleague and say, look what are you teaching in math now? Well, my science colleague, what are you teaching in science? And then [I can] incorporate at the same time those topics. (Angela, interview)*

CLIL therefore appeared to be perceived as providing the same kinds of opportunities for engagement and meaning-focused activities in language classrooms as in subject-area classrooms. There was potential for making connections between the classes, and the teachers were found to be exploring and reflecting on this potential.

8.9 Discussion

A multilingual stance that affirmed cross-curricular language learning and use was clearly evident in the structured CLIL programme. The programme was inclusive in that all students were welcome to opt in, but the greater backdrop of institutional monolingualism in Australia appeared to be an obstacle to student uptake. The two CLIL languages catered both to students with a heritage in a language and students with no familial connection. However, the level of proficiency and confidence of the students observed in the study indicated that students who conversed in the language extensively outside school were not opting in to CLIL, or were very much in the minority. This observation was supported by the principal's speculation regarding the Greek-heritage students. It appeared that students were choosing to study Greek in the language domain but not to engage in cross-curricular use of the language. In the CLIL programme,

8 A Structured, Opt-In Secondary CLIL Programme 223

importance was (understandably) attributed to students' ability to display their knowledge of different subject areas in English because they would be learning these subjects entirely in English in senior secondary school. It is possible that the Greek-heritage students (and their parents) understood that this would not be the case. Exposure to English across the curriculum may have been a priority for them.

From a translanguaging perspective, there is potential in a CLIL programme to make meaning across languages in order to help students understand the subject area (and English) more effectively (cf. Gumperz & Cook-Gumperz, 2005; Martin-Beltrán, 2014). In the study, heightened student engagement with content appeared to be happening at both an affective and cognitive level. Students reported engaging with subject areas more enthusiastically as a result of the crosslinguistic delivery. For the Italian-heritage students, the inclusion of Italian in classes also appeared to be identity-affirming (see Cenoz & Gorter, 2011; García & Li, 2014; Lin & He, 2017) because their pride and general happiness at being able to speak more Italian to members of their family were clear. Valuing Italian in the school domain appeared to be instrumental. The presence of a CLIL language was also found to assist students' understanding of content. This was especially the case for *kanji* in the Japanese CLIL science classroom. The pedagogy that the teacher was using could be considered crosslinguistic, or broader than translanguaging pedagogy, because it relied on direct translation without the additional inclusion of further meaning-making activities (cf. García & Li, 2014). However, students were able to deepen their understanding of content because the translation came back into English differently from the explanation presented by the teacher, or in the textbook. Thus, the translation itself was found to be a useful crosslinguistic exercise in meaning-making for difficult concepts.

Sociopolitical goals associated with the disruption of linguistic hierarchies (García & Li, 2014) did not appear to be a strong consideration of the CLIL programme at the school. However, the very presence of a structured programme in the Australian context can be viewed as a preliminary step towards the disruption of the dominance of English. As in Chap. 7, a teacher-as-co-learner model was taking place: Audrey, the monolingual science teacher, was acting as co-learner of Japanese with the students. The valuing of particular language practices which a teacher does not share—and shows interest in learning—may be able to seed a space and ideas for critical reflection on linguistic inequity. Similar to the discussion in the previous chapter, a teacher's level of comfort related to allowing different ways of knowing into her classroom underpins any real change in teaching and learning practices if these practices are student-centred. Changes can include the active incorporation of other (non-CLIL) languages into the classroom, and the expansion of a multilingual stance to the rest of the school. French, Spanish and Greek, as well as Italian and Japanese, were taught in the languages domain, and various target and heritage languages could be gradually introduced across the curriculum in ways that are relevant to different subject areas. Helping students make meaning in their learning through a focus on crosslinguistic strategies may help legitimise the cross-curricular use of different languages in the eyes of students and parents.

Finally, expectations around the developmental learning of language in formal settings were aided by the structured nature of the programme, and the way language production was understood holistically (and recycled) in relation to the language the students were learning in the language classroom. However, in order to move further along a multilingual stance continuum with regard to commitment to the expansion of students' linguistic repertoire, there appeared to be scope for more communicative language use than required by language curriculum documents. A focus on subject-area vocabulary, structures and concepts in the subject-area classrooms seemed to lead to a relative lack of focus on students' creative self-expression and interactive use of the target language. The language classroom was only an indirect part of the study, but is perhaps the most suitable space for the strategic leveraging of communicative language practices from a translanguaging perspective (see the discussion in Chap. 6). Collaboration between language teachers and subject-area teachers may be able to help create opportunities for students to use the target language more communicatively across the curriculum.

8.10 Conclusion

The structured approach to CLIL in a school that did not have select-entry requirements for the programme was found to be successful: students were extremely positive about the experience and no obstacle to the learning of content was perceived by any of the stakeholders. Expectations appeared to derive from a multilingual stance, and the idea of challenge or that learning languages is difficult was very conspicuous in the data. This challenge was positioned as positive by students who had opted in to CLIL, but was also understood as a reason for student avoidance of this mode of study. Engagement with the cross-curricular use of target languages at school was found to be strong for stakeholders—not only the students, but also the principal, teachers and parents. Staffing and time-tabling, although complicated, were found to be very conducive to professional learning, and pedagogies were found to work with the very low communicative proficiency of students in the target language. The leveraging of content to learn language and language to learn content were both clear. Finding ways to engage more students (and parents) by showing them how meaning-making can be achieved crosslinguistically may be a way to encourage more participation in structured CLIL programmes. This may also provide more space for critical awareness and interrogation of linguistic inequity.

References

Australian Curriculum, Assessment and Reporting Authority (ACARA). (2018). *My school*. Retrieved from https://www.myschool.edu.au/

Braun, V., & Clarke, V. (2008). Using thematic analysis in psychology. *Qualitative Research in Psychology, 3*(2), 77–101.

Cenoz, J., & Gorter, D. (2011). Focus on multilingualism: A study of trilingual writing. *The Modern Language Journal, 95*, 356–369.

Dalton-Puffer, C., Llinares, A., Lorenzo, F., & Nikula, T. (2014). 'You can stand under my umbrella': Immersion, CLIL and bilingual education. A response to Cenoz, Genesee & Gorter (2013). *Applied Linguistics, 35*(2), 213–218.

García, O., & Li, W. (2014). *Translanguaging: Language, bilingualism and education*. New York: Palgrave Macmillan.

Gumperz, J. J., & Cook-Gumperz, J. (2005). Making space for bilingual communicative practice. *Intercultural Pragmatics, 2*(1), 1–23.

Lin, A. M. Y., & He, P. (2017). Translanguaging as dynamic activity flows in CLIL classrooms. *Journal of Language, Identity & Education, 16*, 228–244. https://doi.org/10.1080/15348458.2017.1328283

Martin-Beltrán, M. (2014). What do you want to say? How adolescents use translanguaging to expand learning opportunities. *International Multilingual Research Journal, 8*, 208–230.

Read, J. (1996). Recent developments in Australian late immersion language education. *Journal of Multilingual and Multicultural Development, 17*(6), 469–484.

Smala, S. (2011). *Contexts and agents: Different ways of 'doing' bilingual education in Queensland.* Paper presented at the Language and Diversity Conference, November 22–25, in Auckland, New Zealand.

Smala, S. (2016). CLIL in Queensland: The evolution of immersion. *Babel, 50*(2–3), 20+.

Turner, M. (forthcoming). The positioning of Japanese in a secondary CLIL science classroom in Australia: Language use and the learning of content. *Journal of Immersion and Content-Based Language Education.*

Part III

Synthesis

Part III of this book addresses teaching and learning objectives that can help to ground a holistic student-centred school-based language policy, and also discusses issues related to the opening up of multilingual spaces in formal learning. In Chap. 9, objectives are related to leveraging language as a resource and then to learning language as a goal, and the studies that appeared in Part II are drawn upon to show how each objective relates to what was found to be happening in schools. Multilingual language practices across the curriculum are addressed in Chap. 10. Both chapters aim to show the kinds of thinking and choices that may be involved in the promotion of multilingualism in the mainstream from a perspective that foregrounds students' existing and developing language resources. Chapter 10 ends with a reflection on the use of the framework for bringing together the learning of (and through) a chosen target language across the curriculum at school and the inclusion of non-dominant languages into classes where a dominant language is the medium of instruction.

9

Teaching and Learning Objectives

9.1 Introduction

Identifying different reasons for the incorporation of multilingual practices across the curriculum can help to enhance and develop these practices systemically. The teaching and learning objectives discussed in this chapter are informed by the studies in Part Two, and draw on the three dimensions of multilingual stance, student engagement with languages, and institutional structures and pedagogies. Taking the sociocultural and sociopolitical nature of these dimensions into consideration is important if the overarching goal is to promote meaningful and sustainable navigation of linguistic diversity.

Objectives include the leveraging and use of heritage languages in dominant language-medium classrooms, as well as the cross-curricular learning and use of often prestigious target languages. These different foci can be conceptualised on Cenoz and Gorter's (2015) research continuum of *being multilingual* and *becoming multilingual* respectively. Being multilingual has a principal focus on what people do with their languages, and becoming multilingual focuses on language acquisition (ibid.). Even though these research traditions are considered to be suited to a continuum, there may be a perception in schools that they are com-

© The Author(s) 2019
M. Turner, *Multilingualism as a Resource and a Goal*,
https://doi.org/10.1007/978-3-030-21591-0_9

229

pletely separate. For example, in the European context, Nikula, Dalton-Puffer, Llinares, and Lorenzo (2016, p. 6) pointed out an understanding of 'decisive differences' between immigrant students coming to school with different home languages and students learning a target language across the curriculum. Immigrant students are generally in classes with 'linguistically unaware teachers' who 'place the problem [of working in a less familiar language] entirely with the learners: if only these learners knew better German/Spanish/English/Finnish (the country's majority language) before coming to class, there would be no problem'. CLIL learners 'are seen as mainstream, or even a particularly capable and privileged band of said mainstream'. The teachers often 'see themselves as being in the "same boat" as their students, having to work through the curriculum in a language that they may use with less confidence than their L1' (ibid.).

In schools where students come from diverse linguistic backgrounds, linguistically aware teachers can be even more of an asset than in relatively homogeneous classrooms. Also, in many contexts of cross-curricular language learning, the boundaries between language learners and immigrants can become blurred: the presence of first and second-generation immigrants was clear in the CLIL studies discussed in Part Two. Linguistic awareness is as significant for a CLIL teacher inadvertently silencing a heritage student who may be bored or anxious about knowing much more of the target language than other members of the class as it is for the teacher who, either wittingly or unwittingly, is creating conditions that make language other than the dominant language appear irrelevant or subordinate to students' learning. The premise of this book is that becoming more linguistically aware entails taking a multilingual stance, and focusing in a systemic way on students and what they are bringing to class.

Teaching and learning objectives are thus based on thinking about how to leverage languages—and indirectly encourage heritage-language maintenance—as well as how to learn a target language across the curriculum. The objectives related to the former broadly align with the translanguaging pedagogical goals discussed in Chap. 2: to co-construct knowledge in the classroom and to demonstrate it (e.g., Gumperz & Cook-Gumperz, 2005; Martin-Beltrán, 2014), to promote metalinguistic and crosslinguistic awareness (e.g., García & Kano, 2014; García & Li, 2014; Lewis, Jones, & Baker, 2012; Martin-Beltrán, 2014), to affirm multilingual identities (e.g., Cenoz & Gorter, 2011; de Jong, 2011; Lin & He, 2017) and to support social justice and critical reflection on language inequity (e.g., de Jong, 2011; Flores & García, 2017; García & Li, 2014). The objectives were referenced against the findings of the studies and were also informed by the inclusion of target language use. The affirmation of multilingual identities was a conspicuous finding. The co-construction and demonstration of knowledge overlapped with metalinguistic and crosslinguistic awareness and these are discussed together under general learning and instruction. Critical reflection on language hierarchies and social structures were not as conspicuous in the data but are discussed in relation to possible teaching and learning spaces, and preliminary steps towards the disruption of these hierarchies. The objectives also take into account that heritage students are not necessarily very familiar with their heritage language(s), and students who are only exposed to a target language at school may gain linguistic knowledge from the classroom, but the degree of their investment may be lower than if family members speak the language at home.

Objectives: Leveraging Languages as a Resource for Learning

1. Celebrating and valuing multilingual identities
2. General learning and instruction
3. Reflecting critically on linguistic hierarchies and social structures

Although it can frequently happen at the same time, learning target languages across the curriculum is not necessarily the same as leveraging students' language practices as a resource for general learning. The aim in the case of learning a target language is commonly to expand students' linguistic repertoires through an explicit focus on—or increased exposure to—the language. This focus may not be directly relevant to students' everyday lives and/or high-stakes assessments and, from a sociopolitical perspective, the degree of value placed on a target language can be influential in the uptake of associated language practices. The first objective that relates to the learning of languages is considered to be the integration of content-related target language into different subject areas. The objective links to Meyer, Coyle, Halbach, Schuck, and Ting's (2015) pluri-literacies model and also to Morton's (2012) understanding of language as a curriculum concern (see Chap. 3): it highlights the 'languaging' of subject-specific knowledge and concepts. The second objective relates to the integration of cross-curricular content into language classes. This was evident in the data, and assists in breaking down what Nikula et al. (2016, p. 10) referred to as 'the often taken for granted separation between "language subjects" and "content subjects"'.

For the learning of languages, the use of the target language for everyday communication is categorised as a further objective. This objective includes elements of Morton's (2012) L2 as a tool for learning and L2 as a matter of competence (see Chap. 3) because it is based in classroom discourse and the interactions that students engage in during student-centred learning. This kind of communication emerges as the students seek to express themselves, and it requires their willingness to engage in more spontaneous use of a target language. Although there is plenty of crossover with the other two objectives, this objective focuses on language production that moves away from highly scaffolded situations towards the embedding of more fluent language practices in the students' linguistic repertoire.

Objectives: Learning Languages

1. Learning content-related target language in different subject areas
2. Learning language in language classes via cross-curricular content
3. Using a target language for everyday communication

Each objective will be addressed in turn in the chapter by drawing and expanding on findings from the studies. Although the objectives are explored separately, they are conceptualised as overlapping in their enactment.

9.2 Celebrating and Valuing Multilingual Identities

Of all the teaching and learning objectives, the celebrating and valuing of students' existing multilingual identities was found to come naturally to the participating teachers. The expectation that language maintenance was important was a clear finding in the primary school settings. Previous to the studies, heritage languages that were not target languages in the school were mostly relegated to the community domain, but this appeared more related to feasibility than teachers' willingness to engage. Home use of heritage languages was actively promoted in the generalist primary schools, and this was endorsed by the Victorian Department of Education and Training (2018) where an encouragement to 'speak to your child in the language you know best' appeared on the website. A commitment to language maintenance was further noted in the primary bilingual school, where there also appeared to be a real pride in belonging to a culturally diverse community.

Shifting the teachers' expectation that multilingual identities were something to be promoted in the community domain to something that could be more actively valued in the classroom was made possible in the primary school settings through professional learning around a form of identity text (see Cummins, 2006; Cummins & Early, 2011) called language maps (D'Warte, 2013, 2014). In these texts, or maps, students were given a space where they could visually represent their language practices. The study design, adapted from Somerville, D'Warte, and Sawyer (2016), of giving first the teachers and then the students space to think about what they do with language, with whom and where was found to be a way to affirm multilingual identities, and heritage students' engagement was overwhelmingly positive. Many students chose to visually represent their practices by writing in different languages.

Also, positioning students who had exposure to different languages at home as knowing something of value was found to lead both to positive engagement in the classroom and, for students with only limited exposure, a desire to learn more about their linguistic heritage. Teachers in the generalist primary school setting also saw that home language

234   **M. Turner**

exposure did not necessarily extend to literacy practices, and began to think how they could target these practices. In the primary bilingual setting, heritage students were eager to share their knowledge of scripts such as Russian, Hindi and Korean, thereby evidencing the complexity and richness of their literacy practices: they were learning the three Japanese scripts (*hiragana, katakana* and *kanji*), as well as English, at school.

Increasing the cultural capital of an expanded linguistic repertoire resulted in some neutral or negative engagement from monolingual students in the generalist primary setting, but not in the primary bilingual programme nor in the secondary teacher-driven CLIL setting where advanced Japanese language students were bringing Japanese into the monolingual (in English) history class. Teachers in the generalist classes spoke of strategies such as enlisting the languages teacher to expose monolingual students to an additional language to share with others, as a way to facilitate their engagement. This would have the additional benefit of exposing these students to more language learning. In the primary bilingual programme, students were accustomed to another language (Japanese) being valued across the curriculum at school. In this context, it appeared that an increase in the value attributed to a target language at school was normalising the presence of other languages. In the secondary teacher-driven CLIL setting, the advanced Japanese language students were in the minority in the history class, and the language use was carefully considered in order to control for any anxiety among monolingual students (and teachers). Here, the valuing and celebrating of the linguistic knowledge of the advanced students, along with piquing the curiosity and engaging the majority of students, was an objective. The advanced students were also able to complete the history assessment using Japanese, to give them the opportunity to draw on different aspects of their linguistic repertoire, not only English.

Finally, in two of the studies (the primary bilingual programme and the structured secondary CLIL programme), the desire to celebrate and value multilingual identities at school could be linked to the way many students' heritage languages were being taught as target languages. However, students and families did not always prioritise this kind of cross-curricular inclusion of their heritage language. In the primary bilingual context, where approximately one-third of the students had a

Japanese heritage, a majority of heritage students were conversationally fluent in Japanese and chose to speak it to teachers and to other Japanese-heritage students. However, in the structured secondary CLIL context, the principal reported that the Greek-heritage students at the school were actively learning and speaking Greek in the community, and were choosing to learn Greek as a subject area, but were not choosing to participate in a Greek CLIL programme. In this setting, it appeared that Italian-heritage students who were opting in to an Italian CLIL programme had less exposure to their language in the community, and could see the benefits of the CLIL programme more clearly than students who had a lot of community exposure to their language. The celebrating and valuing of Greek language appeared to be perceived by parents and students as something that mainly belonged to the community domain and to a subject area in a language classroom. In this case, valuing language as a resource at school in concrete, perhaps gradual, ways may help stakeholder understanding of how a language can aid learning in general and not only the learning of the heritage language. This will be discussed in the next section.

9.3 General Learning and Instruction

In some cases, the teaching and learning objective of leveraging students' language resources for general learning was found to be more challenging for the teachers than the affirmation of multilingual identities. For example, the generalist primary teachers spoke of feeling more empowered to incorporate heritage languages in their lessons as a result of the study, but also of the need for support. Making direct and meaningful connections between languages and curriculum content was found to be a powerful, but not necessarily intuitive, process. In the two primary school settings, the studies encouraged thinking around students' language practices, and how they could be related to the curriculum. It was an enhanced understanding of these practices that appeared to open up a student-centred educational space where linguistic resources could be leveraged for learning. In the secondary settings, the design of the studies did not specifically focus on the incorporation of target languages for general learning and instruction, but some teachers were found to be leveraging the target language in this way.

First, in the generalist primary setting, crosslinguistic awareness activities were found to be key to student learning, and to result in the achievement of goals set for English curriculum content. However, although the use of heritage languages was found to be relevant and very engaging for students, it was not always central to meaning-making activities, or students' co-construction of knowledge. In these cases, activities were mainly designed for translation from one language to another as an end in itself, rather than as a means to an end. The incorporation of heritage languages into teaching and learning was new for the teachers, and the translation was found to provide a useful way to begin thinking about embedding languages in the classroom and about making linguistic connections between home and school. It was also found to be a way to work towards the first objective of the celebration and valuing of multilingual identities.

In the primary bilingual setting, there was an extra dimension to the inclusion of Japanese as a heritage language, alongside other heritage languages, into the English-medium classroom because everyone in the class knew at least some Japanese. Crosslinguistic awareness activities aimed at English curriculum content were the focus in this context as well. Nevertheless, the study showed that it may be necessary to be explicit about the teaching and learning objective. If students (and parents) are accustomed to language separation and the use of another language at school as related to the learning of that language, they may assume that the different heritage languages themselves are the object of formal study.

The incorporation of a target language in secondary classrooms was also found to provide opportunities for a deeper understanding of concepts and reinforcement of skills related to different subject areas, and teachers reported searching for linguistic features that would enhance student learning of content. This was especially apparent in the science classroom in the structured CLIL setting where *kanji* was reported to be deepening the students' understanding of scientific concepts. *Kanji* and science content were being learned simultaneously, and the literal meaning of the *kanji* in English presented the concept differently from the explanations provided by the main science teacher.

In the secondary CLIL settings, general learning of subject areas was further aided by the degree of scaffolding for language—often omitted from solely English-medium classrooms—and by enhanced student engagement with subject-area content. For example, in one school in the teacher-driven CLIL setting, the teacher used Japanese as a gentle, indirect and playful way to revise important geography concepts for students struggling to understand. Teachers across the settings sought to work backwards from the content they wanted to teach, and to consider ways they could ask students (or parents) to bring language into the classroom, or they themselves could incorporate language to help students' understanding, and enjoyment, of the subject area.

Leveraging target language practices to enhance learning of content can thus be viewed as a key instructional aim for CLIL teachers as much as for English-medium teachers including students' multilingual practices into lessons. Teachers can take into account the relationship between the target and dominant language for example. This might include cross-linguistic analysis, a direct translation from one language to another that explains a concept differently, or attractive aspects of culture, such as *anime* or *manga*, that can increase engagement with a subject area. Professional learning, especially in the form of collaboration and connections to communities of practice, may be instrumental in thinking about innovations in a systemic way. In the structured secondary CLIL programme, this community of practice appeared to be emerging through a system of mentoring that was found to be formally structured into the programme by the principal via co-teaching.

9.4 Reflecting Critically on Linguistic Hierarchies and Social Structures

The sociopolitical teaching and learning objective of critically reflecting on linguistic hierarchies and social structures was not a direct finding of the studies. Priority was given to exploring how to embed languages in English-medium classes and also how target languages were being used in mainstream contexts across the curriculum. In the Australian context, languages are still commonly viewed as occupying their own domain away from the rest of teaching and learning. As Lucas and Villegas (2013) pointed out in their discussion on linguistically responsive pedagogies for EAL students, languages can get lost under a larger umbrella of culturally responsive pedagogies. This may also be true of discussions aimed at helping students explore language critically. The studies therefore show (or begin to show) the leveraging of language resources in order to highlight languages in a very real, practical way so that critical discussions can incorporate linguistic repertoire, rather than only talk about this repertoire in the dominant language.

An important pedagogical element of Australian schools that appeared to be conducive to the embedding of language as a resource—and a critical discussion of this—was a student-centred approach to learning, especially enquiry-based learning. The idea that students investigate or work with their own material was found to assist primary teachers in devising activities that relied on the students or parents bringing the languages to class. This strategy also relied on the inclusion of the community in children's formal learning—another conspicuous school structure at primary school level in Australia. Parents and grandparents assisted in heritage-language activities devised by the teachers by doing translations, speaking on a video, reading books in the heritage language in class or guiding their child in an activity whereby they had to produce something for homework. Enquiry-based learning could provide a bottom-up way of allowing critical language-based discussions in the classroom. For example, one of the generalist primary teachers found that three Filipino-heritage students came to school each with a different translation of the word 'tropical'. From a critical perspective, this could instigate a discussion on the linguistic diversity and richness of the Philippines. Enquiry-based modules of work were further found to be a useful space for giving humanities content a more specific cultural focus and including it in language classes. The cultural focus could also be a space for critical reflection.

There were signs of linguistic disruption in all four settings, if we understand this disruption as the valuing of more than one language across the curriculum in the context of institutional monolingualism. The greatest commitment to the positioning of other languages as valuable was found in the primary bilingual setting and, even though the target language was

Japanese, there was a very clear sensitivity towards other languages—this will be discussed in the next chapter. The affirmation of students' linguistic repertoire in the primary settings appeared to inject capital into this knowledge and could thus be viewed as a disruption because it positioned the monolingual students differently; they did not know something important rather than something previously considered irrelevant to classroom learning. The dynamic was different—there was less of a disruption—when the majority of the students did not have valued linguistic resources, such as in the combined CLIL/non-CLIL class in the structured CLIL programme or the advanced language students in the history class in the teacher-driven CLIL initiative. In these two cases, the teachers were found to be more accommodating of students who found it harder to participate and/or share knowledge in the language-based activities.

Finally, in the bilingual primary programme and the two secondary settings, a teacher-as-co-learner model was evident. Monolingual (in English) teachers were found to be actively trying to learn Japanese alongside their students. This was a way to affirm the presence of the language in class and position their students (who knew much more than them) as knowing something important. The model could help to create a space where linguistic hierarchies are interrogated because teachers are repositioning themselves. Valuing and leveraging students' linguistic knowledge in the classroom, particularly when it is not shared by the teacher, gives precedence to an extended linguistic repertoire over a potentially more limited one. This is likely only to be temporary—teachers can usually assert their authority in English at any time in Australian schools—but it can be considered a preliminary step towards critical discussions about language.

9.5 Learning Content-Related Target Language in Different Subject Areas

In the settings where target languages were used in different subject areas, students were exposed to the language in a way that corresponded to Dalton-Puffer, Llinares, Lorenzo, and Nikula's (2014) content-driven characteristic of CLIL programmes in Europe. This kind of cross-curricular language use is still not the norm in a majority of Australian mainstream schools, but its increasing adoption may be partially related to the growing autonomy of schools (Spence-Brown, 2014). In the structured CLIL programme, the principal was able to make timetabling and staffing decisions that were beneficial to the programme, such as facilitating co-teaching arrangements and combining CLIL and non-CLIL classes if CLIL student numbers were low. In the primary bilingual programme, leadership had ensured a consistent approach across the English- and Japanese-medium classrooms: themes for enquiry-based learning and approaches to literacy were used across languages as a way to scaffold content learning in Japanese. In the teacher-driven CLIL setting, the reason that CLIL was occurring in one school was to solve the issue of languages losing hours: humanities and languages could be taught at the same time, with humanities driving the assessment.

In two of the three CLIL studies, language teaching and learning objectives deriving from the languages curriculum offered a structured way to recycle and reinforce target language in different subject areas. This approach can also be related to form-focused instruction, or a focus on language items whilst teaching content-driven lessons. It may have been guided by the teachers' training in CLIL pedagogy, because a pedagogical framework associated with CLIL highlights a structured approach to the kind of language that students will need when studying specific content—see Coyle, Hood, and Marsh's (2010) triptych of language of/for/through learning in Chap. 3 for an example. The approach to language lends itself to making links with developmental language learning, as a way to consider structures that make sense to the students. The bilingual primary programme and the structured secondary CLIL programme were explicit about their language focus in the subject-area classrooms. In the teacher-driven CLIL setting, where the target language was used outside the language classroom or in a combined class, vocabulary and *kanji* were found to be the main ways of incorporating language with content, and language rules or patterns were not found to be as emphasised.

Form-focused instruction in subject-area classrooms appeared to help the teachers think through the language they expected the students to produce. Teachers used the target language in their teaching, drawing on multimedia resources and communication strategies such as repetition, speaking clearly and controlling for slang or difficult vocabulary and grammar. In the primary bilingual setting in particular, where the teachers were following the immersion pedagogy of instructional language separation (see Fortune & Tedick, 2008; Hamman, 2018) and consistently communicating in Japanese, there was found to be a significant gap between what the students who had little or no exposure to Japanese outside school could understand in a highly scaffolded classroom, and what they could say or write. Form-focused instruction was thus used to aid language production. In the structured secondary CLIL programme, the teachers differed in the degree to which they incorporated the target language in class, but there was an overall tendency to use at least some English to communicate with the students, and assessments were mostly done in English. Teachers did find ways to include the target language in these assessments, however, and form-focused instruction was found to provide clarity on what to include. Japanese and Italian language use in subject areas was mapped against the developmental learning in the languages classroom in this setting. The language structures could also be used by the secondary teachers to guide their own oral language production in class.

The way teachers structured language into subject-areas sometimes needed to take into account low student engagement in learning languages. Linking the language explicitly to the languages curriculum was a way to rationalise the presence of—as well as make decisions around—the language planned for subject-area lessons. In the secondary settings, the importance of increasing the cultural capital of languages was also clear in the teachers' approach. For example, in the structured secondary CLIL setting, the students who had opted into the programme were very engaged, but they were in the minority. In the combined Year 7 Italian CLIL/non-CLIL class, teachers included all students in presentations and activities where Italian was being used. Non-CLIL students were found to engage positively, and began to produce Italian in scaffolded exercises. Expectations around the extent of target language use in the different settings, and the lack of firm objective around students' language proficiency, other than what would be expected of them if they did not have enhanced exposure to the target language, will be discussed in the next chapter.

9.6 Learning Language in the Language Classroom Via Cross-curricular Content

The language-driven teaching and learning objective relates to the languages domain. The CLIL training course was found to be particularly influential for language teachers in the teacher-driven CLIL setting, not only because of the content of the course but for the confidence and agency it bestowed. School leaders' acceptance and an experimental attitude could be important factors influencing whether or not they were able to use this training in any form. In all three schools in this setting, CLIL-trained teachers instigated the innovations and, in one of the schools, the humanities-based initiative only took place in the languages classroom. The student-centred learning approach in the school assisted with this initiative. In humanities units, students could choose to focus on topics such as a career or a chosen geographical feature. Using aspects of these units, the Japanese language teacher was able to narrow the focus to Japan and work with the same topics. This refining of humanities themes could support and reinforce in the language classroom what students were learning in history and geography. The French teacher in the school then took the same approach for French-speaking countries.

The advantage of the approach was that students were learning language in a way that clearly linked to what they were learning in different subject areas. When content had a cultural focus, teachers were able to engage students in learning more about the customs and lands of people speaking the language, and this kind of advocacy is timely in a country such as Australia, where institutional interest for languages appears to be waning. Stakeholders are also unlikely to struggle with the relevance of cultural content in a languages classroom. However, there did appear to be some friction between the CLIL approach and a more traditional focus on the developmental learning of language. In the teacher-driven CLIL setting in particular, language teachers highlighted students' need for developmental learning, and found the presence of content-driven material in the language

9 Teaching and Learning Objectives 243

classroom to be a challenge, at least for students with very limited language proficiency. This concern is reflected in Dalton-Puffer et al.'s (2014) understanding of CLIL in Europe as taking place in subject-area classrooms, and not replacing language classrooms. The French teacher who was incorporating cultural content into his classes explained how the language needed to talk about the humanities in French could require complicated language items, such as the subjunctive. The teacher of advanced language students at a different school was also found to consider linking language learning to cross-curricular content—in his case a history classroom—to be a way to extend language learning once curriculum-based language-driven expectations had been met. There was evidence in all three settings of a strong institutional expectation to teach language in a developmental, explicit way so that students were able to do well in the languages subject area.

Making learning meaning-focused has long been prioritised in instructed language learning (see Ellis & Shintani, 2014). However, it can require a lot of thought to integrate language learning in a developmental way if a focus on meaning is sustained and not limited to information or opinion-gap activities designed to practise—either implicitly or explicitly—different language items. The Japanese teacher who had spent some time preparing resources for his language classroom was committed to trialling ways to improve the overall Japanese language learning experience by also teaching students about Japan in meaningful, contemporary ways. Similar to the teachers in the bilingual primary setting and the structured secondary CLIL setting, he provided his students with an immersive experience in Japanese, and his resources focused on particular language structures. He began by preparing Japanese reading texts for his students, supplemented by multimedia resources, which he then deconstructed with the students (using Japanese). He then experimented with a more bottom-up approach, which provided developmental linguistic 'building blocks' to scaffold the students' production of the kind of Japanese demanded by a particular humanities activity. This latter approach was found to be favoured by the students.

244   M. Turner

This may not always be the case, but slowly building up key language in an immersive environment before introducing it in content texts may be one way to integrate a focus on the content with the more traditional developmental learning focus of language classrooms. This may help students who receive very limited exposure to the language and/or are not very invested in it to avoid feeling overwhelmed/disengaged. It is also important to note that the approach may require confidence with the target language on the part of the teacher, and also the ability to integrate (and continue to reinforce) language items the students are required to learn whilst focusing on content.

9.7   Using a Target Language for Everyday Communication

The final objective for language learning is communication, or to expand students' linguistic repertoire in a productive way. This may appear obvious, but it is well established that it can be challenging to facilitate student use of the target language, even in contexts of immersion (e.g., Kovelman, Baker, & Petitto, 2008; Tedick & Young, 2016). Communicative expectations around target languages were not found to be high across the three CLIL settings, and were generally aligned with the achievement outcomes of the languages curriculum, which could rely on structured and memorised output. This alignment was inclusive of all students given the mainstream (non-select-entry) nature of the classes, and may have been related to the expectation that use of a target language in class is challenging.

Even in the bilingual primary programme, where there was whole-school commitment, investment in JFL was identified as an issue by the teachers. Students reported liking aspects of Japanese culture, but mostly they were observed to speak Japanese only when asked a direct question or to complete a class activity. Japanese-as-a-foreign-language (JFL) students also had an observed tendency to rely on the Japanese-as-a-heritage-language (JHL) students when they could. The substantial difference in communicative proficiency between the two groups, as well as the heritage status of their peers, may have affected JFL students' sense of themselves as legitimate speakers of Japanese. There was an expectation that the Japanese teachers would speak in Japanese to all students outside class and the JHL students attending the school regularly spoke Japanese to the teachers and to each other. JFL students' relatively low level of proficiency made it challenging for them to enter these conversations, and JHL students routinely swapped to English to speak to them. Despite the challenges, JFL students' understanding of Japanese was generally much higher than if they were attending a traditional language programme.

Issues around language production in this setting were also highlighted by the school's focus on enquiry-based learning because the approach relies on interaction, not only teacher transmission of content. Avoidance of unprompted, communicative use of a target language is much more apparent in a student-centred learning environment, but the existence of this kind of environment also offers opportunities to encourage the students to speak—something the Japanese teachers at the school were actively targeting as they moved from Japanese-medium classes for seven and a half hours of the school week to a 50:50 language distribution in 2018. In the structured secondary CLIL setting and in the CLIL-inspired secondary Japanese language classroom where students received an immersive experience, students' Japanese language use also related to content and/or developmental language learning, and expectations around everyday communication did not appear to be high.

In different kinds of settings, including bilingual programmes where students avoid producing the target language, a translanguaging perspective may help to encourage language production—as discussed at the end of Chap. 6. Working with what the students might want to say, as well as from curriculum-based content, may be a way to facilitate more investment in language use. A translanguaging lens allows a shift towards more unfettered self-expression. Given the need for extensive target language production (see Swain, 1985), it might seem counterintuitive to consider drawing on students' knowledge of the dominant language (English). However, finding spaces where students can use their language practices fluidly while the teacher continues to use the target language may help students use more and more of this language, as they are increasingly able to interact with it. The approach emphasises the importance of the *desire* to engage with certain language practices, and the way that creativity and self-expression might be able to help when investment is low. It also relies on translanguaging practices as a strategic—not ad hoc—focus of the teacher, and the setting up of the kinds of activities that ensure student uptake of useful, interactive target language. The significance of this perspective both to the creation of cross-curricular multilingual spaces and the expansion of students' linguistic repertoire will be discussed in the next chapter.

9.8 Conclusion

Teaching and learning objectives related to the leveraging and learning of languages across the curriculum in mainstream schools were the focus of this chapter. Findings from the application of the multilingual practices framework were discussed as a way of showing the relevance of school-based data to the objectives. Sociocultural and sociopolitical dimensions were given prominence in the framework and provided a point of departure for considering the kinds of benefits and challenges different institutional structures and pedagogies might bring to particular contexts. The main similarity between the settings was the way that one language (English) eclipsed others, although the degree of the eclipse varied, and languages were positioned differently. When confronted both with diversity of student cohort and English dominance, thinking about teaching and learning objectives can be a way to help plan the systemic use and learning of languages across the curriculum.

References

Cenoz, J., & Gorter, D. (2011). Focus on multilingualism: A study of trilingual writing. *The Modern Language Journal, 95*, 356–369.

Cenoz, J., & Gorter, D. (2015). Towards a holistic approach in the study of multilingual education. In J. Cenoz & D. Gorter (Eds.), *Multilingual education: Between language learning and translanguaging* (pp. 1–15). Cambridge: Cambridge University Press.

9 Teaching and Learning Objectives 247

Coyle, D., Hood, P., & Marsh, D. (2010). *CLIL: Content and language integrated learning.* Cambridge: Cambridge University Press.

Cummins, J. (2006). Identity texts: The imaginative construction of self through multiliteracies pedagogy. In O. Garcia, T. Skutnabb-Kangas, & M. E. Torres-Guzman (Eds.), *Imagining multilingual schools: Language in education and glocalization* (pp. 51–68). Toronto: Multilingual Matters.

Cummins, J., & Early, M. (2011). *Identity texts: The collaborative creation of power in multilingual schools.* Staffordshire: Trentham Books.

D'Warte, J. (2013). *Pilot project: Reconceptualising English learners' language and literacy skills, practices and experiences. University of Western Sydney.* Retrieved from http://researchdirect.westernsydney.edu.au/islandora/object/uws:23461

D'Warte, J. (2014). Exploring linguistic repertoires: Multiple language use and multimodal literacy activity in five classrooms. *Australian Journal of Language and Literacy, 37*(1), 21–30.

Dalton-Puffer, C., Llinares, A., Lorenzo, F., & Nikula, T. (2014). 'You can stand under my umbrella': Immersion, CLIL and bilingual education. A response to Cenoz, Genesee & Gorter (2013). *Applied Linguistics, 35*(2), 213–218.

de Jong, E. J. (2011). *Foundations for multilingualism in education: From principles to practice.* Philadelphia, PA: Caslon Publishing.

Department of Education and Training, Victoria. (2018). *Languages.* Retrieved from http://www.education.vic.gov.au/school/teachers/teachingresources/discipline/languages/Pages/default.aspx?Redirect=1

Ellis, R., & Shintani, N. (2014). *Exploring language pedagogy through second language acquisition research.* London: Routledge.

Flores, N., & García, O. (2017). A critical review of bilingual education in the United States: From basements and pride to boutiques and profit. *Annual Review of Applied Linguistics, 37*, 14–29.

Fortune, T. W., & Tedick, D. J. (2008). One-way, two-way and indigenous immersion: A call for cross-fertilization. In T. W. Fortune & D. J. Tedick (Eds.), *Pathways to multilingualism: Evolving perspectives on immersion education* (pp. 3–21). Clevedon: Multilingual Matters.

García, O., & Kano, N. (2014). Translanguaging as process and pedagogy: Developing the English writing of Japanese students in the U.S. In J. Conteh & G. Meier (Eds.), *The multilingual turn in languages education: Benefits for individuals and societies* (pp. 258–277). Clevedon: Multilingual Matters.

García, O., & Li, W. (2014). *Translanguaging: Language, bilingualism and education.* New York: Palgrave Macmillan.

Gumperz, J. J., & Cook-Gumperz, J. (2005). Making space for bilingual communicative practice. *Intercultural Pragmatics, 2*(1), 1–23.

Hamman, L. (2018). Translanguaging and positioning in two-way dual language classrooms: A case for criticality. *Language and Education, 32*(1), 21–42.

Kovelman, I., Baker, S., & Petitto, L. (2008). Age of first bilingual language exposure as a new window into bilingual reading development. *Bilingualism: Language and Cognition, 11*(2), 203–223. https://doi.org/10.1017/S1366728908003386

Lewis, G. W., Jones, B., & Baker, C. (2012). Translanguaging: origins and development from school to street and beyond. *Educational Research & Evaluation, 18*, 641–654.

Lin, A. M. Y., & He, P. (2017). Translanguaging as dynamic activity flows in CLIL classrooms. *Journal of Language, Identity & Education, 16*, 228–244. https://doi.org/10.1080/15348458.2017.1328283

Lucas, T., & Villegas, A. M. (2013). Preparing linguistically responsive teachers: Laying the foundation in preservice teacher education. *Theory Into Practice, 52*(2), 98–109.

Martin-Beltrán, M. (2014). What do you want to say? How adolescents use translanguaging to expand learning opportunities. *International Multilingual Research Journal, 8*, 208–230.

Meyer, O., Coyle, D., Halbach, A., Schuck, K., & Ting, T. (2015). A pluriliteracies approach to content and language integrated learning—Mapping learner progressions in knowledge construction and meaning-making. *Language, Culture and Curriculum, 28*(1), 41–57. https://doi.org/10.1080/07908318.2014.1000924

Morton, T. (2012). *Teachers' knowledge about language and classroom interaction in content and language integrated learning.* Doctoral thesis, Universidad Autónoma de Madrid.

Nikula, T., Dalton-Puffer, C., Llinares, A., & Lorenzo, F. (2016). More than content and language: The complexity of integration in CLIL and bilingual education. In T. Nikula, E. Dafouz, P. Moore, & U. Smit (Eds.), *Conceptualising integration in CLIL and multilingual education* (pp. 1–25). Bristol: Multilingual Matters.

Somerville, M., D'Warte, J., & Sawyer, W. (2016). *Building on children's linguistic repertoires to enrich learning: A project report for the NSW Department of Education.* Retrieved from http://www.uws.edu.au/centre_for_educational_research

Spence-Brown, R. (2014). On rocky ground: Monolingual educational structures and Japanese language education in Australia. In N. Murray &

A. Scarino (Eds.), *Dynamic ecologies, Multilingual education* (pp. 183–198). Dordrecht: Springer.

Swain, M. (1985). Communicative competence: Some roles of comprehensible input and comprehensible output in its development. In S. Gass & C. Madden (Eds.), *Input in Second Language Acquisition* (pp. 235–253). Rowley, MA: Newbury House.

Tedick, D. J., & Young, A. I. (2016). Fifth grade two-way immersion students' responses to form-focused instruction. *Applied Linguistics, 37*(6), 784–807.

10

Multilingual Practices and Opportunities to Learn

10.1 Introduction

The way we think about language has an enormous influence on how cross-curricular language learning and use is conceived and embedded into formal schooling. Language has historically been studied as a system, and this scholarship is reflected in dictionary definitions, such as the *Oxford English Dictionary* (OED) definition offered in Chap. 2 (OED, 2018). This has never been the whole story, even for linguists such as Saussure who chose to study languages as relatively closed, decontextualised, systems. However, although scholars have become increasingly interested in language practices, or what emerges from the speaker, institutions are still generally accustomed to prioritising what counts as a language.

Thinking about languages as static, bounded entities that belong in separate domains can be counterproductive for cross-curricular language and use, especially in contexts where one language (English, in the case of this book) is overwhelmingly dominant. A feeling of deficit, of not being anywhere near good enough at speaking a language is a powerful reason to avoid it, especially if a student speaks English and does not need

© The Author(s) 2019
M. Turner, *Multilingualism as a Resource and a Goal*,
https://doi.org/10.1007/978-3-030-21591-0_10

251

252   M. Turner

another language, either to communicate in society or for any perceived status. It is well-established that language is central to students' identities but, when heritage students are born in an English-speaking country and/or speak English, the dominant language can become the default. Background knowledge that has arrived through other languages may be internally translated by the students, but the institutional message is one of compartmentalisation. Language separation can mean that a rich resource for teaching and learning and engagement in general—students' linguistic repertoire—is not strategically entering the classroom. This is true not only of heritage students but also of students only learning a language in a dedicated subject area.

Finding spaces for multilingual practices across the curriculum does not rule out a focus on language-as-system; both can work together, especially in the context of expanding students' linguistic resources. Rule-based, explicit learning can be a concrete cross-curricular goal and was found to be so in the studies. This way of learning language is deeply entrenched in institutions, and identification of patterns, or rules, can help students learn in formal situations with only limited exposure to a chosen language (see Ellis & Shintani, 2014). However, what students can do with the language(s) they know, and ways that they can feel a sense of belonging through their practices is important on an affective level. Learning language-as-a-system is a tool for building one's repertoire—it is a means to an end, not the end itself. If we take Bakhtin's (1981) dialogic understanding of language as a pull towards what has gone before and a push towards self-expression, the pull can be conceptualised as rule-based instruction, or the students' structured reproduction of a target language that was found in the studies. Finding spaces for students to express themselves in creative ways can then facilitate a 'push' that might help motivate them to engage with another language. If we put languages across the curriculum, they enter the stream of communication; they are not only systems that we understand ourselves to have already acquired or are in the process of acquiring. They are resources that we can call upon to engage in social practices.

The social, situated nature of language is central to this. Rather than an understanding of language as a form of knowledge that expresses itself in statements such as 'I know French' or 'I'm learning French', language-as-practice might express itself as 'I speak Spanish to my grandmother on Skype and I sometimes tell her how to say things in Japanese', 'my Mauritian Dad usually speaks French to me, but I nearly always speak English to him' or 'I speak to my sister in Japanese when I don't want my parents to understand'. Positioning multilingualism as practices in which students engage can facilitate the leveraging of languages in everyday teaching and learning, and help teachers learn more about their students.

The idea of constructing cross-curricular spaces for multilingual practices also includes the expansion of students' capacity for these kinds of practices. If students have little exposure to a particular language, a strong focus on using it at school is likely to be necessary in order to speak it: language practices that have not yet been automatised appear to require greater cognitive demand (see Del Maschio & Abutalebi, 2018). Further, the benefits of cross-curricular language use and learning can (indirectly) include greater community engagement with a language through increased student investment, as well as the use of language(s) as a resource in the classroom.

In this book, multilingual practices at school have been considered in relation to opportunities to learn (see Fig. 10.1), and three dimensions that influence these opportunities have been explored in different settings. Opportunities to learn are understood to be affordances (Greeno & Gresalfi, 2015): the opportunities lie not only in the learning situation or

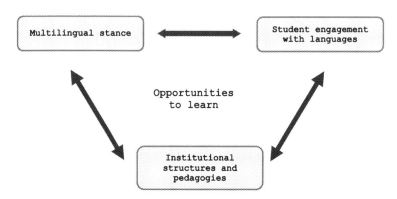

Fig. 10.1 Multilingual practices framework

254   M. Turner

with the individual student but in the relationship between the two. The way institutions and practitioners understand the role(s) of language can be an influential part of the learning context, along with institutional structures and pedagogies. The degree and nature of engagement with languages is an influential aspect of what individual students bring to their learning. This chapter revisits multilingual stance, student engagement with languages and institutional structures and pedagogies, and then discusses three issues that relate to the conceptualisation of learning opportunities through a sociocultural and sociopolitical lens: differentiation, innovation and language hierarchies.

10.2   Multilingual Stance

In order to consider the use and learning of languages across the curriculum, some kind of acceptance of multilingualism in formal learning environments is necessary. It is well-established that home languages can be leveraged as a resource for immigrant students in English-medium classes (e.g., Cummins & Swain, 1986; Lucas & Katz, 1994; Moll, Amanti, Neff, & Gonzales, 1992), and researchers are increasingly exploring what teachers and schools do and how students' linguistic repertoire is incorporated into teaching and learning (e.g., Cenoz & Gorter, 2015; de Jong, 2011; French, 2016; Pacheco, 2018). In this book, I have drawn on the idea of multilingual stance (de Jong, 2011; de Jong & Freeman, 2010) in order to frame the degree of importance institutions and practitioners attribute to the use and learning of other languages in general.

A multilingual stance can be understood on a continuum that begins with passive acceptance and works towards active affirmation (see de Jong, 2018), and it is a policy of affirmation that is advocated in the book. Understanding that languages are a resource for all students at school was an explicit aim in the English-medium classrooms in Chaps. 5 and 6. In all the studies discussed in this book, a majority of students were born in Australia and had spent their school lives learning in English. They could certainly 'survive' without other languages entering the classroom. A multilingual stance is not dependent on necessity, or whether or not students have sufficient command of the dominant language to cope at school. Along with the active, strategic incorporation of students' linguistic repertoire if they *are* struggling to understand, the stance includes a validation and celebration of all students' multilingual language practices. Schools can open up spaces for many learning opportunities, as well as actively support heritage-language maintenance in the community by incorporating these languages into everyday teaching and learning.

Understanding multilingual stance on a continuum may be able to assist in deepening an affirmation orientation, or in embedding this orientation into everyday teaching and learning practices. If the stance is taken to be connected to a concrete goal rather than a state of mind, there may be an assumption on the part of different stakeholders that the inclusion of students' language practices can be a 'one-off' set of identity lessons, or a kind of contained celebration of students' multilingual identities, and then it is back to business as usual in the dominant language. This is a very limited interpretation of multilingual stance. The lesson sequences provided in Chaps. 5 and 6 show a range of possible engagement with the incorporation of heritage languages into different subject areas in primary school classes. As demonstrated across the settings, target languages can also be used as a resource for general learning. For example, secondary subject-area teachers who did not speak the target language saw the value of making language links with the language classroom in practice-focused ways. Literature is increasingly showing that the use of non-dominant languages as a resource in subject-area classes does not require the teacher to speak the language (e.g., Blair, Haneda, & Nebus Bose, 2018; French, 2016; Ollerhead, 2018; Pacheco, 2018).

In this book, a multilingual stance is also inclusive of a focus on the extension of linguistic repertoire at school. This may involve noticing that students who speak languages that are linguistically similar to the target language—as well as heritage students of the language—are positioned differently in class: for example, a Korean-heritage student in a Japanese bilingual programme. It may further involve exploring similarities and differences between various kinds of language practices. The depth and type of attention to language learning is an important element of an affirming multilingual stance if a goal is to emphasise the expansion of students' linguistic repertoire. A sustained focus on cross-curricular language learning appeared to require a certain degree of commitment by schools—this will be discussed in the institutional structures and pedagogies section. However, individual teachers were also finding ways to increase students' exposure to, and engagement with, target languages.

A greater inclusion of implicit learning of a target language, both inside and outside the languages classroom, can be correlated with a greater multilingual stance because it requires meaningful, communicative use of the language (e.g., Krashen, 1981), and thus a greater degree of exposure than rule-based learning. However, an interface position whereby an explicit focus on language is integrated into communicative use is also well established in the literature as being beneficial (e.g., Ellis & Shintani, 2014; Meyer, Coyle, Halbach, Schuck, & Ting, 2015; Morton, 2012; Nikula, Dalton-Puffer, Llinares, & Lorenzo, 2016). In general, teachers' expectations around the cross-curricular role of a target language were found to be explicitly mapped against the languages curriculum for student language production, but there was a substantial range of attention paid to implicit language learning. Careful consideration of what an affirming multilingual stance might look like in relation to students' language learning in different contexts could include enhanced exposure to a target language, as well as spaces for students' self-expression—and general communication—where they gradually incorporate new language practices into their repertoire.

A stance of language affirmation relies on an understanding of—and a willingness to engage with—students' language practices, as discussed in the introduction of this chapter. Making this stance explicit is especially important in contexts of institutional monolingualism. If language separation is the prevailing school-based expectation, and languages are generally limited to language classrooms, incorporating languages into English-medium classes gradually—and for clearly stated teaching and learning objectives—may be a way of showing the effectiveness of a multilingual approach. This thinking applies as much to the use of target languages across the curriculum as to heritage languages. Seeking ways in which languages may be able to assist in enhancing general learning and instruction (see Chap. 9) can be a means to move them gradually across the curriculum.

10.3 Student Engagement with Languages

Student engagement with languages both inside and outside the classroom can also be a significant influence on opportunities to learn. In mainstream contexts, students' desire to use and learn languages across the curriculum cannot be assumed, and understanding and working with a great range of engagement can help to facilitate learning. In the multilingual practices framework, engagement was considered through a broad sociolinguistic lens of motivation (e.g., Motha & Lin, 2014; Norton, 2000; Turner & Lin, 2017) and through perspectives on the power dynamics in social interactions (e.g., Bourdieu & Passeron, 1977; Kramsch, 2012). This literature helped position opportunities to learn as dependent on the relationship between a student and the learning environment. In this relationship, students' desire to engage is important, as a lack of desire might constrain the use and learning of languages.

Increasing the value, or cultural capital (Bourdieu & Passeron, 1977), attached to different language practices by planning them into classroom teaching and learning, as well as explicitly affirming them, can have a positive influence on students' desire to learn. For target languages, this may require teachers to take an advocacy role. For example, it was evident in the teacher-led CLIL initiatives that teachers were actively searching for ways to include interesting aspects of Japanese culture in cross-curricular content. This was also true of the more structured bilingual programmes in the primary bilingual and the secondary CLIL settings. In the former, school promotion of Japanese culture was found to be a very positive experience for the students and, in the latter, advocacy was important as a result of low student numbers in the CLIL programme. Advocacy may not always ignite a strong desire in students to learn the language. However, if student engagement in a particular language is low, showing how the inclusion of languages across the curriculum can be fun and also help learning in general may be able to increase engagement. Even if it does not have a substantial effect on students' ongoing commitment to a particular language, it still has the potential to increase opportunities to learn, as it did with the non-CLIL students learning in Italian with the CLIL students in the structured secondary CLIL setting.

Affirming languages through their active use in the classroom can also positively influence feelings towards a heritage language, and promote community language maintenance in a very tangible way. As well as having a positive effect on student participation in class, the incorporation of languages in English-medium classes was found to influence heritage students' language use and learning. The explicit valuing of languages at school appeared to trigger engagement at home. This was true in the generalist primary setting and also in the secondary structured CLIL setting, where Italian-heritage students who spoke very little Italian accessed the programme, and enjoyed their increasing ability to speak, especially to grandparents. The attribution of value to heritage-language *literacy* practices of students is also an area of importance, and is not necessarily intuitive. For example, one teacher reported that the school encouraged parents to speak their heritage language at home, but had not considered the promotion of literacy. Literacy in a heritage language can provide a sense of familial connection, as well as a tool for learning language in general (see Eisenchlas, Schalley, & Guillemin, 2013).

Along with the attribution of value, student engagement can be considered in relation to feelings of legitimacy, especially in contexts where there is a great range of extracurricular exposure to different languages. If the institutional sanctioning of language practices (see Kramsch, 2012) is granted to an extended—rather than dominant language—repertoire, it may cause feelings of illegitimacy amongst some students. This appeared to be the case in the two primary school settings where heritage-language practices in English-medium classes and Japanese language practices in Japanese-medium classes were explicitly valued, and English monolingual students and non-Japanese-heritage students in the latter setting were learning side by side with heritage students. Kramsch (2012, p. 488) spoke about illegitimacy (and inauthenticity) in relation to an imposture or a gap in 'the fit between an idealized self [...] and the self one really considers oneself to be' (see Chap. 4). In the case of the studies, it seemed that the gap was related to children's comparisons with each other, and a resulting sense for some students that their own linguistic knowledge was inadequate. In the generalist setting, teachers were speaking of enlisting the aid of the language teacher so that the monolingual students could have something of their own to share. In the primary bilingual setting, with the advent of the 50:50 bilingual programme in 2018, teachers found that some of the non-Japanese-heritage students who were more engaged in Japanese were exerting a positive influence on their non-heritage peers' engagement. This appears to highlight the benefits of comparisons which the children did not find overwhelming.

Finally, whether or not to measure the depth and quality of student engagement can be considered in relation to teaching and learning objectives (see Chap. 9). Given the institutional dominance of English in Australian schooling, only linking success to formal language proficiency assessments may inadvertently serve to prioritise select-entry programmes where students are chosen by the school based on predictions of their achievement against enhanced language measures. All the settings discussed in this book were mainstream, and school leaders and teachers were found to take a gentle, value-adding, inclusive approach. Language practices were left relatively unmeasured except against a languages curriculum baseline—the usual achievement standards for a languages classroom in the Australian state of Victoria. As Hüttner, Dalton-Puffer, and Smit (2013, p. 280) noted in the Austrian context, 'one might argue that stakeholders can make CLIL into a success more easily by changing their or their learners' feelings as [target language] speakers, than by changing the language proficiency of a large and mixed cohort of learners'. From a student-centred, engagement perspective, changing the way students feel about language—both for students who have a heritage language (other than English) and students who do not—can be considered an important goal in itself. The current flexibility in Australian classrooms around the use of languages across the curriculum offers a lot of potential for working towards different kinds of teaching and learning objectives, and not only towards formal language assessments. Nevertheless, formal assessments that require enhanced communicative language use may offer a way to increase teachers' expectations around students' language production, especially in more structured bilingual programmes.

10.4 Institutional Structures and Pedagogies

The third influence on students' opportunities to learn in the multilingual practices framework is institutional structures and pedagogies. This dimension focuses on the more practical aspects of what schools and teachers can do to facilitate the cross-curricular use of languages. In the studies, influential structures were found to be professional learning and collaboration, student-centred learning, inclusion of the community and degree of flexibility in the use of a target language. Language-related pedagogies linked closely to these structures. Structures and pedagogies are together in the same dimension because the distinction is somewhat artificial—if institutional structures include the organisation of teaching and learning, they overlap with pedagogies adopted by the school. Those discussed in this book were found to underpin initiatives and programmes in at least more than one setting.

First, it is important to note that professional learning and collaboration were features of the study design in three of the four settings, and it would therefore be strange if they were not conspicuous in the data. They were the initial catalysts for cross-curricular heritage (non-target) language use in the primary generalist and bilingual settings and for target language use in the secondary teacher-driven CLIL initiatives. They were also found to be central in the fourth setting: the structured secondary CLIL programme. The integration of content and language learning or the inclusion of heritage languages in class is not the norm in Australian mainstream schools and does not necessarily feature in teacher education courses. As a result, the professional learning opportunities either encouraged or permitted by the schools were instrumental in cross-curricular language learning and use. Collaboration in the form of mentoring was found to be actively structured into this professional learning, such as the approach taken by the principal in the structured secondary CLIL programme, or it could occur more organically in the teachers' sharing of knowledge and practices, such as in the generalist primary setting (cf. Blair et al., 2018). The way the teachers thought through the process collaboratively in this latter setting most likely contributed to its success, particularly given the shift in thinking that occurred and the joint reflection on how to structure the lesson sequences to leverage heritage languages for learning.

10 Multilingual Practices and Opportunities to Learn   261

Student-centred spaces were also central to opportunities for bringing languages into the classroom across settings. The finding is similar to other studies where heritage languages have been incorporated into English-medium classes, and teachers do not necessarily share the languages of their students (e.g., Blair et al., 2018; French, 2016; Pacheco, 2018). A teacher-centred approach to the inclusion of unknown content—languages, for example—can have the effect of challenging the teacher's knowledge base, and thus her or his professional status (cf. Pacheco, 2018). If a student-centred approach is used, students' knowledge construction is the focus and the teacher's role can be that of facilitator. The teacher can negotiate meaning with students. The way student-centred learning allowed language into class was evident in settings where languages were taught at school and also where they were not; for example, the advanced Japanese language students bringing Japanese to an English monolingual history class in the teacher-driven CLIL setting and heritage languages in the primary English-medium classrooms respectively. In the latter case, spaces could also be viewed as community-centred because students did not always know their heritage language, and family members were able to help them participate. When learning through the medium of a target language, rather than in English-medium classrooms, student-centred learning also presents opportunities because interaction is prioritised, providing spaces for students to practise using the language. However, it can be challenging, as discussed in the final section of Chap. 9. The challenge will be addressed again later in this chapter in relation to crosslinguistic pedagogy and translanguaging.

The degree of flexibility in the use of a target language tended to relate to language choices made at a macro—or school—level (see de Jong, Yilmaz, & Marichal, 2019; Duverger, 2007). On a continuum of school commitment to the cross-curricular use of a target language, structured programmes can deliver more sustained exposure. The active endorsement of school leadership appeared to play an important role in raising stakeholder expectations around this language use. Nevertheless, without a similar level of support, charismatic and committed teachers were found to be able to navigate school structures as best they could and work innovatively with what they found. In the three settings where a target language was a focus of study, the extent to which the school actively structured in cross-curricular target language use varied (see Fig. 10.2).

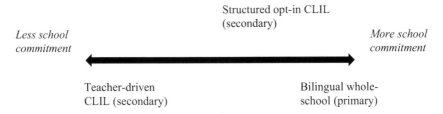

Fig. 10.2 Degree of school commitment to the cross-curricular use of a target language

Sustained language use outside the language classroom was not found in the setting where the initiatives were teacher-driven, and was found to occur the most in the bilingual primary programme.

Thus, considering cross-curricular target language distribution at a macro—or school—level is a way to increase student exposure to the language. Alongside issues of organisation lie pedagogical issues that can be understood at the meso (unit and lesson plan) and micro (lesson plan implementation) levels (see de Jong et al., 2019; Duverger, 2007). As discussed in Chap. 9, one way that all the participating teachers worked with cross-curricular language use was through form-focused instruction, often to help focus on what they wanted the students to produce. They also used language scaffolding strategies, mostly to help students understand material in the target language. The teachers in the primary bilingual setting used genre-based pedagogy—although this could sometimes hide differences in genres between languages—as a way to achieve consistency in the teaching and learning of literacy practices across Japanese and English. Working with these pedagogies aided exposure to, and production of, target languages across the curriculum.

10.5 Crosslinguistic and Translanguaging Pedagogy

In this book, pedagogies that directly relate to the leveraging of students' linguistic repertoire have been referred to as crosslinguistic and translanguaging pedagogies. Although included in the institutional structures and pedagogies dimension in the framework, they are discussed separately here because they are considered to be key to multilingualism as a resource and a goal in mainstream schooling. In contexts of institutional monolingualism, these pedagogies are likely to be the difference between the cross-curricular use of language and a purely monolingual form of schooling outside the languages classroom.

A distinction between crosslinguistic and translanguaging pedagogy was made in order to draw attention to the degree of meaning-making that was included in activities by the teacher. Crosslinguistic pedagogy was used as an umbrella term that could include actively writing students' language practices into English-medium lessons, but in the form of direct translation with no follow-up focus on language. Translanguaging pedagogy highlights the inclusion of students' language practices in class as a tool for making meaning, for example, through discussion of a text written in a particular language, or by linking learning to students' background knowledge so that they can understand more effectively (see García & Li, 2014). Direct translation as an activity in itself was a strategy for bringing other languages into the classroom across different settings. Celebrating the inclusion of languages in the classroom is worthwhile, given the very positive engagement of heritage students with the process. Meaning-making through the incorporation of more than one language into the lesson can be considered on a continuum, with the idea that steps along the way are supported and valued.

Another important element of the multilingual practices framework was to understand the leveraging and expanding of *all* students' linguistic repertoires. Exposure to meaningful use of other languages lies at the heart of the expansion of students' linguistic repertoire. Using a target language across the curriculum can provide this exposure, and the more sustained the use can be, the more likely that students in mainstream contexts will need to engage with it. Thus, in the context of learning a non-dominant target language, crosslinguistic pedagogy needs to be treated with caution because the dominant language can be the default interactive language for students (see Ballinger, Lyster, Sterzuk, & Genesee, 2017). This was found to be the case across the settings: students were mainly found to interact in English unless they were Japanese-heritage students speaking to each other or with the Japanese teacher in the primary bilingual programme.

However, caution might not entail complete language separation. For example, if an opt-in mainstream programme may be more attractive to students because they are assessed in English with peripheral use of target language in these assessments, as appeared to be the case in the structured secondary CLIL setting, this kind of pedagogy might make the programme viable. Also, as discussed for the final teaching and learning objective in the previous chapter, a translanguaging lens, or the encouragement of meaning-making and self-expression through the use of students' complete linguistic repertoire, might help students engage with target language practices, especially if students have limited or no exposure to the language at home. Translanguaging pedagogy can be beneficial where students are struggling to interact in meaningful ways using a target language (and subsequently avoiding its use), as much as where language resources are being recognised holistically in English-medium classes. Student engagement with a language taught at school—including their desire to speak it—requires careful and strategic thought, and a policy of instructional language separation does not preclude a student-centred pedagogy of translanguaging.

In the studies, language reproduction, rather than self-expression or creativity, appeared to be the main driver of connections between the subject areas and language learning. Although translation and the learning of patterns and language structures can be extremely useful, especially in situations of limited exposure to the language, finding spaces for more creative and personalised use of language fits well with a language-as-social practice perspective, and might also gradually help students (want to) use the language more spontaneously. Experimentation and an emphasis on students' language resources to communicate in everyday ways were not highly visible across the different settings. In the case of target language use, sustained collaboration with language teachers might offer a way forward.

10.6 Differentiation

In contexts of diversity, differentiation is central to language use through a student-centred lens because students come to class with various language experiences and attitudes. Differentiation has been discussed in

10 Multilingual Practices and Opportunities to Learn 265

relation to differentiated instruction; for example, in translanguaging pedagogy, content and language might be taught differently to monolinguals, emerging bilinguals and bilinguals (García & Li, 2014). Differentiation might not only equate to differentiated instruction, however. It can also include the idea of actively working with differences in students' linguistic repertoires as a resource for everyone's learning (see Turner, 2017), working with different levels of student engagement with languages and with idiosyncratic characteristics of languages.

First, encouraging students to draw on their (or their family's) language practices without differentiating instruction was found to be a way to meet curriculum objectives in the English-medium classes. For example, two teachers in the generalist primary setting were able to demonstrate how their students had achieved a curriculum objective related to language awareness through the inclusion of different language practices. In this case, not differentiating instruction was a way to disrupt linguistic hierarchies in class. Monolingual student discomfort offered a way to reflect critically with students about how peers who are not proficient in English may feel when their linguistic repertoire is not considered 'enough' in the context of formal learning (cf. Palmer, Cervantes-Soon, Dorner, & Heiman, 2019). Not varying instruction also allowed consideration of how to accommodate students only exposed to the dominant language at home in different ways, such as through promotion of the expansion of their own linguistic repertoire.

Differentiation choices might also rely on what is possible to do in a particular context. For example, differentiating between students' linguistic repertoires, rather than instruction in a subject area, was found to occur in the teacher-driven CLIL setting, where Japanese was brought into the English monolingual history classroom by advanced Japanese language students. There was no cross-curricular opportunity available just for these students at the time of the study and, because the timetable was not going to be changed, two teachers were determined to find a different way to collaborate. On the one hand, the solution did not include as much Japanese language use in the history classroom as it would have with differentiated instruction, or if the dually-qualified Japanese and humanities teacher had been provided the opportunity to teach the history unit to his advanced students. On the other hand, the advanced students' linguistic repertoire was treated as valuable and all students benefited from having some Japanese enter their learning of a Japan-related history topic. In another school, students' linguistic repertoires were *not* differentiated, and the teacher reported the disengagement of her more advanced Japanese language students: they were usually differentiated in that they had their own class, but were combined with other students in the CLIL classes.

The teaching and learning objectives discussed in Chap. 9 provide a way of thinking about reasons for and against differentiated/undifferentiated instruction. A preliminary step in the decision-making process may also be the location of cross-curricular spaces that would explicitly benefit from students' leveraging of linguistic resources through direct relevance to content outcomes. In the studies in this book, these spaces included a cross-curricular focus on Asia in the Australian curriculum and meeting English curriculum objectives. In the primary bilingual setting, the linguistic resources of Japanese-heritage students were also leveraged for their learning in the Japanese-medium classes even though this was not measured through formal assessment. In the Australian curriculum, critical and creative thinking is further prioritised as a cross-curricular capability (see ACARA, 2018); leveraging students' diverse language experiences for this aim as well as for subject content may be another way of considering how to differentiate according to students' linguistic repertoires, and also incorporate target languages across the curriculum. In the studies, strategically leveraging language resources was found to have the effect of helping students understand the importance of what they knew, as well as gain from exposure to their classmates' language practices.

Differentiating between students is also important given that the language experiences students bring to the classroom are not all of the same type, and may be different from what the teacher expects. In the studies, teachers in the generalist setting in particular began to distinguish between oracy and literacy practices over the course of the study—they originally had not considered differences between students' knowledge of these modes of communication. A conspicuous number of students had a heritage language with a different script and they were not literate in the language. All of the English-medium teachers in both the generalist and

10 Multilingual Practices and Opportunities to Learn 267

bilingual primary settings chose ways to incorporate heritage languages that relied on students either reading or writing in their language. The emphasis on literacy reflects both the importance placed on this mode in formal learning in Australia and its global status. However, it may render heritage-language speakers with strong oral traditions more invisible. It may also be difficult for parents with disrupted education to assist their children with literacy. Valuing students' literacy practices in heritage languages whilst not always linking language use in class to these practices is possible through the use of human resources, such as parents/grandparents, and multimedia, such as songs and videos.

Along with attention to various kinds of language resources, differentiation can also be considered according to student engagement. This does not need to mean select entry into a programme—having a certain level of language proficiency or academic achievement—but rather opting in, or *wanting* to participate. For example, in the structured secondary CLIL setting, students who signed up to learn either Japanese or Italian in an enhanced way were placed in a class with similar-minded students. This might not only entail a separate programme. Differentiation based only on student engagement (and not proficiency or ability) was also found in the teacher-driven CLIL initiative in the French language classroom. In this case, the teacher was exploring a way to differentiate between students based on engagement, so that everyone would get more done in a class where the desire to use and learn French was very low.

Finally, differentiating according to the relationship between different languages and the dominant language (English) is worthy of attention because it can influence the way aspects of the language are leveraged for learning. What is useful for one language may not be as useful for another. Different kinds of language characteristics were conspicuous in the studies. For example, there were clear conceptual benefits to the use of Japanese *kanji*; these were discussed in the previous chapter. The leveraging of cognates in Italian was also found to be a useful hook to engage students in classroom activities. Logographic similarities between Chinese and Japanese were additionally noted and leveraged in the history classroom at one school where Japanese was being introduced into class and the majority of the advanced-level students had a Chinese heritage.

10.7 Innovation

Applying a student-centred lens to the cross-curricular leveraging and use of language requires innovation because the approach is context-sensitive. Innovation can include creativity with school structures and pedagogies and also with language. Teachers can be (re)invigorated via the incorporation of different kinds of language practices in class, including practices associated with CLIL, and can think very creatively about the application of these, either individually or in collaboration with others. Examples of innovations have been discussed in this book. Particularly for the inclusion of heritage languages, it may be beneficial for teacher to begin by interrogating how they understand language because the concept of languages operating as whole entities in discrete contexts (language separation) can be powerful, and can manifest in a feeling that the incorporation of heritage languages is a very good idea in theory but is not feasible in practice. Feasibility was a strong theme in the primary settings where heritage languages were included in English-medium classes.

A powerful reason for the cross-curricular use of language is that language lies at the heart of all subject areas, and student comprehension and engagement when confronted with an unfamiliar language (or languages) are even more reliant on effective pedagogy than when a more familiar language is the sole language of instruction. The multilingual practices framework aims to help think about pedagogy in situated ways in different settings. It was an explicit finding of the structured secondary CLIL setting, where subject areas could often rely on textbook teaching, that CLIL had a positive effect on teaching quality. Teachers planned the way language was going to be used, and did not automatically assume comprehension. A positive impact on teaching quality was reported by the principal, teachers and students. Innovations can also be considered across different settings in the school rather than be contained to a particular programme. One teacher reported that she was interested in trialling a CLIL approach in her non-CLIL Italian language classes to connect to what students were studying in different subject areas. Considering cross-curricular use of heritage languages in English-medium classes alongside the learning and use of target languages in schools has the additional potential to increase language awareness among stakeholders and result in innovative teaching.

It is important to note that, as a result of the need to create materials and the increased importance of language scaffolding, this may require greater time investment (see Ball, 2018 in relation to CLIL). The teachers in the primary bilingual setting and also the teacher in the secondary Japanese class who gave his students an immersive experience in Japanese were able to recycle their resources for later groups of students. This could also be true of the structured CLIL programme, but there appeared to be more teacher movement, owing to the complexity of timetabling and staffing, and this was cited by one teacher as a challenge. Teaching innovation in this setting was being nurtured, however, through such initiatives as co-teaching. In the generalist primary context, teachers from one of the schools also reported that the embedding of heritage languages in the students' learning had required a lot of time, and this is a significant reason for making the teaching approach systemic, so teachers can share ideas and resources. Innovation can be time-consuming, but has the potential to become less so with collaboration—both internal and external to the school—and school commitment to a fostering/affirming multilingual stance.

Finally, encouraging creativity with language can also be considered a kind of teaching innovation, and playfulness, transformation and translanguaging as an objective in itself are all cited in translanguaging literature (e.g., Jakonen, Szabó, & Laihonen, 2018; Li, 2011, 2018; Moore & Nikula, 2016; Turner & Lin, 2017). As mentioned earlier in the chapter, this kind of language creativity was not common in the studies, but there is space for reflection on it in language classrooms and also in language arts (English-as-a-subject-area). For example, creativity in writing narratives often arises from thinking up new metaphors. Metaphors in different languages can vary widely, and literal translation can breathe life into storytelling. Encouraging students to draw on their linguistic repertoire in a holistic way, even when they are (ostensibly) writing in one language, and showing them ways they can do this, can be a way to promote creativity.

10.8 Language Hierarchies

English is overwhelmingly dominant in Australia, and an 'English-and-the-rest' hierarchy was evident in all the settings discussed in this book. As explored in Chap. 2, language has long been used as a political tool and linguistic hierarchies are related to this. Institutional monolingualism, or the need to speak English in public life in Australia, is an influential driver of formal schooling. For this reason, a multilingual stance that includes the use of different languages for learning, especially when students can interact in English without any problem, is not necessarily intuitive. Stakeholders may be pro-multilingual (see Fitzsimmons-Doolan, 2018) in that they believe students should continue to speak their heritage languages in the community and learn in English at school. However, treatment of languages by institutions sends a clear message regarding whether a societal (high status) perspective is one of assimilation or integration. The latter aligns with a student-centred perspective and can foster language enrichment and the strategic leveraging of background knowledge and linguistic resources. Enrichment assumes that learning another language is adding to a students' linguistic repertoire rather than transitioning the student from one language to another (see Baker & Wright, 2017).

If integration rather than assimilation is the goal, a critical reflection on linguistic hierarchies and taking steps to disrupt them is important. As discussed in Chap. 9, the need for disruption can be intuitively understood by monolingual English-medium teachers. In the studies, there were some teachers who positioned themselves as language learners in the classroom. This showed positive engagement with the dynamics of linguistic inequity. However, the fostering of a critical consciousness (Freire, 1970) through an interrogation of language hierarchies (see García & Li, 2014) will most likely require a more explicit, openly reflective, focus. For example, there is a practical need to address the issue of disengagement on the part of students whose linguistic repertoire is only related to English, the dominant language, because there is a chance that this disengagement will affect the sustainability of a multilingual approach in an institutional monolingual context. However, many students who have an extended linguistic repertoire but are not very confident with English

10 Multilingual Practices and Opportunities to Learn 271

might disengage in a monolingual (in English) classroom and this can be overlooked by teachers (see Palmer et al., 2019). The inequity between different kinds of language users can—often inadvertently—remain hidden from stakeholders without some kind of reflection. English in schooling is so dominant that it can be taken for granted in Australia, not only by monolinguals but by bi/multilinguals who understand other languages to belong to the community domain.

It is also important to note that a linguistic hierarchy does not only exist between English-and-the-rest; hierarchies between other languages are also in evidence at schools. Choices around target languages, such as Japanese, Italian and French, can be related to the value attributed to them by influential actors (the government, for example). The inclusion of cross-curricular target languages taught at school and (other) heritage languages in the same multilingual practices framework is done not to gloss over language inequities, and subsequent differences in learning opportunities, but to assist in highlighting and engaging critically with them. A multilingual stance positions the leveraging and expansion of students' linguistic repertoire as key to opportunities. Valuing the extent of linguistic repertoire rather than only the knowledge associated with one language is central to the stance. From a multilingual perspective, students who have a greater exposure to different kinds of language practices are better placed to learn (through) languages. Considering exposure to languages in relation to practices is also beneficial because discourse around bi/multilingualism in a country like Australia can be quite narrowly defined and attributed to a high degree of fluency, even amongst heritage speakers (Piller & Gerber, 2018). A focus on language-as-practice, or as a resource for communicating, attempts to address the rather counterproductive idea that people are either bi/multilingual or they are not.

Considering heritage languages alongside languages taught at school as part of the same framework is also useful because school commitment to a target language across the curriculum can support heritage-language maintenance. The primary bilingual setting is a case in point: this was a context where parents who were committed to their heritage languages—not only Japanese—were choosing to send their children. English was dominant, but the school was not institutionally monolingual. In a study on Korean–English bilingual programmes in the US, heritage

272 M. Turner

speakers of other languages (not Korean) were found to cite heritage-language maintenance as a reason for sending their children to the programme (Ee, 2018). In the setting discussed in this book, the clear learning and use of a variety of heritage languages, most conspicuously demonstrated in students' ability to read and write different scripts, as well as the hum of different languages at drop-off and pick-up times at the school, supported this idea of a bilingual programme as a language-sensitive learning environment. Engagement in heritage languages at home was evident in the generalist primary setting, but appeared to be more uneven. Commitment to individual bilingualism can be difficult and some kind of supportive community can be helpful. As Piller and Gerber (2018, p. 12) pointed out, 'the idea that individual bilingualism is a good thing does not have a lot of leverage in the face of entrenched institutional English monolingualism', and generational language attrition is a very clear phenomenon in Australia (see also Eisenchlas et al., 2013).

In brief, some languages are taught in mainstream schools, and considering these from a speaker-centred perspective across the curriculum has the potential to expand students' linguistic repertoire in more sustained and creative ways. However, a majority of languages spoken in a country like Australia are not formally taught. Actively inviting languages into the classroom, supporting and encouraging their use in meaningful ways in the face of a very real risk of language attrition and providing some kind of leverage in a context of English language dominance are feasible. A multilingual orientation to mainstream education has the power to enrich the learning of all students, and there are many spaces across the curriculum that can facilitate the leveraging and expanding of students' linguistic repertoire.

10.9 Conclusion

This chapter has discussed possibilities of engagement with the diversity of students' linguistic experiences through a focus on language-as-social-practice. The idea of language-as-a-system is also considered to have a place, especially in the learning of a target language to which a student is only exposed at school. Multilingual practices, ways to move towards them and the spaces they open up for learning were all the subject of discussion. The multilingual practices framework was discussed in relation to each of its three dimensions—multilingual stance, student engagement with languages, and institutional structures and pedagogies—with emphasis given to crosslinguistic and translanguaging pedagogies. Differentiation, innovation and language hierarchies were also addressed in relation to opportunities to learn (through) languages.

References

Australian Curriculum, Assessment and Reporting Authority (ACARA). (2018). *Australian curriculum: English.* Retrieved from https://www.australiancurriculum.edu.au/f-10-curriculum/english/

Baker, C., & Wright, W. E. (2017). *Foundations of bilingual education and bilingualism* (6th ed.). Bristol: Multilingual Matters.

Bakhtin, M. M. (1981). *The dialogic imagination: Four essays by M.M. Bakhtin* (C. Emerson & M. Holquist, Trans. & M. Holquist, Ed.). Austin, TX: University of Texas Press.

Ball, P. (2018). Innovations and challenges in CLIL materials design. *Theory Into Practice, 57,* 222–231.

Ballinger, S., Lyster, R., Sterzuk, A., & Genesee, F. (2017). Context-appropriate crosslinguistic pedagogy: Considering the role of language status in immersion education. *Journal of Immersion and Content-Based Language Education, 5*(1), 30–57.

Blair, A., Haneda, M., & Nebus Bose, F. (2018). Reimagining English-medium instructional settings as sites of multilingual and multimodal meaning making. *TESOL Quarterly, 52*(3), 516–538.

Bourdieu, P., & Passeron, J. (1977). *Reproduction in education, society, and culture.* London and Beverly Hills, CA: Sage Publications.

Cenoz, J., & Gorter, D. (2015). Towards a holistic approach in the study of multilingual education. In J. Cenoz & D. Gorter (Eds.), *Multilingual education: Between language learning and translanguaging* (pp. 1–15). Cambridge: Cambridge University Press.

Cummins, J., & Swain, M. (1986). *Bilingualism in education: Aspects of theory, research and practice.* Harlow: Longman.

de Jong, E. J. (2011). *Foundations for multilingualism in education: From principles to practice*. Philadelphia, PA: Caslon Publishing.

de Jong, E. J. (2018, Keynote). *Taking a multilingual stance: Quality education for ELLs*. Minneapolis, MN: Minnesota-TESOL.

de Jong, E. J., & Freeman, R. (2010). Bilingual approaches. In C. Leung & A. Creese (Eds.), *English as an additional language. Approaches to teaching linguistic minority students* (pp. 108–122). New York: Sage.

de Jong, E. J., Yilmaz, T., & Marichal, N. (2019). A multilingualism as a resource orientation in dual language education. *Theory Into Practice*. https://doi.org/10.1080/00405841.2019.1569375

Del Maschio, N., & Abutalebi, J. (2018). Neurobiology of bilingualism. In D. Miller, F. Bayram, J. Rothman, & L. Serratrice (Eds.), *Bilingual cognition and language: The state of the science across its subfields* (pp. 325–345). Amsterdam: John Benjamins Publishing.

Duverger, J. (2007). Didactiser l'alternance des langues en cours de DNL. *Tréma, 28*, 81–88.

Ee, J. (2018). Exploring Korean dual language immersion programs in the Unites States: Parents' reasons for enrolling their children. *International Journal of Bilingual Education and Bilingualism, 21*(6), 690–709. https://doi.org/10.1080/13670050.2016.1208144

Eisenchlas, S., Schalley, A., & Guillemin, D. (2013). The importance of literacy in the home language: The view from Australia. *SAGE Open, 3*(4), 1–14. https://doi.org/10.1007/2158244013507270

Ellis, R., & Shintani, N. (2014). *Exploring language pedagogy through second language acquisition research*. London: Routledge.

Fitzsimmons-Doolan, S. (2018). Language ideology change over time: Lessons for language policy in the U.S. state of Arizona and beyond. *TESOL Quarterly, 52*(1), 34–61.

Freire, P. (1970). *Pedagogy of the oppressed*. New York: Herder & Herder.

French, M. (2016). Students' multilingual resources and policy-in-action: An Australian case study. *Language and Education, 30*, 298–316. https://doi.org/10.1080/09500782.2015.1114628

García, O., & Li, W. (2014). *Translanguaging: Language, bilingualism and education*. New York: Palgrave Macmillan.

Greeno, J. G., & Gresalfi, M. S. (2015). Opportunities to learn in practice and identity. In P. A. Moss, D. C. Pullin, J. P. Gee, E. H. Haertel, & L. Jones (Eds.), *Assessment, equity and opportunity to learn*. Cambridge: Cambridge University Press.

10 Multilingual Practices and Opportunities to Learn 275

Hüttner, J., Dalton-Puffer, C., & Smit, U. (2013). The power of beliefs: Lay theories and their influence on the implementation of CLIL programmes. *International Journal of Bilingual Education and Bilingualism, 16*(3), 267–284.

Jakonen, T., Szabó, T. P., & Laihonen, P. (2018). Translanguaging as playful subversion of a monolingual norm in the classroom. In G. Mazzaferro (Ed.), *Translanguaging as everyday practice* (pp. 31–48). Dordrecht: Springer.

Kramsch, C. (2012). Authenticity and legitimacy in multilingual SLA. *Critical Multilingualism Studies, 1*, 107–128.

Krashen, S. (1981). *Second language acquisition and second language learning.* Oxford: Pergamon.

Li, W. (2011). Moment analysis and translanguaging space. *Journal of Pragmatics, 43*, 1222–1235.

Li, W. (2018). Translanguaging as a practical theory of language. *Applied Linguistics, 39*(1), 9–30.

Lucas, T., & Katz, A. (1994). Reframing the debate: The roles of native languages in English-only programs for language minority students. *TESOL Quarterly, 28*, 537–561. https://doi.org/10.2307/3587307

Meyer, O., Coyle, D., Halbach, A., Schuck, K., & Ting, T. (2015). A pluriliteracies approach to content and language integrated learning—Mapping learner progressions in knowledge construction and meaning-making. *Language, Culture and Curriculum, 28*(1), 41–57. https://doi.org/10.1080/07908318.2014.1000924

Moll, L., Amanti, C., Neff, D., & Gonzales, N. (1992). Funds of knowledge for teaching: Toward a qualitative approach to connect homes and classrooms. *Theory Into Practice: Qualitative Issues in Educational Research, 3*(2), 132–141.

Moore, P., & Nikula, T. (2016). Translanguaging in CLIL classrooms. In T. Nikula, E. Dafouz, P. Moore, & U. Smit (Eds.), *Conceptualising integration in CLIL and multilingual education* (pp. 211–234). Bristol: Multilingual Matters.

Morton, T. (2012). *Teachers' knowledge about language and classroom interaction in content and language integrated learning.* Doctoral thesis, Universidad Autónoma de Madrid.

Motha, S., & Lin, A. M. Y. (2014). 'Non-coercive rearrangements': Theorizing desire in TESOL. *TESOL Quarterly, 48*(2), 331–359.

Nikula, T., Dalton-Puffer, C., Llinares, A., & Lorenzo, F. (2016). More than content and language: The complexity of integration in CLIL and bilingual education. In T. Nikula, E. Dafouz, P. Moore, & U. Smit (Eds.),

Conceptualising integration in CLIL and multilingual education (pp. 1–25). Bristol: Multilingual Matters.

Norton, B. (2000). *Identity and language learning: Gender, ethnicity and educational change*. Harlow: Pearson Education/Longman.

Ollerhead, S. (2018). Teaching across semiotic modes with multilingual learners: Translanguaging in an Australian classroom. *Language and Education.* https://doi.org/10.1080/09500782.2018.1516780

Oxford English Dictionary. (2018). *Definition of 'language'.* Retrieved February 26, 2018, from https://en.oxforddictionaries.com/definition/language

Pacheco, M. (2018). Spanish, Arabic, and 'English-Only': Making meaning across languages in two classroom communities. *TESOL Quarterly, 52*(4), 1–27. https://doi.org/10.1002/tesq.446

Palmer, D. K., Cervantes-Soon, C., Dorner, L., & Heiman, D. (2019). Bilingualism, biliteracy, biculturalism and critical consciousness for all: Proposing a fourth fundamental goal for two-way dual language education. *Theory Into Practice, 58*(2), 121–133. https://doi.org/10.1080/00405841.2019.1569376

Piller, I., & Gerber, L. (2018). Family language policy between the bilingual advantage and the monolingual mindset. *International Journal of Bilingual Education and Bilingualism.* https://doi.org/10.1080/13670050.2018.1503227

Turner, M. (2017). Integrating content and language in institutionally monolingual settings: Teacher positioning and differentiation. *Bilingual Research Journal, 40*(1), 70–80.

Turner, M., & Lin, A. M. Y. (2017). Translanguaging and named languages: Productive tension and desire. *International Journal of Bilingual Education and Bilingualism.* https://doi.org/10.1080/13670050.2017.1360243

Conclusion

In this book, I have focused on multilingualism as a resource and a goal against a backdrop of institutional monolingualism. My main aim has been to consider what might be feasible for the implementation of a sustainable school-level language policy, especially when students have a great range of experiences with different languages. Alongside the leveraging of language resources for learning, the expansion of linguistic repertoire, or the learning of a target language at school, has been highlighted. The language policy is that of an affirming multilingual stance, and the rest of the multilingual practices framework offered in this book, along with teaching and learning objectives, relates to its enactment. I have also sought to keep in mind teachers who would like to implement a multilingual language policy in their classrooms without necessarily enjoying school commitment to a multilingual approach.

My point of departure has been that there is a strong relationship between how we think about language and how we use it. This is true for all stakeholders: school leaders, teachers, students and parents. Moving along a multilingual continuum might be imagined as a gradual process when monolingual approaches to language are prevalent in schools. The multilingual practices framework takes this into account. Institutional

© The Author(s) 2019
M. Turner, *Multilingualism as a Resource and a Goal*,
https://doi.org/10.1007/978-3-030-21591-0

278 Conclusion

structures and pedagogies associated with bilingual education and the incorporation of different languages into English-medium classrooms are unlikely to be effective without attention both to the multilingual stance of practitioners and to student engagement with languages. In the framework, opportunities to learn (through) languages arise from the influence of all three dimensions. The incorporation of heritage languages and bilingual education may appear beyond contemplation, and in need of more community will than often exists, at least in Australian schools. However, I have not found this to be the case in the course of my research. A shift of focus from languages to the students themselves has the potential to enhance the prospects for such incorporation. What students do with languages, and/or what teachers (and school leaders) would like them to do, and why, can help create a pathway for their gradual integration into predominantly monolingual systems.

Moving towards a systemic shift of focus is important. Initiatives in schools can be short-lived if they are not embedded in something larger— a bigger picture that can act as a guide when logistics prevent implementation of a particular kind of programme, for example, or students (and other stakeholders) do not engage as anticipated. Experimentation can be assisted by clarity of objectives and a way to communicate these to the school community. A multilingual orientation to teaching and learning can be used as an umbrella for both the affirmation and leveraging of linguistic diversity and the imperative to move monolingual students— including students disengaged with their linguistic heritage—away from a taken for granted belief that the dominant language is the only one of value. An orientation that is actively inclusive of everyone is likely to be more sustainable in settings where monolingualism is rewarded in high stakes testing regimes, and students are ultimately not required to engage with other languages in order to succeed academically. Embedding multilingual practices in everyday teaching and learning has the potential to demonstrate to students and other stakeholders the benefits of language learning and use.

The multilingual practices framework represents my effort to grapple systemically with what I was seeing in schools (and what I was not seeing). My perspective was influenced by contemporary thinking from sociocultural, sociolinguistic, second language acquisition, school-based bilingual education and TESOL research. I considered a multilingual stance in relation to schools and teachers because I conceptualised this stance as language policy, or a school's expectations—made explicit—around multilingual practices. Teachers' and school leaders' engagement with particular languages was not always required for the effective incorporation of languages across the curriculum. Practitioners' positioning towards, and use of, different languages can be viewed as a multilingual stance, or part of school or classroom policy. Students' engagement with languages, on the other hand, cannot be considered in this way because there are aspects of this engagement that fall outside a teacher's or a school's sphere of influence, especially in mainstream settings. Ideally, a multilingual stance can drive the normalisation of multilingual practices for all students, as much as possible, through teaching and learning practices and objectives. The examples given in the institutional structures and pedagogies dimension of the multilingual practices framework were guided by the studies, and serve to illustrate what might be practical in the design of programmes and lessons.

None of the studies in this book had a specific focus on English language learners, but there is no reason why the multilingual practices framework would not be appropriate for students who are still becoming fluent in English. As discussed in the book, there is a growing body of research that shows the benefits of guiding students' use of their expanded linguistic resources to make meaning in formal language environments; just because students do not know content in one language does not necessarily mean that they do not know it in any language. A multilingual stance includes the expansion of a linguistic repertoire and, for EAL students, it is English that they are adding to their repertoire. Thus, if there are students from a homogeneous language group who are avoiding the use of English in class, this avoidance can be compared with majority language speakers who are reluctant to use a target language in a bilingual education programme. In this case, the strategic application of crosslinguistic and translanguaging pedagogy might include students' increased productive use of English, and guiding them towards new English language practices. It can be a logical reaction for schools to implement a *de facto* English-only policy in these situations, but this reaction negates a significant resource that students are bringing to their (language) education.

In sum, approaching cross-curricular language use in a holistic way provides opportunities for all students to learn. This learning incorporates communicative, cognitive, creative and affective dimensions. It also includes critical reflection on linguistic hierarchies and a respect for the linguistic and cultural knowledge of others that moves beyond rhetoric and into institutional spaces in systemic ways. Encouraging students to identify with more than one language group can be a gentle, insistent and potentially powerful way to bring people together and, in the world in which we live, this would appear to be an increasingly urgent endeavour.

References

Ahmed, S. (2010). *The promise of happiness.* Durham, NC: Duke University Press.

Alexander, R. J. (2001). *Culture and pedagogy: International comparisons in primary education.* Oxford: Blackwell.

Alexander, R. J. (2008). *Towards dialogic teaching: Rethinking classroom talk.* York: Dialogos.

Anderson, B. (1991). *Imagined communities: Reflections on the origin and spread of nationalism* (revised ed.). New York: Verso.

Anderson, T., & Shattuck, J. (2012). Design-based research: A decade of progress in education research? *Educational Researcher, 41*(1), 16–25.

Arkoudis, S. (2006). Negotiating the rough ground between ESL and mainstream teachers. *International Journal of Bilingual Education and Bilingualism, 9*, 415–433.

Arkoudis, S., & Creese, A. (2006). Introduction. *International Journal of Bilingual Education and Bilingualism, 9*(4), 411–414.

Árva, V., & Medgyes, P. (2000). Native and non-native teachers in the classroom. *System, 28*, 355–372.

Australian Curriculum, Assessment and Reporting Authority (ACARA). (2011). *The shape of the Australian curriculum: Languages.* Retrieved from http://docs.acara.edu.au/resources/Languages__Shape_of_the_Australian_Curriculum_new.pdf

© The Author(s) 2019
M. Turner, *Multilingualism as a Resource and a Goal,*
https://doi.org/10.1007/978-3-030-21591-0

282 References

Australian Curriculum Assessment and Reporting Authority (ACARA). (2015). *Asia and Australia's engagement with Asia.* Retrieved from http://www.acara.edu.au/curriculum/cross_curriculum_priorities.html

Australian Curriculum, Assessment and Reporting Authority (ACARA). (2018a). *My school.* Retrieved from https://www.myschool.edu.au/

Australian Curriculum, Assessment and Reporting Authority (ACARA). (2018b). *Australian curriculum: English.* Retrieved from https://www.australiancurriculum.edu.au/f-10-curriculum/english/

Baker, C. (2001). *Foundations of bilingual education and bilingualism* (3rd ed.). Bristol: Multilingual Matters.

Baker, C. (2003). Biliteracy and transliteracy in Wales: Language planning and the Welsh national curriculum. In N. H. Hornberger (Ed.), *Continua of biliteracy: An ecological framework for educational policy, research, and practice in multilingual settings.* Clevedon: Multilingual Matters.

Baker, C., & Wright, W. E. (2017). *Foundations of bilingual education and bilingualism* (6th ed.). Bristol: Multilingual Matters.

Bakhtin, M. M. (1981). *The dialogic imagination: Four essays by M.M. Bakhtin* (C. Emerson & M. Holquist, Trans. & M. Holquist, Ed.). Austin, TX: University of Texas Press.

Ball, P. (2018). Innovations and challenges in CLIL materials design. *Theory Into Practice, 57,* 222–231.

Ballinger, S. (2015). Linking content, linking students: A cross linguistic pedagogical intervention. In J. Cenoz & D. Gorter (Eds.), *Multilingual education: New perspectives* (pp. 35–60). Cambridge: Cambridge University Press.

Ballinger, S., Lyster, R., Sterzuk, A., & Genesee, F. (2017). Context-appropriate crosslinguistic pedagogy: Considering the role of language status in immersion education. *Journal of Immersion and Content-Based Language Education, 5*(1), 30–57.

Bandura, A. (1997). *Self-efficacy: The exercise of control.* San Francisco: W.H. Freeman.

Banegas, D. L. (2014). An investigation into CLIL-related sections of EFL coursebooks: Issues of CLIL inclusion in the publishing market. *International Journal of Bilingual Education and Bilingualism, 17*(3), 345–359.

Beatens Beardsmore, H. (2009). Bilingual education: Factors and variables. In O. García (Ed.), *Bilingual education in the 21st century: A global perspective* (pp. 137–158). Malden, MA: Wiley-Blackwell.

Behan, L., Turnbull, M., & Spek, W. (1997). The proficiency gap in late immersion (extended French): Language use in collaborative tasks. *Le journal de l'immersion, 20,* 41–42.

References   283

Bell, D. A. (1980). Brown v. board of education and the interest convergence dilemma. *Harvard Law Review, 93*, 518–533.

Bialystok, E. (2001). *Bilingualism in development: Language, literacy and cognition.* Cambridge: Cambridge University Press.

Blackledge, A., & Creese, A. (2010). *Multilingualism: A critical perspective.* London, UK: Continuum.

Blair, A., Haneda, M., & Nebus Bose, F. (2018). Reimagining English-medium instructional settings as sites of multilingual and multimodal meaning making. *TESOL Quarterly, 52*(3), 516–538.

Blommaert, J. (2010). *The sociolinguistics of globalization.* Cambridge: Cambridge University Press.

Boaler, J., & Greeno, J. G. (2000). Identity, agency, and knowing in mathematics worlds. In J. Boaler (Ed.), *Multiple perspectives on mathematics teaching and learning* (pp. 171–200). Westport, CT: Ablex Publishing.

Bourdieu, P. (1977). The economics of linguistic exchanges. *Social Science Information, 16*(6), 645–668.

Bourdieu, P. (1991). *Language and symbolic power.* London: Polity Press.

Bourdieu, P., & Passeron, J. (1977). *Reproduction in education, society, and culture.* London and Beverly Hills, CA: Sage Publications.

Braun, V., & Clarke, V. (2008). Using thematic analysis in psychology. *Qualitative Research in Psychology, 3*(2), 77–101.

Bucholz, M. (2003). Sociolinguistic nostalgia and the authentication of identity. *Journal of Sociolinguistics, 7*, 398–416.

Butzkamm, W. (2003). We only learn language once. The role of the mother tongue in FL classrooms: Death of dogma. *Language Learning Journal, 28*, 29–39.

Cammarata, L., & Tedick, D. (2012). Balancing content and language in instruction: The experience of immersion teachers. *The Modern Language Journal, 96*(2), 251–269. https://doi.org/10.1111/j.1540-4781-2012.01330.x

Canagarajah, S. (1999). *Resisting linguistic imperialism.* Oxford: Oxford University Press.

Canagarajah, S. (2011). Translanguaging in the classroom: Emerging issues for research and pedagogy. *Applied Linguistics Review, 2*, 128.

Canagarajah, S. (2013). *Translingual practice: Global Englishes and cosmopolitan relations.* New York: Routledge.

Cazden, C. (1981). Performance before competence: Assistance to child discourse in the zone of proximal development. *Quarterly Newsletter of the Laboratory of Comparative Human Cognition, 3*, 5–8.

284 References

Cenoz, J. (2015). Content-based instruction and content and language integrated learning: The same or different? *Language, Culture and Curriculum, 28*(1), 8–24.

Cenoz, J., Genesee, F., & Gorter, D. (2014). Critical analysis of CLIL: Taking stock and looking forward. *Applied Linguistics, 35*(3), 243–226.

Cenoz, J., & Gorter, D. (2011). Focus on multilingualism: A study of trilingual writing. *The Modern Language Journal, 95*, 356–369.

Cenoz, J., & Gorter, D. (2015). Towards a holistic approach in the study of multilingual education. In J. Cenoz & D. Gorter (Eds.), *Multilingual education: Between language learning and translanguaging* (pp. 1–15). Cambridge: Cambridge University Press.

Chamot, A. U., & O'Malley, J. M. (1987). The cognitive academic language learning approach: A bridge to the mainstream. *TESOL Quarterly, 21*(2), 227–249.

Chamot, A. U., & O'Malley, J. M. (1994). *CALLA handbook: Implementing the cognitive academic language learning approach.* Reading, MA: Addison-Wesley.

Cho, D. W. (2012). English-medium instruction in the university context of Korea: Trade-off between teaching outcomes and media-initiated university ranking. *Journal of Asia TEFL, 9*(4), 135–163.

Chomsky, N. (1957). *Syntactic structures.* The Hague: Mouton.

Chomsky, N. (1986). *Knowledge of language: Its nature, origin and use.* New York: Praeger.

Chomsky, N. (2000). *New horizons in the study of language and mind.* Cambridge: Cambridge University Press.

Christie, F. (2005). *Language and education in the primary school.* Sydney: UNSW Press.

Cobb, P., Confrey, J., diSessa, A., Lehrer, R., & Schauble, L. (2003). Design experiments in educational research. *Educational Researcher, 32*(1), 9–13.

Collier, V. P., & Thomas, W. P. (2004). The astounding effectiveness of dual language education for all. *NABE Journal of Research and Practice, 2*(1), 1–20.

Conteh, J., & Meier, G. (Eds.). (2014). *The multilingual turn in languages education: Opportunities and challenges.* Bristol: Multilingual Matters.

Coyle, D. (2007). Content and language integrated learning: Towards a connected research agenda for CLIL pedagogies. *International Journal of Bilingual Education and Bilingualism, 10*(5), 543–562.

Coyle, D., Hood, P., & Marsh, D. (2010). *CLIL: Content and language integrated learning.* Cambridge: Cambridge University Press.

Creese, A. (2002). The discursive construction of power in teacher partnerships: Language and subject specialists in mainstream schools. *TESOL Quarterly, 36*(4), 597–616.

Creese, A. (2005). Is this content-based language teaching? *Linguistics and Education, 16*(2), 188–204.

Creese, A. (2010). Content-focused classrooms and learning English: How teachers collaborate. *Theory Into Practice, 49*(2), 99–105.

Creese, A., & Blackledge, A. (2010). Translanguaging in the bilingual classroom: A pedagogy for learning and teaching? *The Modern Language Journal, 94*, 103–115.

Creese, A., Blackledge, A., & Takhi, J. (2014). The ideal 'native speaker' teacher: Negotiating authenticity and legitimacy in the language classroom. *The Modern Language Journal, 98*(4), 937–951.

Cross, R. (2015). Defining content and language integrated learning for languages education in Australia. *Babel, 49*(2), 4–15.

Cross, R., & Gearon, M. (2013). *Research and evaluation of the content and language integrated learning (CLIL) approach to teaching and learning languages in Victorian schools.* Melbourne: Melbourne Graduate School of Education, The University of Melbourne.

Cummins, J. (2005). A proposal for action: Strategies for recognizing heritage language competence as a learning resource within the mainstream classroom. *The Modern Language Journal, 89*(4), 585–592.

Cummins, J. (2006). Identity texts: The imaginative construction of self through multiliteracies pedagogy. In O. Garcia, T. Skutnabb-Kangas, & M. E. Torres-Guzman (Eds.), *Imagining multilingual schools: Language in education and glocalization* (pp. 51–68). Toronto: Multilingual Matters.

Cummins, J. (2007). Rethinking monolingual instructional strategies in multilingual classrooms. *Canadian Journal of Applied Linguistics (CJAL), 10*(2), 221–240.

Cummins, J. (2017). Teaching minoritised students: Are additive approaches legitimate? *Harvard Educational Review, 87*(3), 404–425.

Cummins, J., & Early, M. (2011). *Identity texts: The collaborative creation of power in multilingual schools.* Staffordshire: Trentham Books.

Cummins, J., & Swain, M. (1986). *Bilingualism in education: Aspects of theory, research and practice.* Harlow: Longman.

D'Warte, J. (2013). *Pilot project: Reconceptualising English learners' language and literacy skills, practices and experiences. University of Western Sydney.* Retrieved from http://researchdirect.westernsydney.edu.au/islandora/object/uws:23461

286 References

D'Warte, J. (2014). Exploring linguistic repertoires: Multiple language use and multimodal literacy activity in five classrooms. *Australian Journal of Language and Literacy, 37*(1), 21–30.

D'Warte, J. (2015). Building knowledge about and with students: Linguistic ethnography in two secondary school classrooms. *English in Australia, 50*(1), 39–48.

Dagenais, D., & Jacquet, M. (2008). Theories of representation in French and English scholarship on multilingualism. *International Journal of Multilingualism, 5*(1), 41–52. https://doi.org/10.2167/ijm019.0

Dale, L., Oostdam, R., & Verspoor, M. (2018). Searching for identity and focus: Towards an analytical framework for language teachers in bilingual education. *International Journal of Bilingual Education and Bilingualism, 21*(3), 366–383. https://doi.org/10.1080/13670050.2017.1383351

Dalton-Puffer, C. (2013). A construct of cognitive discourse functions for conceptualizing content and language integration in CLIL and multilingual education. *European Journal of Applied Linguistics, 1*(2), 216–253.

Dalton-Puffer, C. (2016). Cognitive discourse functions: Specifying an integrative interdisciplinary construct. In E. Dafouz & T. Nikula (Eds.), *Conceptualising integration in CLIL and multilingual education* (pp. 29–54). Bristol: Channel View Publications.

Dalton-Puffer, C. (2018). Postscriptum: Research pathways in CLIL/immersion instructional practices and teacher development. *International Journal of Bilingual Education and Bilingualism, 21*(3), 384–387.

Dalton-Puffer, C., Llinares, A., Lorenzo, F., & Nikula, T. (2014). 'You can stand under my umbrella': Immersion, CLIL and bilingual education. A response to Cenoz, Genesee & Gorter (2013). *Applied Linguistics, 35*(2), 213–218.

Dalton-Puffer, C., & Smit, U. (2013). Content and language integrated learning: A research agenda. *Language Teaching, 46*(4), 545–559.

Dardot, P., & Laval, C. (2013). *The new way of the world: On a neoliberal society.* London: Verso.

Day, E., & Shapson, S. (1991). Integrating formal and functional approaches to language teaching in French immersion: An experimental study. *Language Learning, 41*, 25–58.

de Graaff, R., Koopman, G. J., Anikina, Y., & Westhoff, G. (2007). An observation tool for effective L2 pedagogy in content and language integrated learning (CLIL). *International Journal of Bilingual Education and Bilingualism, 10*(5), 603–624.

de Jong, E. J. (2011). *Foundations for multilingualism in education: From principles to practice.* Philadelphia, PA: Caslon Publishing.

de Jong, E. J. (2016). Two-way immersion for the next generation: Models, policies, and principles. *International Multilingual Research Journal, 10*(1), 6–16. https://doi.org/10.1080/19313152.2016.1118667

de Jong, E. J. (2018, Keynote). *Taking a multilingual stance: Quality education for ELLs*. Minneapolis, MN: Minnesota-TESOL.

de Jong, E. J., & Freeman, R. (2010). Bilingual approaches. In C. Leung & A. Creese (Eds.), *English as an additional language. Approaches to teaching linguistic minority students* (pp. 108–122). New York: Sage.

de Jong, E. J., & Howard, E. (2009). Integration in two-way immersion education: Equalising linguistic benefits for all students. *International Journal of Bilingual Education and Bilingualism, 12*, 81–99.

de Jong, E. J., Li, Z., Zafar, A. M., & Wu, C. (2016). Language policy in multilingual contexts: Revisiting Ruiz's 'language-as-resource' orientation. *Bilingual Research Journal, 39*(3–4), 200–212. https://doi.org/10.1080/1523 5882.2016.1224988

de Jong, E. J., Yilmaz, T., & Marichal, N. (2019). A multilingualism as a resource orientation in dual language education. *Theory Into Practice*. https://doi.org/ 10.1080/00405841.2019.1569375

de Saussure, F. (1907/1983). *Course in general linguistics*. La Salle, IL: Open Court.

Del Maschio, N., & Abutalebi, J. (2018). Neurobiology of bilingualism. In D. Miller, F. Bayram, J. Rothman, & L. Serratrice (Eds.), *Bilingual cognition and language: The state of the science across its subfields* (pp. 325–345). Amsterdam: John Benjamins Publishing.

Deleuze, G., & Guattari, F. (1977). *Anti-Oedipus: Capitalism and schizophrenia*. New York: Viking Press.

Department of Education and Training. (2017). *EAL learners in mainstream schools*. Retrieved from http://www.education.vic.gov.au/school/teachers/ support/diversity/eal/Pages/ealschools.aspx

Department of Education and Training, Victoria. (2016). *Languages provision in Victorian Government schools, 2016*. Retrieved February 26, 2018, from http://www.education.vic.gov.au/Documents/school/teachers/teachin-gresources/discipline/languages/2016_Languages_provision_report.pdf

Department of Education and Training, Victoria. (2018). *Languages*. Retrieved from http://www.education.vic.gov.au/school/teachers/teachingresources/ discipline/languages/Pages/default.aspx?Redirect=1

Derewianka, B. (2011). *A new grammar companion for teachers* (2nd ed.). Newtown: Primary English Teaching Association.

288   References

Derewianka, B., & Jones, P. (2016). *Teaching language in context* (2nd ed.). Melbourne: Oxford University Press.

Deutscher, G. (2005). *The unfolding of language*. London: Macmillan.

Djité, P. G. (2011). Language policy in Australia: What goes up must come down? In C. Norrby & J. Hajek (Eds.), *Uniformity and diversity in language policy: Global perspectives* (pp. 53–67). Bristol: Multilingual Matters.

Duff, P. (2007). Second language socialization as sociocultural theory: Insights and issues. *Language Teaching, 40*, 309–319.

Durán, L., & Palmer, D. (2014). Pluralist discourses of bilingualism and translanguaging talk in classrooms. *Journal of Early Childhood Literacy, 14*(3), 367–388.

Duverger, J. (2007). Didactiser l'alternance des langues en cours de DNL. *Tréma, 28*, 81–88.

Eccles, J. S. (2005). Subjective task value and the Eccles et al. model of achievement-related choices. In A. J. Elliott & C. S. Dweck (Eds.), *Handbook of competence and motivation* (pp. 105–121). New York: Guilford.

Echevarría, J., Vogt, M., & Short, D. J. (2008). *Making content comprehensible for English learners: The SIOP model* (3rd ed.). Boston: Pearson.

Ee, J. (2018). Exploring Korean dual language immersion programs in the Unites States: Parents' reasons for enrolling their children. *International Journal of Bilingual Education and Bilingualism, 21*(6), 690–709. https://doi.org/10.1080/13670050.2016.1208144

Eisenchlas, S., Schalley, A., & Guillemin, D. (2013). The importance of literacy in the home language: The view from Australia. *SAGE Open, 3*(4), 1–14. https://doi.org/10.1007/2158244013507270

Elliot, A. J., & Dweck, C. S. (Eds.). (2005). *Handbook of competence and motivation*. New York: Guilford.

Ellis, R. (1994). A theory of instructed second language acquisition. In N. Ellis (Ed.), *Implicit and explicit learning of languages* (pp. 79–114). San Diego, CA: Academic Press.

Ellis, R. (2001). Investigating form-focused instruction. *Language Learning, 51*(Suppl. 1), 1–46.

Ellis, R., & Shintani, N. (2014). *Exploring language pedagogy through second language acquisition research*. London: Routledge.

Ethnologue. (2018). *Languages of the world*. Retrieved February 26, 2018, from https://www.ethnologue.com/

European Commission. (2002). *CLIL/EMILE the European dimension: Actions, trends and foresight potential*. Brussels: Brussels European Unit, Public Services Contract 2001-3406/001-001.

References **289**

Eurydice. (2006). *Content and language integrated learning (CLIL) at school in Europe*. Brussels: Eurydice.

Fitts, S. (2006). Reconstructing the status quo: Linguistic interaction in a dual-language school. *Bilingual Research Journal, 30*(2), 337–365.

Fitzsimmons-Doolan, S. (2018). Language ideology change over time: Lessons for language policy in the U.S. state of Arizona and beyond. *TESOL Quarterly, 52*(1), 34–61.

Flores, N. (2014). *Let's not forget that translanguaging is a political act*. Retrieved 12 November, 2018, from https://educationallinguist.wordpress.com/2014/07/19/lets-not-forget-that-translanguaging-is-a-political-act/

Flores, N., & García, O. (2017). A critical review of bilingual education in the United States: From basements and pride to boutiques and profit. *Annual Review of Applied Linguistics, 37*, 14–29.

Fortune, T. W., & Tedick, D. J. (2008). One-way, two-way and indigenous immersion: A call for cross-fertilization. In T. W. Fortune & D. J. Tedick (Eds.), *Pathways to multilingualism: Evolving perspectives on immersion education* (pp. 3–21). Clevedon: Multilingual Matters.

Fortune, T. W., & Tedick, D. J. (2015). Oral proficiency assessment of English-proficient K-8 Spanish immersion students. *Modern Language Journal, 99*(4), 637–655.

Foucault, M. (1980). *Power/knowledge: Selected interviews and other writings 1972–1977* (C. Gordon, Trans.). New York: Pantheon Books.

Freire, P. (1970). *Pedagogy of the oppressed*. New York: Herder & Herder.

French, M. (2016). Students' multilingual resources and policy-in-action: An Australian case study. *Language and Education, 30*, 298–316. https://doi.org/10.1080/09500782.2015.1114628

Gajo, L. (2014). From normalization to didactization of multilingualism: European and Francophone research at the crossroads between linguistics and didactics. In J. Conteh & G. Meier (Eds.), *The multilingual turn in languages education: Opportunities and challenges* (pp. 131–175). Bristol: Multilingual Matters.

García, O. (2009a). *Bilingual education in the 21st century: A global perspective*. Malden, MA: Wiley-Blackwell.

García, O. (2009b). Livin' and Teachin' la lengua loca: Glocalizing U.S. Spanish ideologies and practices. In R. Salaberry (Ed.), *Language allegiances and bilingualism in the United States* (pp. 151–171). Clevedon: Multilingual Matters.

García, O., Ibarra Johnson, S., & Seltzer, K. (2017). *The translanguaging classroom: Leveraging student bilingualism for learning*. Philadelphia, PA: Caslon.

290 References

García, O., & Kano, N. (2014). Translanguaging as process and pedagogy: Developing the English writing of Japanese students in the U.S. In J. Conteh & G. Meier (Eds.), *The multilingual turn in languages education: Benefits for individuals and societies* (pp. 258–277). Clevedon: Multilingual Matters.

García, O., & Kleifgen, J. (2010). *Educating emergent bilinguals: Policies, programs, and practices for English language learners*. New York: Teachers College Press.

García, O., & Li, W. (2014). *Translanguaging: Language, bilingualism and education*. New York: Palgrave Macmillan.

García, O., & Lin, A. M. Y. (2016). Translanguaging in bilingual education. In O. García, A. M. Y. Lin, & S. May (Eds.), *Bilingual and multilingual education (Encyclopedia of language and education)* (pp. 117–130). Cham: Springer.

García, O., & Sylvan, C. (2011). Pedagogies and practices in multilingual classrooms: Singularities in pluralities. *The Modern Language Journal, 95*, 385–400.

Gee, J. P. (2004). *Situated language and learning: A critique of traditional schooling*. New York: Routledge.

Genesee, F. (1981). A comparison of early and late second language learning. *Canadian Journal of Behavioral Science, 13*, 115–127. https://doi.org/10.1037/h0081168

Genesee, F. (1983). Bilingual education of majority-language children: The immersion experiments in review. *Applied Psycholinguistics, 4*(1), 1–46.

Genesee, F. (1987). *Learning through two languages: Studies of immersion and bilingual education*. Cambridge, MA: Newbury House.

Genesee, F. (2015). Canada: Factors that shaped the creation and development of immersion education. In P. Mehisto & F. Genesee (Eds.), *Building bilingual education systems: Forces, mechanisms and counterweights* (pp. 43–56). Cambridge: Cambridge University Press.

Gibbons, P. (2002). *Scaffolding language, scaffolding learning*. Portsmouth: Heinemann.

Gibbons, P. (2003). Mediating language learning: Teacher interactions with ESL students in a content-based classroom. *TESOL Quarterly, 37*(2), 247–273.

Gibbons, P. (2009). *English learners academic literacy and thinking: Learning in the challenge zone*. Portsmouth: Heinemann.

Gibson, J. (1977). *The ecological approach to visual perception*. Hillsdale, NJ: Lawrence Erlbaum.

Gill, M. (2011). Authenticity. In J. O. Östman & J. Verschueren (Eds.), *Pragmatics in practice* (pp. 46–61). Philadelphia, PA: John Benjamins.

González, N., Moll, L. C., & Amanti, C. (Eds.). (2005). *Funds of knowledge: Theorizing practices in households, communities and classrooms*. Mahwah, NJ: Lawrence Erlbaum.

References   291

Greeno, J. G., & Gresalfi, M. S. (2015). Opportunities to learn in practice and identity. In P. A. Moss, D. C. Pullin, J. P. Gee, E. H. Haertel, & L. Jones (Eds.), *Assessment, equity and opportunity to learn*. Cambridge: Cambridge University Press.

Gumperz, J. J., & Cook-Gumperz, J. (2005). Making space for bilingual communicative practice. *Intercultural Pragmatics, 2*(1), 1–23.

Hall, G., & Cook, G. (2011). Own-language use in language teaching and learning. *Language Teaching, 45*(3), 271–308.

Halliday, M. A. K. (1993). Towards a language-based theory of learning. *Linguistics and Education, 5*(2), 93–116.

Halliday, M. A. K. (2009). *The essential Halliday*. London: Continuum.

Hamman, L. (2018). Translanguaging and positioning in two-way dual language classrooms: A case for criticality. *Language and Education, 32*(1), 21–42.

Hammond, J. (2012). Hope and challenge in the Australian curriculum: Implications for EAL students and their teachers. *Australian Journal of Language and Literacy, 35*, 223–240.

Hammond, J., & Gibbons, P. (2005). Putting scaffolding to work: The contribution of scaffolding in articulating ESL education. *Prospect, 20*(1), 6–30.

Harley, B. (1989). Functional grammar in French immersion: A classroom experiment. *Applied Linguistics, 10*, 331–359.

Harley, B. (1998). The role of form-focused tasks in promoting child L2 acquisition. In C. Doughty & J. Williams (Eds.), *Focus on form in classroom second language acquisition* (pp. 156–174). Cambridge: Cambridge University Press.

Harper, C. A., de Jong, E. J., & Platt, E. J. (2008). Marginalizing English as a second language teacher expertise: The exclusionary consequence of *No Child Left* Behind. *Language Policy, 7*, 267–284. https://doi.org/10.1007/s10993-008-9102-y

Harris, R. (1981). *The language myth*. London: Duckworth.

Heller, M. (2007). *Bilingualism: A social approach*. New York: Palgrave Macmillan.

Heller, M., & Duchêne, A. (2012). Pride and profit. Changing discourses of language, capital and nation-state. In A. Duchêne & M. Heller (Eds.), *Language in Late Capitalism* (pp. 1–21). London: Routledge.

Hickey, D. T., & Granade, J. B. (2004). The influence of sociocultural theory on our theories of engagement and motivation. In D. McInerney & S. Van Etten (Eds.), *Big Theories Revisited* (pp. 223–247). Connecticut: Information Age Publishing.

Holland, D., & Lachicotte, W. (2015). Vygotsky, Mead, and the new sociocultural studies of identity. In H. Daniels, M. Cole, & J. V. Wertsch (Eds.), *The Cambridge companion to Vygotsky* (pp. 101–135). Cambridge: Cambridge University Press.

292   References

Holliday, A. (2006). Key concepts in ELT: Native-speakerism. *ELT Journal, 60*(4), 385–387.

Hornberger, N., & Link, H. (2012). Translanguaging in today's classrooms: A biliteracy lens. *Theory Into Practice, 51,* 239–247.

Hornberger, N. H. (2017). *Honoring Richard Ruiz and his work on language planning and bilingual education.* Bristol: Multilingual Matters.

Huang, G. (1995). Self reported biliteracy and self esteem: a study of Mexican American 8th graders. *Applied Psycholinguistics, 16*(3), 271–291.

Hummel, K. (2010). Translation and short-term L2 vocabulary retention: Hindrance or help? *Language Teaching Research, 14*(1), 61–74.

Hüttner, J., Dalton-Puffer, C., & Smit, U. (2013). The power of beliefs: Lay theories and their influence on the implementation of CLIL programmes. *International Journal of Bilingual Education and Bilingualism, 16*(3), 267–284.

Hymes, D. H. (1962). The ethnography of speaking. In T. Gladwin & W. C. Sturtevant (Eds.), *Anthropology and human behavior* (pp. 15–53). Washington, DC: Anthropological Society of Washington.

Hymes, D. H. (1972). On communicative competence. In J. B. Pride & J. Holmes (Eds.), *Sociolinguistics: Selected readings* (pp. 269–293). Harmondsworth: Penguin.

Jakonen, T., Szabó, T. P., & Laihonen, P. (2018). Translanguaging as playful subversion of a monolingual norm in the classroom. In G. Mazzaferro (Ed.), *Translanguaging as everyday practice* (pp. 31–48). Dordrecht: Springer.

Kalantzis, M., & Cope, B. (2008). *New learning: Elements of a science of education.* Cambridge: Cambridge University Press.

Kanno, Y. (2003). *Negotiating bilingual and bicultural identities: Japanese returnees betwixt two worlds.* Mahwah, NJ: Lawrence Erlbaum.

Kaufman, D., & Crandall, J. (2005). Standards- and content-based instruction: Transforming language education in primary and secondary schools. In D. Kaufman & J. Crandall (Eds.), *Content-based instruction in primary and secondary school settings.* Alexandria: Teachers of English to Speakers of Other Languages.

Kim, S. H., & Elder, C. (2008). Target language use in foreign language classrooms: Practices and perceptions of two native speaker teachers in New Zealand. *Language, Culture and Communication, 21*(2), 167–185.

Kong, S. (2014). Collaboration between content and language specialists in late immersion. *The Canadian Modern Language Review/La Revue Canadienne Des Langues Vivantes, 70*(1), 103–122.

Kovelman, I., Baker, S., & Petitto, L. (2008). Age of first bilingual language exposure as a new window into bilingual reading development. *Bilingualism: Language and Cognition, 11*(2), 203–223. https://doi.org/10.1017/ S1366728908003386

Kramsch, C. (1986). From language proficiency to interactional competence. *The Modern Language Journal, 70*(4), 366–372.

Kramsch, C. (1997). The privilege of the nonnative speaker. *PMLA, 112*, 359–369.

Kramsch, C. (2012). Authenticity and legitimacy in multilingual SLA. *Critical Multilingualism Studies, 1*, 107–128.

Krashen, S. (1981). *Second language acquisition and second language learning.* Oxford: Pergamon.

Kravchenko, A. V. (2007). Essential properties of language, or, why language is not a code. *Language Sciences, 29*(5), 650–671.

Kyriacou, C., & Issitt, J. (2008). *What characterizes effective teacher-pupil dialogue to promote conceptual understanding in mathematics lessons in England in key stages 2 and 3?* EPPI-centre report no. 1604R, Social Science Research Unit, Institute of Education, University of London.

Lacan, J. (1977). *The mirror stage as formative of the I. écrits: A selection* (A. Sheridan, Trans.). New York: W.W. Norton.

Lankshear, C., & Knobel, M. (2003). *New literacies: Changing knowledge and classroom learning.* Buckingham: Open University Press.

Lapkin, S., Hart, D., & Swain, M. (1991). Early and middle French immersion programs: French language outcomes. *Canadian Modern Language Review, 48*(1), 11–41.

Lasagabaster, D., & Ruiz de Zarobe, Y. (2010). *Spain: Implementation, results and teacher training.* Newcastle-upon-Tyne: Cambridge Scholars Publishing.

Lasagabaster, D., & Sierra, J. M. (2010). Immersion and CLIL in English: More differences than similarities. *ELT Journal, 64*(4), 367–375.

Lave, J. (1988). *Cognition in practice: Mind, mathematics and culture in everyday life.* New York: Cambridge University Press.

Lave, J., & Wenger, W. (1991). *Situated learning: Legitimate peripheral participation.* Cambridge: Cambridge University Press.

Lemke, J. L. (2016). *Translanguaging and flows.* Unpublished research manuscript.

Letiche, H., & Lissack, M. (2009). Making room for affordances. *Emergence: Complexity and Organization, 11*(3), 61–72.

294 References

Lewis, G. W., Jones, B., & Baker, C. (2012). Translanguaging: origins and development from school to street and beyond. *Educational Research & Evaluation, 18*, 641–654.

Li, W. (2000). Dimensions of bilingualism. In W. Li (Ed.), *The bilingualism reader* (pp. 3–25). New York: Routledge.

Li, W. (2011). Moment analysis and translanguaging space. *Journal of Pragmatics, 43*, 1222–1235.

Li, W. (2018). Translanguaging as a practical theory of language. *Applied Linguistics, 39*(1), 9–30.

Li, W., & Zhu, H. (2013). Translanguaging identities and ideologies: Creating transnational space through flexible multilingual practices amongst Chinese university students in the UK. *Applied Linguistics, 34*(5), 516–535.

Lin, A. M. Y., & He, P. (2017). Translanguaging as dynamic activity flows in CLIL classrooms. *Journal of Language, Identity & Education, 16*, 228–244. https://doi.org/10.1080/15348458.2017.1328283

Lin, A. M. Y. (2008). Code-switching in the classroom: Research paradigms and approaches. In K. A. King & N. H. Hornberger (Eds.), *Encyclopedia of language and education: Vol. 10. Research methods in language and education* (pp. 273–286). New York: Springer.

Lin, A. M. Y. (2013). Classroom code-switching: Three decades of research. *Applied Linguistics Review, 4*(1), 195–218.

Lin, A. M. Y. (2015). Conceptualizing the potential role of L1 in content and language integrated learning (CLIL). *Language, Culture and Curriculum, 28*(1), 74–89.

Lin, A. M. Y. (2016). *Language across the curriculum and CLIL in English as an additional language contexts: Theory and practice*. Singapore: Springer.

Lin, A. M. Y., & Lo, Y. Y. (2017). Trans/languaging and the triadic dialogue in content and language integrated learning (CLIL) classrooms. *Language and Education, 31*(1), 26–45.

Lin, A. M. Y., & Wu, Y. M. (2015). 'May I speak Cantonese?'—Co-constructing a scientific proof in an EFL junior secondary Science classroom. *International Journal of Bilingual Education and Bilingualism, 18*(3), 289–305.

Lin, A. M. Y., Wu, Y. M., & Lemke, J. L. (forthcoming). 'It takes a village to research a village': Conversations with Jay Lemke on contemporary issues in translanguaging. In S. Lau & S. V. V. Stille (Eds.), *Critical plurilingual pedagogies: Struggling toward equity rather than equality*. Cham: Springer. http://www.grape.uji.es/wordpress/wpcontent/uploads/2018/11/Lin-Wu-Lemke_Conversations-with-Jay-Lemke-on-Translanguaging_Clean-Version-1.pdf.

Lindholm-Leary, K., & Genesee, F. (2014). Student outcomes in one-way, two-way, and indigenous language immersion education. *Journal of Immersion and Content-Based Language Education, 2*(2), 165–180.

Lindholm-Leary, K. J. (2001). *Dual language education.* Avon: Multilingual Matters.

Lindholm-Leary, K. J. (2005). The rich promise of two-way immersion. *Educational Leadership, 62*(4), 56–59.

Lindholm-Leary, K. J., & Howard, E. R. (2008). Language development and academic achievement in two-way immersion programs. In T. W. Fortune & D. J. Tedick (Eds.), *Pathways to multilingualism: Evolving perspectives on immersion education* (pp. 177–200). Oxford: Blackwell.

Littlewood, W., & Yu, B. H. (2011). First language and target language in the foreign language classroom. *Language Teaching, 44*, 64–77.

Liu, Y., Fisher, L., Forbes, K., & Evans, M. (2017). The knowledge base of teaching linguistically diverse contexts: 10 grounded principles of multilingual classroom pedagogy for EAL. *Language and Intercultural Communication,* 1–18. https://doi.org/10.1080/14708477.2017.1368136

Lo, Y. Y. (2014). A glimpse into the effectiveness of L2-content cross-curricular collaboration in content-based instruction programmes. *International Journal of Bilingual Education and Bilingualism, 16*(3), 375–388.

Lo Bianco, J. (2001). *Language and literacy policy in Scotland—SCILT.* Retrieved from http://www.scilt.org.uk/Portals/24/Library/publications/languageandliteracy/Language%20and%20literacy%20policy%20in%20Scotland_full%20document.pdf

Lo Bianco, J. (2014). Foreword. In J. Conteh & G. Meier (Eds.), *The multilingual turn in languages education: Opportunities and challenges* (pp. 16–17). Bristol: Multilingual Matters.

Lucas, T., & Katz, A. (1994). Reframing the debate: The roles of native languages in English-only programs for language minority students. *TESOL Quarterly, 28*, 537–561. https://doi.org/10.2307/3587307

Lucas, T., & Villegas, A. M. (2013). Preparing linguistically responsive teachers: Laying the foundation in preservice teacher education. *Theory Into Practice, 52*(2), 98–109.

Luk, J., & Lin, A. M. Y. (2015). Voices without words: Doing critical literate talk in English as a second language. *TESOL Quarterly, 49*(1), 67–91.

Lyster, R. (2004). Research on form-focused instruction in immersion classrooms: Implications for theory and practice. *Journal of French Language Studies, 14*(3), 321–341.

296 References

Lyster, R. (2007). *Learning and teaching languages through content: A counterbalanced approach.* Amsterdam: John Benjamins.

Lyster, R. (2011). Content-based second language teaching. In E. Hinkel (Ed.), *Handbook of research in second language teaching and learning.* New York: Routledge.

Lyster, R., Collins, L., & Ballinger, S. (2009). Linking languages through a bilingual read-aloud project. *Language awareness, 18,* 366–383. https://doi.org/10.1080/09658410903197322

Lyster, R., & Mori, H. (2006). Interactional feedback and instructional counterbalance. *SSLA, 28,* 269–300.

Lyster, R., & Ranta, L. (1997). Corrective feedback and learner uptake. *Studies in Second Language Acquisition, 19*(1), 37–66.

MacSwan, J. (2017). A multilingual perspective on translanguaging. *American Educational Research Journal, 54*(1), 167–201.

Makoni, S., & Pennycook, A. (2007). Disinventing and reconstituting languages. In S. Makoni & A. Pennycook (Eds.), *Disinventing and reconstituting languages* (pp. 1–41). Clevedon: Multilingual Matters.

Marian, V., Shook, A., & Shroeder, S. R. (2013). Bilingual two-way immersion programs benefit academic achievement. *Bilingual Research Journal, 36*(2), 167–186. https://doi.org/10.1080/15235882.2013.818075

Marsh, D. (Ed.). (2002). *CLIL/EMILE the European Dimension: Actions, trends and foresight potential.* University of Jyväskylä. Retrieved from https://jyx.jyu.fi/handle/123456789/47616

Martin, J. R. (1985). *Factual writing: Exploring and challenging social reality.* Geelong, VIC: Deakin University Press. (Republished by Oxford University Press, 1989).

Martin, J. R. (1991). Types of writing in infants and primary schools. In *Working with genre: Papers from the 1989 LERN conference* (pp. 33–44). Leichhardt: Common Ground.

Martin, J. R. (1994). Macro-genres: The ecology of the page. *Network, 21,* 29–52.

Martin, J. R. (2009). Genres and language learning: A social semiotic perspective. *Linguistics and Education, 20,* 10–21.

Martin, J. R., & Matthiessen, C. (2014). Modelling and mentoring: Teaching and learning from home to school. In A. Mahboob & L. Barratt (Eds.), *Englishes in multilingual contexts* (pp. 137–163). Dordrecht: Springer.

Martin-Beltrán, M. (2014). What do you want to say? How adolescents use translanguaging to expand learning opportunities. *International Multilingual Research Journal, 8,* 208–230.

References   297

Martínez-Roldan, C. M. (2015). Translanguaging practices as mobilization of linguistic resources in a Spanish/English bilingual after-school program: An analysis of contradictions. *International Multilingual Research Journal, 9*(1), 43–58. https://doi.org/10.1080/19313152.2014.982442

Mäsch, N. (1993). The German model of bilingual education: An administrator's perspective. In H. B. Beardsmore (Ed.), *European models of bilingual education* (pp. 155–172). Clevedon: Multilingual Matters.

May, S. (Ed.). (2014). *The multilingual turn: Implications for SLA, TESOL and bilingual education*. London: Routledge.

McCaslin, M. (2009). Co-regulation of student motivation and emergent identity. *Educational Psychologist, 44*(2), 137–146.

Mehisto, P., Marsh, D., & Frigols, M. J. (2008). *Uncovering CLIL*. London: Macmillan Education.

Meyer, O., Coyle, D., Halbach, A., Schuck, K., & Ting, T. (2015). A pluriliteracies approach to content and language integrated learning—Mapping learner progressions in knowledge construction and meaning-making. *Language, Culture and Curriculum, 28*(1), 41–57. https://doi.org/10.1080/07908318.2014.1000924

Moll, L., Amanti, C., Neff, D., & Gonzales, N. (1992). Funds of knowledge for teaching: Toward a qualitative approach to connect homes and classrooms. *Theory Into Practice: Qualitative Issues in Educational Research, 3*(2), 132–141.

Moore, H. (2007). Non-language policies and ESL: Some connections. *TESOL Quarterly, 41*(3), 573–583.

Moore, P., & Nikula, T. (2016). Translanguaging in CLIL classrooms. In T. Nikula, E. Dafouz, P. Moore, & U. Smit (Eds.), *Conceptualising integration in CLIL and multilingual education* (pp. 211–234). Bristol: Multilingual Matters.

Morton, T. (2012). *Teachers' knowledge about language and classroom interaction in content and language integrated learning*. Doctoral thesis, Universidad Autónoma de Madrid.

Morton, T. (2018). Reconceptualizing and describing teachers' knowledge of language for content and language integrated learning (CLIL). *International Journal of Bilingual Education and Bilingualism, 21*(3), 275–286.

Motha, S., & Lin, A. M. Y. (2014). 'Non-coercive rearrangements': Theorizing desire in TESOL. *TESOL Quarterly, 48*(2), 331–359.

Moussu, L., & Llurda, E. (2008). Non-native English-speaking English language teachers: history and research. *Language Teaching, 41*(3), 315–348.

Murphy, P. K. (2007). The eye of the beholder: The interplay of social and cognitive components in change. *Educational Psychologist, 42*(1), 41–53.

298 References

Navés, T. (2002). Successful CLIL programmes. In G. Langé & P. Bertaux (Eds.), *The CLIL professional development course* (pp. 93–102). Milan: Ministero della' Instruzione della' Universitá e della Ricerca.

Newman, K., Samimy, K., & Romstedt, K. (2010). Developing a training program for secondary teachers of English language learners in Ohio. *Theory Into Practice, 49*(2), 152–161.

Nikula, T., Dafouz, E., Moore, P., & Smit, U. (Eds.). (2016). *Conceptualising integration in CLIL and multilingual education*. Bristol: Multilingual Matters.

Nikula, T., Dalton-Puffer, C., Llinares, A., & Lorenzo, F. (2016). More than content and language: The complexity of integration in CLIL and bilingual education. In T. Nikula, E. Dafouz, P. Moore, & U. Smit (Eds.), *Conceptualising integration in CLIL and multilingual education* (pp. 1–25). Bristol: Multilingual Matters.

Nolen, S., Horn, I., & Ward, C. (2015). Situating motivation. *Educational Psychologist, 50*(3), 234–247.

Nolen, S., Ward, C. J., & Horn, I. S. (2011). Motivation, engagement, and identity: Opening a conversation. In D. McInerney, R. A. Walker, & G. A. Liem (Eds.), *Sociocultural theories of learning and motivation: Looking back, looking forward* (Vol. 10, pp. 109–135). Charlotte, NC: Information Age.

Norton, B. (2000). *Identity and language learning: Gender, ethnicity and educational change*. Harlow: Pearson Education/Longman.

Norton, B., & Toohey, K. (2011). Identity, language learning, and social change. *Language Teaching, 44*(4), 412–446.

Norton Peirce, B. (1995). Social identity, investment, and language learning. *TESOL Quarterly, 29*(1), 9–31.

Ó Ceallaigh, T. J., Ní Mhurchú, S., & Ní Chróinín, D. (2017). Balancing content and language in CLIL: The experiences of teachers and learners. *Journal of Immersion and Content-Based Language Education, 5*(1), 58–86.

Ó Murchadha, N., & Flynn, C. J. (2018). Educators' target language varieties for language learners: Orientation toward 'native' and 'nonnative' norms in a minority language context. *The Modern Language Journal, 102*(4), 797–813. https://doi.org/10.1111/modl.125140026-7902/18

O'Malley, J., & Chamot, A. (1990). *Learning strategies in second language acquisition*. Cambridge: Cambridge University Press.

Oliver, R., Rochecouste, J., & Nguyen, B. (2017). ESL in Australia—A chequered history. *TESOL in Context, 26*(1), 7–26.

Ollerhead, S. (2018). Teaching across semiotic modes with multilingual learners: Translanguaging in an Australian classroom. *Language and Education*. https://doi.org/10.1080/09500782.2018.1516780

Ortega, L. (2009). *Understanding second language acquisition*. London: Hodder Education.

Otheguy, R., García, O., & Reid, W. (2015). Clarifying translanguaging and deconstructing named languages: A perspective from linguistics. *Applied Linguistics Review, 6*(3), 281–307.

Ovando, C., Combs, M., & Collier, V. (2006). *Bilingual and ESL classrooms: Teaching in multilingual contexts* (4th ed.). Boston, MA: McGraw Hill.

Oxford English Dictionary. (2018). *Definition of 'language'*. Retrieved February 26, 2018, from https://en.oxforddictionaries.com/definition/language

Pacheco, M. (2018). Spanish, Arabic, and 'English-Only': Making meaning across languages in two classroom communities. *TESOL Quarterly, 52*(4), 1–27. https://doi.org/10.1002/tesq.446

Pacheco, M., & Smith, B. E. (2015). Across languages, modes, and identities: Bilingual adolescents' multimodal codemeshing in the literacy classroom. *Bilingual Research Journal, 38*(3), 292–312. https://doi.org/10.1080/152358 82.2015.1091051

Palmer, D. K., Ballinger, S., & Lizette, P. (2014). Classroom interaction in one-way, two-way, and indigenous immersion contexts. *Journal of Immersion and Content-Based Language Education, 2*(2), 225–240.

Palmer, D. K., Cervantes-Soon, C., Dorner, L., & Heiman, D. (2019). Bilingualism, biliteracy, biculturalism and critical consciousness for all: Proposing a fourth fundamental goal for two-way dual language education. *Theory Into Practice, 58*(2), 121–133. https://doi.org/10.1080/00405841.2019.1569376

Pennycook, A. (1994). *The cultural politics of English as an international language*. London: Longman.

Pennycook, A. (2001). Lessons from colonial language policies. In R. D. González (Ed.), *Language ideologies: Critical perspectives on the official English movement* (Vol. 2, pp. 195–219). Urbana, IL: National Council of Teachers of English.

Pennycook, A. (2017). Translanguaging and semiotic assemblages. *International Journal of Multilingualism, 14*(3), 269–282.

Pérez-Cañado, M. L. (2012). CLIL research in Europe: Past, present, and future. *International Journal of Bilingual Education and Bilingualism, 15*(3), 315–341.

Pérez-Cañado, M. L. (2016a). Teacher training needs for bilingual education: In-service teacher perceptions. *International Journal of Bilingual Education and Bilingualism, 19*(3), 266–295.

Pérez-Cañado, M. L. (2016b). Are teachers ready for CLIL? Evidence from a European study. *European Journal of Teacher Education, 39*(2), 202–221. https://doi.org/10.1080/02619768.2016.1138104

300 References

Piller, I., & Gerber, L. (2018). Family language policy between the bilingual advantage and the monolingual mindset. *International Journal of Bilingual Education and Bilingualism.* https://doi.org/10.1080/13670050. 2018.1503227

Polio, C. G., & Duff, P. A. (1994). Teachers' language use in university foreign language classrooms: A qualitative analysis of English and target language alternation. *The Modern Language Journal, 78*(3), 313–326.

Potowski, K. (2004). Student Spanish use and investment in a dual immersion classroom: Implications for second language acquisition and heritage language maintenance. *The Modern Language Journal, 88*(1), 75–101.

Potowski, K. (2007). *Language and identity in a dual immersion school.* Clevedon: Multilingual Matters.

Prasad, G. (2015). Beyond the mirror towards a plurilingual prism: Exploring the creation of plurilingual 'identity texts' in English and French classrooms in Toronto and Montpellier. *Intercultural Education, 26*(6), 497–514.

Prasad, G. (2018). How does it look and feel to be plurilingual? Analyzing children's representations of plurilingualism through collage. *International Journal of Bilingual Education and Bilingualism.* https://doi.org/10.1080/136 70050.2017.1420033

Reid, J. (1996). Recent developments in Australian late immersion education. *Journal of Multilingual and Multicultural Development, 17*(6), 469–484.

Rojas-Drummond, S., & Mercer, N. (2004). Scaffolding the development of effective collaboration and learning. *International Journal of Educational Research, 39,* 99–111.

Rose, D. (2012). Integrating SFL theory with literacy teaching. In Z. Yan, J. Webster, & F. Yan (Eds.), *Developing systemic functional linguistics: Theory and application.* London: Equinox.

Rose, D. (2015). Building a pedagogical metalanguage II: Knowledge genres. In J. R. Martin (Ed.), *Applicable linguistics and academic discourse* (pp. 29–58). Shanghai: Shanghai Jiao Tong University Press.

Rose, D., & Martin, J. R. (2012). *Learning to write, reading to learn: Genre, knowledge and pedagogy in the Sydney school.* London: Equinox.

Rubinstein-Avila, E. (2002). Problematizing the "dual" in a dual immersion program: A portrait. *Linguistics and Education, 13*(1), 65–87.

Rubio Mostacero, M. D. (2009). Language teacher training for non-language teachers: Meeting the needs of Andalusian teachers for school plurilingualism projects. In *Design of a Targeted Training Course.* Jaén: Universidad de Jaén.

Ruiz, R. (1984). Orientations in language planning. *NABE Journal, 8*(2), 15–34.

References 301

Rumlich, D. (2014). Prospective CLIL and non-CLIL students' interest in English (classes): A quasi-experimental study on German sixth-graders. *Utrecht Studies in Language and Communication, 28*, 75–95.

Rymes, B. (2010). Classroom discourse analysis: A focus on communicative repertoires. In N. Hornberger & S. McKay (Eds.), *Sociolinguistics and language education* (pp. 528–546). Buffalo, NY: Multilingual Matters.

Rymes, B. (2014). Communicative repertoire. In C. Leung & B. V. Street (Eds.), *The Routledge companion to English studies* (pp. 287–301). London: Routledge.

Säljö, R. (2009). Learning, theories of learning, and units of analysis in research. *Educational Psychologist, 44*(3), 202–208.

San Isidro, X. (2018). Innovations and challenges in CLIL implementation in Europe. *Theory Into Practice, 57*, 185–195.

Scarino, A. (2014). Situating the challenges in current languages education policy in Australia—Unlearning monolingualism. *International Journal of Multilingualism, 11*(3), 289–306.

Schecter, S., & Cummins, J. (Eds.). (2003). *Multilingual education in practice: Using diversity as a resource.* Portsmouth, NH: Heinemann.

Schleppegrell, M. J. (2004). *The language of schooling: A functional linguistics perspective.* Mahwah, NJ: Lawrence Erlbaum.

Schmidt, R. (1983). Interaction, acculturation and the acquisition of communication competence. In M. Wolfson & E. Judd (Eds.), *Sociolinguistics and second language acquisition.* Rowley, MA: Newbury House.

Schmidt, R. (1990). The role of consciousness in second language learning. *Applied Linguistics, 11*(2), 129–158.

Seedhouse, P. (1999). Task-based interaction. *ELT Journal, 53*(3), 149–156.

Seedhouse, P. (2005). 'Task' as research construct. *Language Learning, 55*(3), 533–570.

Skehan, P. (1998). *A cognitive approach to language learning.* Oxford: Oxford University Press.

Skehan, P. (2011). *Researching tasks: Performance, assessment and pedagogy.* Shanghai: Shanghai Foreign Language Education Press.

Smala, S. (2011). *Contexts and agents: Different ways of 'doing' bilingual education in Queensland.* Paper presented at the Language and Diversity Conference, November 22–25, in Auckland, New Zealand.

Smala, S. (2016). CLIL in Queensland: The evolution of immersion. *Babel, 50*(2–3), 20+.

Somers, T., & Surmont, J. (2012). CLIL and immersion: How clear-cut are they? *ELT Journal, 66*(1), 113–116.

302   References

Somerville, M., D'Warte, J., & Sawyer, W. (2016). *Building on children's linguistic repertoires to enrich learning: A project report for the NSW Department of Education.* Retrieved from http://www.uws.edu.au/centre_for_educational_research

Spence-Brown, R. (2014). On rocky ground: Monolingual educational structures and Japanese language education in Australia. In N. Murray & A. Scarino (Eds.), *Dynamic ecologies, Multilingual education* (pp. 183–198). Dordrecht: Springer.

Spolsky, B., Green, J., & Read, J. (1974). *A model for the description, analysis, and perhaps evaluation of bilingual education.* Navajo Reading Study Progress Report 23. University of New Mexico, Albuquerque, NM.

Swain, M. (1985). Communicative competence: Some roles of comprehensible input and comprehensible output in its development. In S. Gass & C. Madden (Eds.), *Input in Second Language Acquisition* (pp. 235–253). Rowley, MA: Newbury House.

Swain, M. (2000). French immersion research in Canada: recent contributions to SLA and Applied Linguistics. *Annual Review of Applied Linguistics, 20,* 199–212.

Swan, M. (2005). Legislation by hypothesis: The case of task-based instruction. *Applied Linguistics, 26*(3), 376–401.

Tarone, E., & Swain, M. (1995). A sociolinguistic perspective on second language use in immersion classrooms. *The Modern Language Journal, 79,* 166–178.

Tedick, D. J., & Weseley, P. M. (2015). A review of research on content-based foreign/second language education in US K-12 contexts. *Language, Culture and Curriculum, 28*(1), 25–40.

Tedick, D. J., & Young, A. I. (2016). Fifth grade two-way immersion students' responses to form-focused instruction. *Applied Linguistics, 37*(6), 784–807.

Tedick, D. J., & Young, A. I. (2017). Two-way immersion students' home languages, proficiency levels, and responses to form-focused instruction. *International Journal of Bilingual Education and Bilingualism, 21*(3), 1–16. https://doi.org/10.1080/13670050.2017.1383354

Teo, P. (2008). Outside in/inside out: Bridging the gap in literacy education in Singapore classrooms. *Language and Education, 22*(6), 411–431. https://doi.org/10.1080/09500780802152721

The New London Group. (1996). A pedagogy of multiliteracies: Designing social futures. *Harvard Educational Review, 66*(1), 60–92. https://doi.org/10.17763/haer.66.1.17370n67v22j160u

Thibault, P. J. (2011). First-order languaging dynamics and second-order language: The distributed language view. *Ecological Psychology, 23*(3), 210–245.

References 303

Thomas, W. P., & Collier, V. P. (2002). *A national study of school effectiveness for language minority students' long-term academic achievement*. Santa Cruz, CA: University of California at Santa Cruz, Center for Research on Education, Diversity, and Excellence.

Tsung, L. (2014). *Language power and hierarchy: Multilingual education in China*. London: Bloomsbury Academic.

Turnbull, M., Lapkin, S., Hart, D., & Swain, M. (1998). Time on task and immersion graduates' French proficiency. In S. Lapkin (Ed.), *French second language education in Canada: Empirical studies* (pp. 31–55). Toronto: University of Toronto Press.

Turner, M. (2017). Integrating content and language in institutionally monolingual settings: Teacher positioning and differentiation. *Bilingual Research Journal, 40*(1), 70–80.

Turner, M. (forthcoming). The positioning of Japanese in a secondary CLIL science classroom in Australia: Language use and the learning of content. *Journal of Immersion and Content-Based Language Education*.

Turner, M., & Lin, A. M. Y. (2017). Translanguaging and named languages: Productive tension and desire. *International Journal of Bilingual Education and Bilingualism*. https://doi.org/10.1080/13670050.2017.1360243

Ur, P. (1996). *A course in language teaching: Practice and theory*. Cambridge: Cambridge University Press.

Vadeboncoeur, J., Vellos, R., & Goessling, K. (2011). Learning as (one part) identity construction: Educational implications of a sociocultural perspective. In D. McInerney, R. Walker, & G. Liem (Eds.), *Sociocultural theories of learning and motivation: Looking back, looking forward* (pp. 223–251). Charlotte, NC: Information Age Publishing.

Valadez, C., MacSwan, J., & Martínez, C. (2002). Toward a new view of low achieving bilinguals: A study of linguistic competence in designated 'semilinguals. *Bilingual Review, 25*(3), 238–248.

Valdés, G. (2003). *Expanding definitions of giftedness: The case of young interpreters from immigrant communities*. Mahwah, NJ: Lawrence Erlbaum.

Van de Pol, J., Volman, M., & Beishuizen, J. (2012). Promoting teacher scaffolding in small-group work: A contingency perspective. *Teaching and Teacher Education, 28*, 193–205.

Van Lier, L. (2004). *The ecology and semiotics of language learning: A sociocultural perspective*. New York: Kluwer Academic.

Vásquez, A., Hansen, A., & Smith, P. (2013). *Teaching language arts to English language learners* (2nd ed.). New York: Routledge.

Velasco, P., & García, O. (2014). Translanguaging and the writing of bilingual learners. *Bilingual Research Journal, 37*(1), 6–23.

References

Vrikki, M., Wheatley, L., Howe, C., Hennessy, S., & Mercer, N. (2018). Dialogic practices in primary classrooms. *Language and Education.* https://doi.org/10.1080/09500782.2018.1509988

Vygotsky, L. S. (1960). *Razvitie vysshyke psikhichekikh funktsii [The development off higher mental functions].* Moskow: Izdatel'stvo Akademii Pedagogicheskikh Nauk.

Vygotsky, L. S. (1978). *Mind in society: The development of higher psychological processes.* Cambridge, MA: Harvard University Press.

Vygotsky, L. S. (1987). *The collected works of L. S. Vygotsky. Volume 1: Problems of general psychology. Including the volume thinking and speech* (N. Minick, Ed. & Trans.). New York: Plenum.

Weedon, C. (1997). *Feminist practice and poststructuralist theory* (2nd ed.). London: Blackwell.

Wenger, E. (1998). *Communities of practice: Learning, meaning, and identity.* Cambridge: Cambridge University Press.

Wertsch, J. V. (1991). *Voices of the mind: A sociocultural approach to mediated action.* Cambridge, MA: Harvard University Press.

Wertsch, J. V. (2015). Mediation. In H. Daniels, M. Cole, & J. V. Wertsch (Eds.), *The Cambridge companion to Vygotsky* (pp. 178–192). Cambridge: Cambridge University Press.

West, C. (1992). A matter of life and death. *October, 61*(Summer), 20–23.

Williams, C. (1994). *Arfaniad oDdulliau Dysgu ac Addysgu yng Nghyd-destun Addysg Uwchradd Ddwyieithog [An evaluation of teaching and learning methods in the context of bilingual secondary education].* Unpublished Doctoral Thesis, University of Wales, Bangor.

Williams, C. (1996). Secondary education: Teaching in the bilingual situation. In C. Williams, G. Lewis, & C. Baker (Eds.), *The language policy: Taking stock* (pp. 39–78). Llangefni: CAI.

Wilson, D. M. (2011). Dual language programs on the rise. *Harvard Education Letter, 27*(2). Retrieved from http://hepg.org/hel-home/issues/27_2/helarticle/dual-language-programs-on-the-rise

Wood, D., Wood, H., & Middleton, D. (1978). An experimental evaluation of four face-to-face teaching strategies. *International Journal of Behavioral Development, 1*, 131–147.

Zentella, A. C. (1997). The Hispanophobia of the official English movement in the US. *International Journal of Society and Language, 127*, 71–86.

Zitlali Morales, P., & Maravilla-Cano, J. V. (2019). The problems and possibilities of interest convergence in a dual language school. *Theory Into Practice.* https://doi.org/10.1080/00405841.2019.1569377

Index

A

Advocacy, 175–177, 194, 242, 257
Affordance, 82, 83, 253

C

Challenge, 33, 53, 56, 152, 153,
    166, 177, 181, 184, 186, 192,
    194, 204–206, 208, 210, 212,
    213, 217, 225, 243, 245, 246,
    261, 269
Code-switching, 31–32, 65
Collaboration, 53, 57, 65, 81, 94,
    96, 97, 100, 112, 127, 128,
    143, 170, 178, 182–184, 195,
    212, 224, 237, 260, 264, 265,
    268, 269
Content and language integrated
    learning (CLIL), 5, 10–12,
    45, 50–55, 63, 64,
86–88, 95, 96, 169–195,
    197–225, 230, 234–237,
    239–243, 245, 257–261,
    264–269
Crosslinguistic pedagogy, 35, 46, 49,
    58, 65–69, 99, 127–130, 137,
    157, 160, 183, 184, 192, 193,
    213, 215, 221, 261, 263
Cultural capital, 90, 91, 101, 126, 138,
    180, 190, 208, 234, 241, 257

D

Desire, 6, 49, 68, 82, 89, 90,
    93, 94, 100, 123, 131, 155,
    160, 179, 184, 192, 208,
    233, 234, 246, 257, 264, 267
Dialogic approach, 63, 98
Differentiation, 12, 137, 181, 254,
    264–267, 273

© The Author(s) 2019
M. Turner, *Multilingualism as a Resource and a Goal*,
https://doi.org/10.1007/978-3-030-21591-0

306 Index

E

English-as-an-additional-language (EAL), 10–12, 49, 55, 58, 61–63, 84, 85, 88, 96, 137, 238

Enquiry-based learning, 156, 238, 240, 245

Everyday communication, 163, 209, 232, 244–246, 253, 255, 264

F

Form-focused instruction, 46, 58–60, 88, 99, 157, 187, 212, 215, 240, 241, 262

Functional language, 60–62, 88, 99

H

Heritage languages, 3–5, 9, 10, 12, 30, 37, 38, 65, 67, 79, 84, 85, 91, 96, 98, 100, 111–138, 141, 143, 148–149, 152–153, 155–156, 160, 162–167, 175, 179, 180, 189, 192, 194, 204, 224, 229, 231, 233–236, 238, 255, 256, 258–261, 266–272, 278

Heteroglossic practices, 56

I

Implicit and explicit learning of language, 86, 194

Innovation, 12, 51, 170, 172, 175, 193, 194, 237, 242, 254, 268–269, 273

Instructed language learning, 87, 243

Investment, 89, 90, 92, 122, 123, 125, 126, 136, 138, 152–155, 162, 163, 167, 179, 180, 208, 209, 231, 244–246, 253, 269

L

Language
maps, 58, 63, 67, 112–116, 122, 126, 129, 130, 143, 155, 160–162, 233, 241, 256
policy, 4, 8, 55, 79, 80, 83, 100, 254, 264, 277, 279
scaffolding, 46, 58, 61–64, 68, 96, 99, 100, 159, 171, 183, 186, 189, 191, 213, 215, 262, 269
separation, 3, 5, 6, 9, 22, 23, 25, 26, 30, 45–50, 53, 55, 66, 119, 127, 162, 166, 236, 241, 252, 256, 264, 268

Language-as-resource, 36, 37

Language-as-system, 22, 252

Legitimacy, 89–92, 123, 135, 136, 154, 245, 258

Linguistic hierarchies, 3, 36, 137, 166, 193, 223, 231, 237–239, 265, 270, 280

Literacy, 30, 47, 55, 61, 94, 95, 121–122, 124, 125, 144, 152, 157, 162, 234, 240, 258, 262, 266, 267

M

Mental grammars, 31

Monoglossic practices, 25–28, 30

Motivation, 35, 82, 89, 90, 153, 182, 210, 257

Multilingualism-as-resource, 37
Multilingual stance continuum, 86,
    135, 224, 254–256, 270, 271

P

Professional learning, 67, 94–97,
    100, 113, 119, 127, 128, 143,
    182–184, 212–214, 225, 233,
    237, 260
Pro-monolingual ideology, 84, 99
Pro-multilingual ideology, 83, 270

S

Student-centred learning, 3, 5, 12,
    65, 79, 94, 99, 127–131,
    157–159, 166, 232, 235, 238,
    242, 245, 260, 261
Swain's output hypothesis, 49, 98

T

Target languages, 2, 3, 9–11, 34,
    45–48, 50–55, 58–69, 79,
    85, 86, 88, 90, 95, 96, 100,
    122, 128, 131, 138, 141,
    150, 158, 162, 164–166,
    169, 171, 172, 175, 185,
    189, 192, 194, 195, 197,
    204, 206, 207, 218, 224,
    225, 229–238, 241, 244–246,
    252, 255–257, 259–264, 266,
    269, 271, 272, 277, 279
Teaching English to speakers of
    other languages (TESOL), 5,
    9, 25, 30, 46, 111, 112,
    279
Translanguaging pedagogy, 27–38,
    54, 65–69, 91, 93, 136, 137,
    166, 167, 193, 223, 230, 245,
    246, 262–265, 279